WOMEN IN
A Feminist Lis...
Jo Camp...

editorial advisory group

Maria Brenton, *University College, Cardiff*; Phillida Bunckle, *Victoria University, Wellington, New Zealand*; Miriam David, *Polytechnic of the South Bank*; Leonore Davidoff, *University of Essex*; Janet Finch, *University of Lancaster*; Jalna Hanmer, *University of Bradford*; Beverley Kingston, *University of New South Wales, Australia*; Hilary Land, *University of Bristol*; Diana Leonard, *University of London Institute of Education*; Susan Lonsdale, *Polytechnic of the South Bank*; Jean O'Barr, *Duke University, North Carolina, USA*; Arlene Tigar McLaren, *Simon Fraser University, British Columbia, Canada*; Jill Roe, *Macquarie University, Australia*; Hilary Rose, *University of Bradford*; Susan Sellers, *Centre D'Etudes Feminines, Université de Paris*; Pat Thane, *Goldsmiths' College, University of London*; Jane Thompson, *University of Southampton*; Clare Ungerson, *University of Kent at Canterbury*; Judy Walkowitz, *Rutgers University, New Jersey, USA*.

The 1970s and 1980s have seen an explosion of publishing by, about and for women. This new list is designed to make a particular contribution to this process by commissioning and publishing books which consolidate and advance feminist research and debate in key areas in a form suitable for students, academics and researchers but also accessible to a broader general readership.

As far as possible books will adopt an international perspective incorporating comparative material from a range of countries where this is illuminating. Above all they will be interdisciplinary, aiming to put women's studies and feminist discussion firmly on the agenda in subject-areas as disparate as law, physical education, art and social policy.

WOMEN IN SOCIETY
A Feminist List edited by
Jo Campling

Homeworking

Myths and Realities

Sheila Allen
and
Carol Wolkowitz

**MACMILLAN
EDUCATION**

First published 1987

Published by
MACMILLAN EDUCATION LTD
Houndmills, Basingstoke, Hampshire RG21 2XS
and London
Companies and representatives
throughout the world

Printed in Hong Kong

British Library Cataloguing in Publication Data
Allen, Sheila
Homeworking: myths and realities.
1. Home labour
I. Title II. Wolkowitz, Carol
331.2   HD2333
ISBN 0-333-42363-1 (hardcover)
ISBN 0-333-42364-X (paperback)

Series Standing Order

If you would like to receive future titles in this series as they are
published, you can make use of our standing order facility. To place a
standing order please contact your bookseller or, in case of difficulty,
write to us at the address below with your name and address and the
name of the series. Please state with which title you wish to begin your
standing order. (If you live outside the United Kingdom we may not
have the rights to your area, in which case we will forward your order
to the publisher concerned.)

Customer Services Department, Macmillan Distribution Ltd,
Houndmills, Basingstoke, Hampshire, RG21 2XS, England.

*For the homeworkers of
West Yorkshire and elsewhere*

Contents

List of Tables and Figures

Tables

Figure

Acknowledgements

This book could not have been written without the active interest of many women. Our thanks go first to the homeworkers in West Yorkshire who generously gave of their time to describe their working lives and in particular to Margaret who had the courage to give evidence to the Select Committee, knowing full well the probable consequences, but in the belief that while it may not do her 'any good', it would help the next generation of homeworkers. We hope that in some measure our work will repay the debt we owe them.

To all our friends, colleagues, students, neighbours and family members who have recalled for us their own homeworking experiences or that of others, stretching over a period from the middle 1930s to the present day, especially Marjorie McKenny and Marie Allsopp, we are very grateful.

Discussions with women from North and South America, India, Pakistan and Bangladesh, Norway, West Germany and Bulgaria, and in many cases access to their unpublished work, have enabled us to see how widespread homeworking is and how similar the conditions under which it is undertaken. To all of them we express our thanks.

The University of Bradford and the Economic and Social Research Council provided much appreciated financial help which enabled us to carry out the survey work, the data analysis and the writing up.

The contribution made by Janie Newton-Moss and Julia Graham as research assistants in the early years of the research in West Yorkshire, together with the team of women interviewers, was invaluable and is gratefully acknowledged.

To all those we have come to know through their involvement

with 'Homework Campaigns' and who have shared ideas and information with us, many thanks.

Rita Jones, while secretary to the ESRC-financed project (1980–1) gave invaluable assistance on many aspects of the work in addition to her excellent typing. Since then Margaret Ellis, Judith Hammond, Win Healey and Sue Bentley have contributed to the typing of earlier drafts and to the production of the final typescript. For their good humour and efficient support we are extremely grateful and it is a pleasure to acknowledge how much we owe them.

Finally to Vic, Sophie and Lucy Allen, who for the past five years have endured the home-based production of papers on home-working and who have given unfailing domestic and intellectual support, many thanks.

SHEILA ALLEN
CAROL WOLKOWITZ

Introduction

Homeworking is the supply of work to be performed in domestic premises, usually for piecework payment. Known also as outwork, it is a global phenomenon. In highly industrialised countries such as Britain or the United States, women working at home produce everything from clothes, shoes and quilts to windscreen wipers and industrial transmission belts. They process insurance claims, peel vegetables, and do company accounts. In India and Bangladesh homeworkers assemble electrical components, roll cigarettes, and make cane furniture and many other goods. Homeworking takes place under most kinds of political systems, in vastly different economic circumstances, using traditional craft skills and highly sophisticated computer technologies. How can one explain it? Who supplies the work? How is it organised? Are homeworkers predominantly women, and if so why? Does homeworking require regulation, and if so of what kind? This book attempts to answer some of these questions.

In the period before the First World War homeworking was the subject of public investigation and legislation in the United States, in Britain and several countries in Western Europe. But then it became virtually invisible until the 1970s. Even now its existence is usually simply denied or ignored. It is one of the peculiarities of homeworking that although many people have friends, relatives and neighbours who do homework or have done it themselves, they tend to see the work as only isolated instances and are unaware of its extent. So pervasive are the common conceptions of 'real work' or a 'real job' that people do not integrate their knowledge or experience of homeworking into their image of work or jobs. One of the authors of this book, for instance, had always assumed that her grandfather, a trouser-maker and active trade unionist, had been a factory worker. She only discovered that he had been a home-

1

worker when the book was nearing completion. In contrast some women, learning of our interest in homeworking, were surprised that anyone would need to write a book about it, since they, their mothers and sisters knew it to be part of everyday life. Their taken-for-granted experience of homework lies, however, outside the dominant conceptions of work.

Since the mid 1970s homeworking has again begun to receive a modicum of attention. Part of the reason for this has been the increasing concern of women's organisations with demands for improvements in the pay and working conditions of women. Such demands have received considerable support from the work of feminist scholars who, by bringing women to the forefront of their analyses, have added a new dimension to the study of work. By demonstrating the gap between dominant conceptions of women primarily as housewives and the reality of women as waged workers, they have shown the inadequacy of models of work based only on men's employment patterns. Feminist researchers have asked new questions about waged and unwaged work, the social relations through which these are controlled and the ways in which they are rewarded and measured.

Until the 1980s, homeworking tended to lag behind the other concerns of feminist researchers, with a few exceptions (Allen, 1981a; 1981b; Hope, *et al.*, 1976). This is due in part to the influence of certain ideas derived from Marxist analyses, in particular the assumption that waged work takes place outside the home and liberates women from the constraints of domestic life. The neglect of homeworking in feminist research is also due to the fact that when feminists have focused on the home, they have been mainly concerned about women's unpaid domestic labour and the relations between family members. Too often, moreover, they have accepted *as fact* the ideology of the isolated nuclear family, and ignored the role of outsiders in organising the waged work that goes on within the home. The study of homeworking serves as an important corrective to any view which separates the home from waged labour.

The increasing public visibility of homeworking in the 1970s was due more to studies such as those undertaken by the Low Pay Unit. Its interest in homeworking was part of a broader attempt to document the persistence of a large, low-paid labour force, which had been overlooked in the period of post-war economic growth and rising standards of living. The surveys of homeworkers sponsored by the Low Pay Unit, the Fabian Society and others (Bolton, 1975; Brown, 1974; Crine, 1979a; Field, 1979b; Jordan, 1978) were widely quoted in the press and in women's magazines. As a result the image of homeworkers as housewives supported by a husband's wage, seeking a bit of 'pin money' for work in their spare time, was challenged by factual accounts of women who were forced by economic need to undertake long hours of work at home for appalling wages. Some trade unions also began to look more closely at homeworking within industries they organised and investigations in certain Wages Councils were undertaken. Campaigns were launched by the Low Pay Unit, the Leicester Outwork Campaign and trade unions, and led to two Parliamentary bills in 1979 and 1981 which sought to regulate homeworking and improve the employment status of homeworkers. But with the defeat of these bills the issue again languished.

By the early 1980s the economic situation had changed markedly and to some observers homeworking began to look a more attractive proposition. The contraction of manufacturing and steeply rising unemployment led futurologists to be concerned about 'the future of work'. Along with some social scientists they have argued that an expansion of homeworking, as well as increases in self-employment, part-time work and temporary contracts, is not only changing the nature of work in advanced capitalist societies but offers advantages over full-time work outside the home (Atkinson, 1984; Burns, 1977; Gershuny, 1979; Gershuny and Pahl, 1979–80; Handy, 1984; IMS, 1984; R. E. Pahl, 1980; Postgate, 1984; Rose, 1983; Toffler, 1980). Homeworking, for instance, is seen as a boon for women, who need to adjust their paid work around family responsibilities; an advantage to firms seeking to lower overheads and labour costs in order to meet foreign competition; and a way of combating demoralisation by enabling enterprising individuals to take up rewarding work as part of new, home-centred life styles. In the United States it is being argued that restrictions on homeworking 'deprive untold numbers of individuals, such as the mothers of young children' of the opportunity to be gainfully employed and prevent others from taking advantage of the new opportunities presented by electronic information processing technology (*Telecommuting Review*, 1985). In Britain any criticism of homeworking is seen by some as an old-fashioned, rear-guard attempt to hold back the emergence of 'new' structures of work and income generation.

By the mid-1980s, therefore, homeworking had become the subject of conflicting assumptions, evaluations and claims. It is still dismissed by many as a minor problem affecting only a few unfortunate women during their child-rearing years; others portray it as a women's issue or one primarily affecting women from ethnic minorities; others welcome it as a new field of opportunity. What is the reality behind these diverse images? There is clearly a need for fuller, more accurate information about homeworking and the conditions homeworkers experience. As women comprise the vast majority of homeworkers in many societies this aspect must be given close attention in the analysis and explanations put forward.

This book has two aims. One is to provide an account of what is involved in being a homeworker and the second is to identify and explain the processes which create and sustain homeworking in the modern economy. On the first we seek to demonstrate that many of the assumptions about who does homework and why they do it and how it is combined with other responsibilities, are false. Accurate information is essential both in order to assess whether homework is likely to provide new opportunities for those increasingly without outside employment and, more prosaically, to argue for greater priority to be given to measures which will protect homeworkers. The gap between existing misconceptions and the reality of the homeworkers' situation also points to much wider issues. Assumptions about homeworkers are not simply *ad hoc* beliefs about a particular category of women workers. They reflect much more fundamental and widespread misconceptions about women's relation to paid work. Women's struggles to establish their rights as workers, including the right to equal pay, come up against interpretations of work still dominated by the myth of the male family breadwinner, in which women's waged work is assumed to be temporary, intermittent and of secondary importance to individual households and the economy as a whole. In documenting homeworkers' position as permanent members of the waged labour force making a critical contribution to production, we are pointing to many aspects of women's waged work more generally. Many women who are not themselves homeworkers will recognise much about their own situation in the accounts which homeworkers have given of their working lives.

The second aim, we argue, is a different question from why women, rather than men, do homework and thus cannot be answered solely with reference to feminist concepts designed to understand gender divisions. Homeworking is characterised not only by its location in the home, but by the conditions of employment which in many respects resemble certain other forms of employment. It is one of several types of employment in which the workforce is effectively casualised. Casualised workers are those who, though in reality permanent members of the labour force, are treated as temporary workers to whom the employer owes no legal obligations. Many are workers who, because they are forced to switch jobs or suffer spells of unemployment, are thought to have a lower attachment to paid work than other workers. Women are often defined as a casual labour force because some of them leave employment to have children or to care for other members of the family. But the casualised labour force actually includes men and women, and their ideological construction as casual workers stems from the jobs they do, not from their individual characteristics. Many enterprises employ labour on a seasonal basis, or at such low wages that employees seek to change to jobs which are marginally better paid. Because such workers are never able to qualify as permanent employees, they do not enjoy the rights to which full-time permanent workers are entitled. In other cases contracts of employment are designed to ensure that the workers concerned never qualify as permanent employees. Examples are to be found not only among manual workers but also in secretarial, clerical and professional employment. In the 1970s attention was drawn to the situation of office 'temps' and some attempt made to regulate the employment agencies for whom they worked. Since then there has been a noticeable increase in the number of teachers, nurses and other professional workers who are offered only a succession of temporary contracts.

Still other workers never acquire employment rights because their jobs are defined as part-time. In order to qualify they need to remain in their jobs even longer than those defined as full-time workers. Still others, like homeworkers, are not considered to be employees at all, because they are defined as self-employed. In other words, large sections of the labour force lack employment rights and security, and their numbers appear to be growing, among both women and men.

Many of these changes in conditions of employment and methods of work are related to shifts in wider political and economic forces. It is only within these that ideologies of gender and employment and more specifically the construction of women as an appropriate homeworking labour force can be analysed. The balance of power between capital and labour, the level of unemployment, the part played by the state in conditions of employment and income maintenance, and the potential created by technological changes are a few of the factors which are relevant to understanding homeworking.

In Chapter 1, we consider historical and contemporary approaches to homeworking in terms of how these contribute to an understanding of its persistence. While many elements in the feminist challenge to dominant conceptions of the sexual division of labour have opened up investigations into the relationships between women, work and household, the concepts developed in such analysis are not sufficient. Theoretical perspectives which link waged labour in the home with the wider economy, including the literature on the role of the informal sector in the Third World economies, are also necessary. The persistence of homeworking cannot be understood only in terms of – for instance – gender relations, or migrant communities, nor in terms of racial minorities, though these may have particular significance in specific periods. The persistence is to be analysed in terms of the relations between capital and labour and the conditions under which surplus value (or profit) is produced.

In Chapter 2 we look at the attempts which have been made, particularly in Britain, to quantify the extent of homeworking, as regards both the number of workers and the number of suppliers. It can well be argued that knowledge of these numbers is not necessary for legal reform, or for understanding homeworking as a method of production, or for a more adequate appreciation of what it is like to be a homeworker. But in practice, how much homeworking there is, and particularly the question of how many people do it, is a primary source of disagreement – and for some is the main measure of how seriously it should be treated. Gaining accurate figures is therefore important for those seeking legal reform and political support in organising homeworkers.

The question of whether or not homeworking is of only marginal importance also arises in relation to what sort of work homeworkers do. The most common view, which associates homework with clothing or textiles, was challenged by the wide range of work uncovered in the 1970s. With the advent of new technology, however, the argument has shifted to the issue of the relative proportions of what is frequently termed 'traditional' as compared with 'new' homeworking.

The various ways in which homeworking has been defined and the importance of these definitions to the issue of homeworkers' employment status is also discussed in Chapter 2. The focus of campaigning for reform towards the end of the 1970s was the employment status of homeworkers under the law, when it was agreed that bringing homeworkers within the scope of legislation governing employees' rights and benefits was a key factor in improving homeworkers' pay and conditions. However, homeworking, which is a form of disguised waged labour, has been confused in some official publications in the 1980s with other forms of work *at* or *from* home in an all-embracing category of 'home-based workers'. This, we argue, does more to cloud than to clarify the distinctions which are relevant to legislative change, including an analysis of the relations between capital and labour.

In Chapter 3 we evaluate common images of homeworkers and common assumptions about why women become homeworkers. These are assumptions about women's responsibilities for the care of young children, about the cultures of ethnic minorities or their attitudes towards women's employment outside the home, and about homeworkers' income requirements. Using British data, including that collected in four areas of West Yorkshire on homeworkers' socio-economic status and household composition, we show that the reasons for doing homework cannot be understood so simply, nor couched in terms of the circumstances of individual women.

Chapters 4 and 5 analyse various aspects of the labour process in homeworking. Chapter 4 looks at the organisation of homeworking, its advantages for the supplier of work, and its role in the modern economy. This is followed in Chapter 5 by an assessment of the widely held belief that homework confers an autonomy and freedom in choosing when to work and how much to do not enjoyed by those who 'go out to work'.

The problems of collective organisation and the indifference of most governments to the situation of homeworkers form the context of the discussion of organising for change in Chapter 6. Over ninety years ago the conditions and pay of homeworkers provoked so many expressions of moral outrage in Britain that eventually reforms were introduced to regulate minimum payment and to register homework suppliers in some sweated trades. However small the actual changes proved to be, at least the politicians of the time recognised that there was a need for legislation. The low pay and poor conditions revealed in the 1970s brought no such recognition. As mentioned above, the two bills put before Parliament were defeated. Moreover, the recommendations made by a House of Commons Select Committee in 1981, like the proposals for Health and Safety regulations on homeworking produced in the 1970s, were not acted on by the government. In fact the abolition of the Fair Wages Clause and the attack on the Wages Councils have brought about a worsening of the situation for those seeking improvement through parliamentary means. In consequence the emphasis has changed towards locally-based activities and organisation, while the interest and support shown by some local authorities has increased and the official trade union position has been revised.

Homeworking provides a long-standing example of casualised employment, where there is no effective regulation of the suppliers and where the worker has no security, no rights and relatively, if not absolutely, poor pay. In Chapter 7 it is discussed as an extreme form of low-paid, unprotected labour in a socio-economic environment where there are strong political pressures to casualise broader sections of the labour force. High unemployment, industrial restructuring and the removal or non-implementation of regulatory mechanisms form the background against which an increase in and spread of homeworking is being predicted, and within which its implications must be assessed.

From the early 1980s there were a number of predictions of increases in homeworking in Britain. The numbers of homeworkers was thought to be growing and the range of work in which they were involved was claimed to be extending into new areas, especially through the use of computer terminals and microprocessors. In the existing state of knowledge about homeworking in many societies such predictions remain guesses about the future. But they have succeeded in at least focusing attention on homeworking. Some local authorities have been prompted to fund projects which aim to organise homeworkers, to provide them with information about their rights, to explore the possible health and safety hazards their work involves, to give training in relevant skills and improve health care facilities. If there is an increase in homeworking it is more necessary than ever to understand why firms use it, what it entails for those who do it, and what changes are required so that homeworkers enjoy the rights accorded to those defined as workers.

More than this, however, predictions of an increase in home-working coincide with a rise in the number of workers who are concerned about the effects of deregulation on their wages, health and safety at work, and employment security. The following chapters seek to show how waged workers share common interests, and that homeworkers represent only one aspect of the struggle for decent wages and working conditions.

1
Approaches to homeworking

For those who seek to understand homeworking, one of the most intriguing questions is how it became invisible in the public domain. In Britain, for instance, between the passage of the first Trades Board Act in 1909 and the first Low Pay survey in the mid-1970s, economists, sociologists and historians who could have been expected to take some account of it, simply failed to do so. Bythell, for instance, concludes his study of sweated trades in the eighteenth and nineteenth centuries with the optimistic statement that: 'Outwork is rightly relegated to one of the darkest chapters of economic history; and now that it is virtually dead, none should regret its passing' (Bythell, 1978, p. 254).

Those concerned with social policy appear to have been equally ignorant of its existence. Since it is difficult to see how those like social workers, health visitors or district nurses could not have known about it, perhaps it would be more accurate to say that those who wrote about social welfare or made decisions on social policy either remained ignorant of homeworking or considered it irrelevant. Or perhaps they took it for granted as something women did, or assumed that nothing could be done. Homeworking was raised on occasions at the Trades Union Congress in resolutions from hosiery or garment or boot and shoe trade union branches, but these made little or no impression either on the trade union movement or the Labour Party. Those national and local agencies with the statutory authority to record and monitor some of the trades in which it was practised did not apply the powers they had, and political representatives who presumably could have asked for information did not do so.

The invisibility of homework was, and continues to be, constructed partly by the methods of collecting statistical data used by official bodies. Their methods of recording and measuring economic activity not only allow but give credence to the belief that homeworking, if it exists at all, is an activity peripheral to the modern industrial economy. There have been significant changes in the definition of the employed population over time. For instance, married women were at first excluded from, and later encouraged to opt out of, the social insurance schemes from which the numbers of those employed were calculated. Since the Second World War, of course, the number and variety of instruments for measuring employment have increased. These are discussed more fully in Chapter 2. Here we need only note that despite these changes the collection of statistics remains heavily biased towards full-time employees, employed on a regular basis and working outside the home. Similarly, the recording of production, by volume or value, is not amenable to disaggregation to show the contribution of homeworking to either profits or products.

This lack of statistical records is one of the symptoms of the dominant ideological constructions of work and production relations found on both a common-sense level and in the major theories of economics and sociology. These have marginalised many forms of economic activity, particularly those at the level of the household and those involving patterns of work which do not conform to an institutionalised employer–full-time employee relationship. Consequently, tackling the invisibility of homeworking has to begin not with a description of homeworking itself, but by reconsidering the beliefs and theories within which its existence has been denied or ignored. Only in this way is it possible to stop treating homeworking as if it were a marginal, isolated phenomenon and begin investigating it as a normal part of economic life.

It would greatly enhance the analyses we present were we able to place homeworking in a full historical and comparative perspective. This is not only an enormous undertaking, but is one which is premature, for the empirical evidence is still too fragmentary and the necessary reconceptualisation barely begun. In this chapter we indicate the kind of evidence which is relevant, review some of the models and theories which have obscured the persistence of homeworking production, and look at certain attempts to reconceptualise the relationships within which work is carried out. The purpose is to show that any analysis of homeworking is closely connected with how one understands the relationship between household and production. The dominant conceptualisation is to separate these as spheres of analysis. To understand homeworking, however, it is necessary to focus on the penetration of households by capitalist labour processes, in forms which facilitate and reinforce patriarchal relations.

The evidence: personal recollections

Since homeworking is almost absent in official surveys of work, it is necessary to turn to other, more fragmentary, sources. These provide illuminating evidence of the persistence of homeworking from the 1920s through to the 1960s. One source are the biographies and autobiographies of women whose working lives illustrate patterns of paid labour which, though often continuous and crucial as a material contribution to the upkeep of their families, are very unlikely to have been part of statistical records. Another source is oral history. Local history projects are recording information which has previously been lost. More anecdotal evidence is also useful. In talking with family, friends and neighbours, through listening in shops, doctors' surgeries and hospital wards, as well as through the discussions following the presentation of papers on homeworking, we have been told about homeworking carried out over this period. Many take for granted their knowledge about homework, which has been part of their own lives and those of their mothers and grandmothers. Women without direct experience of it know of it through friends, neighbours or relatives.

We have tried to record examples as systematically as possible. They are only fragments of a social and economic history which has yet to be written. They are not necessarily representative of the work or workers involved in homeworking over the period and they tell us little about those who supplied the work. What they suggest, however, is that homeworking has been an integral part of women's paid work (frequently involving their children) throughout the twentieth century.

To take but a few of these examples, let us start with the North American academic who in 1982 began by querying the existence of homeworking on any scale, but then remembered that as a child refugee in Britain in the late 1930s she had been set to work assembling jewellery in the home of her hosts. When she later went to Rhode Island in the United States she continued to 'make jewellery' to be sold in local stores, including Woolworths. She received no direct payment for the work, which was simply one, among many, household activities.

A wide range of homework in Britain has been recalled by other women. In the 1930s in part of Lincolnshire the kitchen floors were covered with dried peas delivered by the sack for sorting. The women had to return both good and bad peas and were paid by weight. Women in the same area also attached string to labels for a printing firm and were paid 2d. per gross (J. and J. A. McKenny, personal communication). Homeworkers produced decorations, streamers, flags and bunting for the 1937 coronation, and during the 1939–45 war made camouflage nets for army lorries, in their kitchens. In 1940 they were paid 1s. 6d. per net for a large lorry (M. McKenny, personal communication). This work was apparently done voluntarily in some other parts of the country (see Longmate, 1973). No history of homeworking in the 1939–45 war has been written but it appears to have been extensive. The Ministry of Information reported that:

> housebound women and elderly relatives assembled parts of aeroplanes or guns, or anything that could be made with small tools like screwdrivers and pliers, in the sitting room. Small groups would work together not just for company, but also to economise on light bulbs and fuel. One firm . . . was able to save 1,800 factory hours in three weeks in this way . . .. Women out-workers in surrounding villagers managed to reach the astounding triple production level by May (1943).   (Minns, 1980, p. 34)

Instances of homeworking after the war which have been brought to our attention include burling and mending for the textile trade, which was very common in parts of West Yorkshire in the 1940s and 1950s. It is claimed the worst work was given to homeworkers (Shipley and Baildon women). Rainwear, aprons, overcoats and garment making were, as they are now, widespread (Saltaire, Shipley and Wakefield women). In the 1960s women were assembling components for electrical goods (Barnsley women), sorting elastic suspenders and assembling shoe heels (M. Allsopp, Leicester), while in Co. Down, Ulster women hem-stitched handkerchiefs by hand, some of them for as long as forty years (M. Hughes, personal communication). Reports like these suggest that home-working did not disappear over the period, and for some women was part of the everyday experience of earning a living.

Women, home and work

Why is documenting the existence of homeworking in the past and understanding its persistence in the present so difficult? The simplest explanation of the invisibility of homework is that it was, and is, women's work. Women's work is consistently ignored or undervalued, not only in industrial society but often also in less sophisticated societies in which the division of labour is less complex (Bradby, 1977). Yet this kind of explanation can only take us so far, for it lacks historical specificity.

In industrialised societies the invisibility of homework is closely related to the ways in which the division of labour is characteristi-cally interpreted. The dominant conceptualisation of social activi-ties in industrialised societies, which is reinforced by the legal system, persistently distinguishes home and work as separate spheres, the one being labelled 'private' and the other 'public' or 'social'. These are assumed to be divided spatially, to entail different types of social relationships, and to require separate investigation.

The emergence of home and work as separate spheres is one of the central tenets of theories developed to describe and explain the process of industrialisation. These theories were developed mainly in the late nineteenth century and were elaborated in the early years of the twentieth century. They assume that with industrialisation the locus of work moved outside the home; that work came to encompass only activities remunerated through the wage relation; and that the link between the family and the economy became confined to the work of only some household members, notably the husband/father, unmarried sons, and, on occasions, unmarried daughters.

There is of course much to be said for these constructions, in particular the centrality given to the wage relation. When the ownership and control of the means of production is concentrated in a few hands, the majority can provide for their material subsistence only through selling their labour. But the perception of the centrality of the wage relation has been accompanied by an ideological construction of the division of labour which domesticates women. The movement of production outside the home is assumed to exclude women from participating in production as wage earners and to restrict their roles to the care of the family as wives and mothers. By the mid-twentieth century Parson's analysis of the kinship system of industrial societies elevated the analytical division between home and production to a high level of abstraction, and his perception of the isolated character of the nuclear family influenced several generations of observers and analysts of work and the family (Parsons, 1943).

There are a number of problems in the assumption that industrialisation separates work and the household, even apart from what it posits about the sexual division of labour. Long before industrialisation, much work in Britain was in fact carried on outside the household, in mining and ship-building for instance, and in agriculture many workers were already employed as waged day labourers. Other work continued to be located within the household until well into the twentieth century, including the employment of many agricultural as well as domestic servants. Such workers were remunerated by an annual payment which included bed and board in the employer's household. It was not a straightforward wage relation, and was deeply enmeshed in household relations. The analytical separation of home and work is so pervasive that most people forget how extensive these forms of employment were, and how recently they persisted.

Examples like these pale into insignificance, however, when we consider how theories about industrialisation have distorted women's paid labour, inside and outside the home. The majority of women were rarely either exclusively housewives/mothers or paid workers, but combined both kinds of work. Waged labour and household work were not alternatives for working-class women. How they were divided among female relatives in part depended on their numbers and ages and in part on the character of the local labour market. Married women in the textile industries, for instance, worked full-time, leaving their daughters to knead the bread which they baked on returning home. Giving birth to children between shifts was not uncommon.

The social and economic theories which assume a neat division between home and work make no place for this kind of pattern. In these theories the relationship between the spheres of work and home was through men who earned wages to support the family. This is also the presumption built into the family wage ideology, which assumed that men earned, or needed to earn, a wage sufficient to support their economically dependent wives and children (Barrett, 1980; Land, 1980). Those who were not employed outside the home were assumed to be non-workers outside the system of production.

The construction of separate spheres of work and home in the analysis of nineteenth-century and twentieth-century industrialism has also distorted the character of social relationships within them. The family as a locus of affective ties is contrasted with the alienation experienced in the public sphere of 'work'. One of the outcomes has been a failure to acknowledge the material relationships which both bind and divide family members, and the inequalities of power which exist within households. A completely separate set of categories and concepts has evolved with which to analyse social relationships in the two spheres.

Translated into the everyday world these conceptions are pervasive, enmeshing all family members, particularly as regards work performed within the home. Homework is not only devalued by others but women themselves see this waged work as 'not a real job' or see themselves as doing it 'for the sake of the children'. This construction of homework, which implies that women can choose between caring for the old, sick, handicapped and young children and engaging in waged work, ignores the actual character of the relation between them. As Young argues, women's labour is 'devalued both because of their "real" role and because this role itself places constraints on the type of work they can undertake' (Young, 1978).

Assumptions about the relationship of women to work and the character of intra-household relations have been extensively criticised by feminist researchers, but their work has not been fully taken on board by other sociologists and economists. One still frequently encounters phrases like 'the work of women increased by *x* per cent between 1951 and 1971' or 'mothers of young children do not work'. Yet as Cynthia Daniels (1985) has remarked, three generations of women in her own family had worked, and she thought that they were not exceptions, despite the theories of social scientists.

However, it has to be said that the vocabulary adopted by many feminist scholars to aid understanding of women's work has not given much scope for improving our understanding of homeworking or documenting its extent. Feminists define unpaid domestic labour in the home as work, and have given considerable attention to documenting women's participation in waged labour. But many feminists continue to distinguish home and production as separate spheres, using phrases like 'waged work' and 'work outside the home' interchangeably. To conceptualise work which women do inside the home they have used the term 'reproduction', which refers in part to women's unpaid domestic work. This formulation has considerable merits, as it makes it possible to link the family and production not simply through the earnings of waged workers, but also through the dependence of production on the women's unwaged domestic labour in reproducing the labour force. But it is a formulation which leaves little room for analysing forms of production which are located in the home, like homework, and tends rather to conflate them with unpaid domestic labour.

It is only by analysing the variety of labour relationships and household forms that an adequate understanding and explanation of the persistence and possible increase in homeworking is possible. The large-scale social, economic and political changes brought about by capitalism cannot be assumed to have had a uniform impact on the relations between men and women or their relation to waged labour. This is clear from several research developments which, while taking place at about the same time, have drawn on different theoretical traditions and have been concerned with different bodies of empirical data. Students of family history, for instance, have cautioned against accepting a necessary relation between modes of production and particular family forms. They have argued that the assumption that the private, kin-based, nuclear family with a male breadwinner is a necessary concomittant of capitalist development is open to both theoretical and empirical question. Although this familial ideology has an impressive dominance, the practices of everyday life in the majority of working-class households did not and could not conform to it (Poster, 1978). Other initiatives which can illuminate the analysis of homeworking are to be found in the work of social historians, in attempts to theorise Third World economies, and in research on informal work in the context of the restructuring of advanced industrial economies. It is impossible to consider all of them in any detail, or to do justice to the variety of theoretical positions adopted in them. But while it has to be said that in these areas sometimes too little attention is given to the relevance of the sexual division of labour, we need to take account of their research on household production and their insights into the variety of ways it is related to the wider economy.

The integration of homeworking in social production

Bridging the conventional analytical division of home and work so as to account for homeworking and to make it visible is only part of the problem. Equally important is the need to challenge the tendency to marginalise homeworking as a form of economic activity, not simply through assumptions about its extent, but also through presuppositions about the nature of the work and the character of suppliers and the work-force. Only in this way is it possible to grasp the wider theoretical implications of homeworking as a form of production under capitalism.

Historical continuities

Comprehending the role of homeworking within social production as a whole is somewhat easier for the nineteenth century, when one can turn to the analyses of both contemporary observers and historians of the period. While for much of the twentieth century homework appears to have been women's work, in the nineteenth century it was widely recognised as extensive and as involving both men and women and their children as workers.

Perhaps for this reason those writing of the period gave much more attention to the connections between homeworking and the wider economy than is usual nowadays. In discussing the putting-out system of developing capitalism, Karl Marx analysed the 'so-called' domestic workers in the clothing industry as 'an external department of the manufacturers, warehouses and even of the workshops of the smaller masters' (Marx, 1958, p. 471), and saw them as tied to factory production through 'invisible threads':

Besides the factory operatives, the manufacturing workmen and the handicraftsmen, whom it concentrates in large masses at one spot, and directly commands, capital also sets in motion, by means of invisible threads, another army; that of the workers in domestic industries, who dwell in large towns and are scattered over the face of the country. (Marx, 1958, pp. 461–2)

Historians in our own day have also highlighted the part played by homeworking in nineteenth-century production. Stedman Jones, for instance, describes not only the continuation of homeworking in London, but its rapid extension in the late nineteenth century through the advent of a mass market for consumption goods, technological changes such as the sewing machine, and the competitive pressures underlying sweated outwork and homework. He argues that the 'vertical disintegration' of production was possible because of 'a cheap, over-filled, unskilled labour pool of women and immigrants who were prepared to work at sub-subsistence wages' (Stedman Jones, 1976, p. 22).

Bythell's study of homeworking in the eighteenth and nineteenth centuries distinguishes it from petty commodity production by artisans. He describes it as integral to capitalist production, involving a minute sub-division of processes to achieve mass production through labour-intensive methods. He argues that the work was on the whole simple, repetitive and needed little training. Middlemen tapped supplies of suitable labour first in rural localities and later in urban areas. He comments that as there were few institutional or legal obstacles to prevent it, sweated outwork was a common form of production relations. But his carefully researched account of the nineteenth-century homeworker as 'insecure, exploited, undefended, often unnoticed' concludes, much as Marx did, that as it became increasingly dominated by factory production the capitalist system of production would witness the demise of the domestic system (Bythell, 1978).

That this is not the case is evident both in studies of present-day Britain, other industrialised societies and Third World economies. Very often, however, these studies have concentrated simply on describing the low pay and poor working conditions in homeworking. While this is a perfectly understandable approach from those seeking legislative reform, it is far from adequate for explanations of the continued existence of homework and the conditions associated with it. To understand the place of homeworking in the modern economy one needs to focus on those who supply the work and their relations with other enterprises.

The usual picture of the supplier as typically a small businessman or market trader struggling in a highly competitive market is not only a very partial one but one that marginalises homeworking. Much homework is in fact the result of sub-contracting, and local agents are only the last in a chain of relationships through which labour-intensive processes or specialist skilled work are devolved out of large firms into the home. Whether or not this arrangement enables 'the ambitious small man to get a first foothold in the lower rungs of the entrepreneurial ladder' is a matter of some debate (Bythell, 1978, p. 112). For the nineteenth century, Bythell argues that this claim remains unproven. So far as some contemporary homework is concerned, however, possibilities for entrepreneurial initiatives have been perceived. Anwar, for instance, describes the stages of the process among Pakistanis in and around the Manchester and Rochdale areas in relation to clothing manufacture (Anwar, 1979, pp. 130–5). He emphasises their access to cheap, encapsulated labour, direct selling on local markets and to the wholesale businesses where the profit, retained at all stages, can be used for expansion. He stresses the resources not only of kinship but of village networks, and draws a comparison with Jewish migrants to the areas in the late nineteenth and early twentieth centuries. However, several queries are to be noted here. First, there is no record of the proportion of those using homework labour, who, however ambitious they might be, remain petty traders or factory employees and fail to move through the various stages to become economically successful businessmen. Secondly, the part played by injections of capital, in the form of credit, by existing large business or financial institutions cannot be ignored. The relative importance of homeworking in the building of capitalist enterprise remains a question (see also Bythell, 1978, pp. 250–1).

A further point needs to be made in response to the ease with which homeworking, both in terms of the workers and suppliers, has been equated with minority populations. This can be found in discussions of homeworking earlier in this century as well as in contemporary Britain and the United States. This is discussed more fully in Chapter 3. Here it is sufficient to indicate that homeworking is much too widespread to be explained in terms of the ethnicity of the workers or suppliers. Whether or not it is found disproportion-ately in Britain among, for instance, Muslim women (a view frequently expressed) is an open question. Even if homework were found to be disproportionately a job done by minority women, the explanation is more complex than colour or 'ethnicity' or the cultural values supposedly associated with them. Jayaben Desai was reported to have become a homeworker after the end of the dispute at Grunwick, in order 'to keep body and soul together'. And Anwar Ditta, who sustained a long struggle for the admission of her children to Britain, was also a homeworker. The racism faced by black or immigrant women in the labour market is a factor too often ignored by those who rely on cultural or ethnic explanations of homeworking.

As far as suppliers, particularly middlemen or agents, are concerned, the facts about their ethnicity remain unknown in any systematic way. Innumerable examples of Asian or Cypriot suppliers, for instance, can be found, as earlier this century Jewish suppliers were frequently cited. It is very unlikely that any of these are (or were) a majority of those supplying homework. In our research in West Yorkshire this was certainly not the case. Even in London there is no hard evidence to support the view that ethnic minority suppliers play a disproportionate role. Since the supply of homeworking is so under-researched, it is not possible to assess with any certainty the extent to which suppliers from minority groups are involved compared with those from the majority population. What is clear, however, is that – as with homeworkers – suppliers are *believed* to be migrants. This is a comfortable and easy way of marginalising homework production and displacing the responsibil-ity for its existence, low pay and poor conditions on to minority groups.

The categories of industrial sociology

The literature of industrial sociology and applied economics may be useful as a way of understanding homework. Such concerns as the control of labour and output, the determination of wages and costs of producton, orientations to work and worker behaviour, labour market theories of recruitment, segmentation, segregation and mobility, institutional developments of work organisation and resistance, legal restraint and employer/managerial strategies are a few of the areas material to understanding why homeworking persists and how it is structured. Unfortunately, few if any of these are ordinarily applied to homeworking, except negatively, in order to exclude it. This is not altogether surprising, since even such commonplace notions as working time or the working day are usually conceptualised so that they are inappropriate for analysing many forms of labour organisation. Consequently, in order to provide a useful framework for analysing homework some of the basic concepts in this literature need to be substantially revised and elaborated. This is, in any case, a necessary development if any kind of women's work is to be adequately dealt with in this literature (Dex, 1985).

In general there has been little attempt to understand work outside circumscribed milieu. For instance, whether or not the ways in which work in factory or office is measured are adequate for measuring work outside them has not been investigated by social scientists. Since work came to be measured in terms of the twelve or ten or eight hours spent in factory or office, the working day has been assumed to be finite, with a single time of beginning and a conclusive finish (E. P. Thompson, 1967). But this assumption of a finite working day leads to many kinds of distortions about homework production and indeed about women's work generally, which does not conform to this kind of measurement. Though important for some work locations, the assumption of a finite working day also hides or distorts the analysis of many work patterns which though different are as constrained as one full-time job outside the home. Only when this assumption is challenged is it possible to begin to see not a 'housewife' fitting in a job on the side, but how unpaid labour is combined with externally controlled homework in terms of the extension of the working day. This challenge also enables a recognition of patterns of multiple jobs, including the combination of full-time work with a second job, two or more part-time jobs, or a part-time job, homeworking and child-minding. All or any of these may, particularly for women, be associated with the constraints imposed by the unpaid labour of social reproduction.

Another example of the inadequacy of the existing models drawn from industrial sociology and labour economics to deal with homeworking is with regard to the understanding of pay levels. Especially in economics wage differentials, including those between men and women, are attributed to differences in productivity, which are in turn perceived to derive from differences in human capital, such as education and training and length of work experience (see Dex, 1985, for an extensive critique). These are a poor basis for understanding the widespread differences between men's and women's wages, or between homeworkers' and other workers',or among homeworkers themselves.

From our data it appears that wage levels were not usually related, as one might expect, to levels of skill or type of supplier or product, although there is some indication that certain kinds of 'new' homeworking command better rates. Where there are inworkers doing comparable work or ex-employee homeworkers carrying out the same or similar work ar home, relative standards can be established, but for much homeworking this is not possible. The difficulty of establishing comparable rates is readily exploited by the supplier. There is fragmentary evidence of suppliers using their local knowledge of the homeworkers' circumstances to push down rates, with the consequence that those most in need of the income are paid the least, but how widespread this practice is remains unknown.

The low pay associated with homework obviously reflects the general wage differentials between men and women, which can be traced to, among other factors, discrimination, the conventional definitions of skill and training which are thought to justify it and to the existence of segregated labour markets. More particularly, the casualised relation between the supplier of work and the homeworker allows the supplier to use homework over long periods whenever necessary without incurring fixed wage costs which increase over time, through (for instance) employee seniority or improved skill levels. In homeworking, therefore, factors like experience, training and skill, which human capital theorists see as determining wage differentials, play almost no part.

Beyond raising such questions, however, knowledge of the rate of pay and the differentials in homeworking is still at a descriptive level and will remain so until much more is known about employers' use of homework, whether directly or through sub-contracting. Indeed it has to be said that the implications of casualised relations of this kind for theories in industrial economics and sociology are only beginning to be taken on board. Homework, which is for the most part legally and ideologically defined as self-employment, is one of several forms of economic activity which do not exhibit many of the features associated with the conventional employer–employee relationship usually investigated by economists and sociologists. Others – in industrial societies – include seasonal workers, as well as some who are described as self-employed or sub-contract labour. In Chapter 7 we discuss the debates surrounding the alleged increase in forms of casualisation in the context of economic recession.

Homework as commodity production

The forms through which domestic production is incorporated as economic activity vary. Homeworking is a form of commodity production. It is distinguished from other forms of production located in the home by the waged character of the relation between homeworker and the supplier of work.

Both the attention given to forms of irregular and informal economic activity in industrial societies over the last decade and studies of Third World economies have addressed issues which are relevant to our understanding of homework. Studies of Third World economies and the regional 'peripheries' of some industrialised economies have, for instance, given rise to theories about many forms of working patterns and relationships which are directly situated within the capitalist mode of production or subordinated to it through relations of unequal exchange. All of these reject theories which conceive of such economies as composed of a traditional backward sector and an advanced industrial sector, or as characterised by a formal-informal dualism. (See, for instance, Bromley and Gerry, 1979; Moser, 1978; Portes and Walton, 1981.) There is no simple relation between modes of capitalist penetration in subsistence economies, nor is the use of non-capitalist forms homogeneous. Nevertheless it is apparent that one form of capitalist penetration results in homeworking which is remarkably similar to that found in the West (Baud, 1983, 1985; Rao and Husain, 1983; Watanabe, 1972). This is waged employment carried out at home for export or domestic industries. The homeworker, almost invariably a woman, does not sell the product but is paid at piece-rates by a supplier, working to a design determined by him with materials he supplies.

When goods produced in the home are marketed through commercial export agencies for consumption in the West, traditional skills are employed and transformed. The skills of those who produce pottery, clothes, jewellery, enamelware, and cane and leather goods are no longer devoted to production for use in local communities or for sale by the artisan producers themselves. They become instead objectified in commodity production. The sense of loss and alienation the worker experiences in this process are well expressed in Harriet Arnow's novel *The Dollmaker*, which traces the degradation of a poor white woman's skills within the relations of patriarchy and capitalism in the United States of the 1940s (Arnow, 1972). The skills, for instance, of quilt-makers in the Upper South of the USA, glove-knitters in Vermont and Tromso in Norway, jewellery-makers in India, or potters and cane-workers in Bangladesh have become incorporated into the production, at low piece-work rates, of commodities which are then sold at high prices in national and international markets.

In other cases, traditional skills are not involved and homeworkers are employed by the industrial sector to manufacture clothing and shoes as well as components for new technology industries (Roldán, 1985). Studies of the Third World and the peripheries of the advanced industrial world show how women's work is largely construed as invisible, while at the same time it is being incorporated by capital, directly and indirectly, in a complexity of production relations.

Homeworking (or more precisely the putting-out system) was investigated by historians in the 1970s and 1980s in order to assess both its historical role in capital accumulation and industrial expansion in western Europe and its relevance to economic development in the Third World (Bythell, 1978; Head, 1961; Mendels, 1972; Tilley and Tilley, 1971). There was little agreement on its historical role. In some interpretations domestic production is seen as a significant factor in providing employment, increasing productivity and creating an adaptable, disciplined labour force as well as in accumulating entrepreneurial capital, while in others evidence that it delayed or obstructed industrial development is emphasised.

The question of whether homeworkers can provide the basis for an expansion of entrepreneurial activity was mentioned above. The role of homeworking in Third World development, as far as indigenous capital accumulation is concerned, is even more complex, as it has to be viewed in relation to the role played by international capital. International capital may employ homeworking labour through direct investment or through indigenous entrepreneurs, but in either case where the surplus is exported there will be no local accumulation. Even where only indigenous capital is involved, the pattern of re-investment in the range of industries and different-sized enterprises using homeworking labour cannot be assumed but requires further investigation. From the evidence available on the conditions of Third World homeworkers their situation can be described in the same terms Bythell used to assess nineteenth-century outwork in England.

> Outwork, . . . was one of the least acceptable of many disagreeable aspects of private capitalism [in which] 'labour' was a mere factor of production . . . to be acquired in the cheapest market without any regard for its human dimension [and] where [there was] little 'honest' independence, no communal exchange and hardly any job satisfaction in most of the homework carried on at the behest of capitalists . . . instead there is only hard work, insecurity, and low paid drudgery in circumstances which contributed nothing to domestic comfort or personal happiness. (Bythell, 1978, p. 253)

Theorisation of the role of household production in advanced capitalist economies only began to be undertaken in the 1970s, when increasing unemployment in the recorded labour force and the decentralising potential of some forms of new technology brought a new (or perhaps re-emerging) focus on forms of economic activity ignored for decades by sociologists and economists (Gershuny, 1979; Gershuny and Pahl, 1979/80; Jenkins and Sherman, 1979). These included work which was paid and unpaid, legal and illegal, done at, from, or outside the home. Leaving aside normal domestic labour, they may be summarised as work for household provisioning (for instance, growing, freezing and preserving fruit and vegetables; 'do it yourself', home maintenance and improvements); reciprocal exchanges of goods and services between kin, household and neighbours (baby-sitting, repairs and the exchange of tools, plants and clothing); illegal work (work for cash income undeclared for tax or insurance purposes, work done by children under the permitted legal age, as well as criminal activities); informal work unrecorded by the employer or self-employed individual (for instance, unregistered child-minding, window-cleaning, part-time shop work, and commission selling).

These activities and those involved in them are not easily compartmentalised. In fact the problem of defining the informal sector was recognised in the middle 1970s (Bremen, 1976) and the shifting divisions between paid and unpaid work and the continuity over a long period in forms of self-provisioning among the working class has been commented upon (Allen, 1980, 1983a). Despite the difficulties of conceptualising all these forms of work and a tendency to assume that many of them are new, the break from the restrictive, conventional equation of work with formally recorded employment has produced a new emphasis and understanding by sociologists of, among other things, women's paid and unpaid labour (Bell, 1982; McKee and Bell, 1986; Mingione, 1985; R. E. Pahl, 1984; Pahl and Wallace, 1985). Instead of homeworking being portrayed as a marginal activity, as informal sector work or even confused with unpaid domestic, reproductive labour, it came to be increasingly recognised as part of the capitalist labour process carried out in the main in households with at least one member in full-time employment.

In contrast, the 'discovery' of home-based work in the 1980s is being interpreted in official and some political circles as representing a viable future pattern of work, and as a source of economic regeneration. This view is in serious danger of reviving a crude variation of a very old idea, and by ignoring the institutional framework of advanced capitalism on several counts, portrays an illusion. It does this by ignoring the basic, collectively provided infrastructure which enables the reproduction of labour to take place; and by taking as given technologies which, whatever their merits, create a majority of the population as surplus to economic requirements. It fails to confront this contradiction and the implications of embodying in state policy a political philosophy which – by attempting to de-regulate the production of goods and services in health, housing, education and land use, as well as in manufacturing and food production – brings into question the viability of the productive system itself.

Conclusions

The frameworks within which work is usually analysed tend to marginalise homeworking and perpetuate its invisibility. The sexual division of labour characteristic of industrial capitalism, for instance, has generally been assumed to confine women to the home, thereby excluding them from waged employment. So far as the analysis of homeworking is concerned, the feminist challenge to this assumption has so far been rather partial. Although feminists have emphasised the domestic sphere as a location of women's unpaid labour, the separation of home and waged employment is still generally taken for granted. This is scarcely surprising, for some of the basic concepts used in industrial sociology and applied economics rely upon just such a distinction. But it would seem that one conclusion of the discussion so far is that a consideration of homeworking is useful in elaborating a feminist critique of these models and in developing alternatives.

As we have tried to show in this chapter, looking at homeworking makes it apparent that in some respects the line separating home and waged work is an artificial one. This has so far been appreciated mainly by some of those researchers concerned with work in the Third World, where work at home – waged and unwaged – is, though unrecorded, now generally recognised as comprising an important sector of the economy. However, this does not mean that all work done at home should be analysed as a single category. Homeworking must be examined as waged labour incorporated into capitalist relations of production. This means challenging the many ways in which homework is disguised by its superficial similarity to other forms of work done at home. It is separate from the various kinds of work such as 'normal' domestic labour, self-provisioning or production for barter which are outside the constraints of the market. Nor should it be confused with petty commodity production by artisans, who sell their own products, or with the work of those, like musicians or scriptwriters, who produce work for clients, or with the work of consultants, who charge a fee for their services. The relations between homeworker and supplier differentiate homework from all these other forms of work.

Homeworking is a form of casualised employment but is nevertheless *waged* employment. Empirical investigation of homework should therefore be set within this context. Rather than assuming that homeworkers differ from other workers, we need to view them in relation to participation in the labour market more generally. As we document in this book, if homeworkers are compared with those doing similar jobs outside the home there do not appear to be any marked differences. Similarly, we need to ask whether the firms which supply homework differ substantially from firms which employ in-workers. Here again we have demonstrated that the suppliers of homework are to be found in most industrial sectors and range from small to very large national and international firms. In other words, rather than isolating homework as a subject of investigation, thereby replicating assumptions about its marginality or uniqueness, we have tried to produce an analysis which locates homeworking as an integral part of the wider economy.

2

The incidence and range of homeworking

How many people do homework, what kind of work they do and whether it is increasing are the first questions people ask about homeworking in Britain. They also want to know who supplies homework, and how many suppliers there are. None of these questions have a simple answer, for each gives rise to yet another: how would we know? Comparatively little is known about these aspects of homeworking in quantitative terms, and this makes it all the more necessary to examine how existing estimates of the extent of homeworking have been calculated. Otherwise there is, in our experience, a marked tendency to assume certain kinds of answers to these questions, and to rely on them in making arguments about the scale and nature of homeworking in Britain.

In this chapter we take up these and related questions. The number of homeworkers is a matter of some debate, and we consider the widely varying estimates which have been made and views on its growth or decline. We then turn to information on the types of suppliers, and to those estimates which have been made of their numbers. Finally, we look at the range of work in which homeworking features. While no discussion of this can be exhaustive, since more examples come to light constantly, we present as comprehensive a view as possible, and assess the usefulness of categorising some kinds of homework as new and others as traditional.

Why, it may be asked, is homework so hidden as a form of production that comprehending its scope and extent is such a complicated business? As one union official stated about his own industry. 'We have no idea of the degree of homework, let alone who is participating in it' (House of Commons Select Committee on Employment, 1981b, 14 April, para. 236). Part of the answer lies in the fact that in Britain, as in many other societies, homework is inadequately recorded in official indices of economic activity, both in terms of the number of firms supplying homework and the number of workers carrying it out. In the Introduction to this book we pointed out that it has been characterised both as marginal to productive activity *and* as playing a novel and increasingly important part in changing patterns of work. As long as so little is known about the real incidence of homeworking, images like these will be difficult to challenge and will continue to appear in diverse guises. This chapter is therefore necessarily largely descriptive in presenting what is known about the extent and range of homeworking from official and other sources. But it attempts to go beyond this to consider how distorted constructions of homeworking are related to, and arise out of, inadequacies in the way homework is measured by official statistics.

In the early 1980s, in an attempt to fill the gaps left by official statistics, a variety of estimates of the number of homeworkers were made. The latest appeared in 1984 and 1985, based on data collected in 1980 and 1981 (Hakim, 1984a, 1984b, 1985). Before they can be considered, however, it is necessary to make some observations about the production and use of official statistics in relation to the labour force and those who employ homeworkers. For the invisibility of homework and homeworkers arises in part from the purposes for which data on economic activity are sought by official agencies, the methods used for collecting and analysing them, and the forms in which they are published. Unfortunately these issues, which are important in considering the adequacy of numerical estimates of homeworking and of official constructions of it, have not been taken on board in even the more recent studies.

Official sources

Social scientists who use official statistics of any kind have to evaluate them not only in terms of the techniques used, but in relation to their adequacy as basic information which can further the understanding and explanation of forms of economic and social organisation and patterns of change. For, as Hindess has argued, official statistics 'are rarely collected with the interests of science as their primary concern' (Hindess, 1973, p. 47). A statement in 1981 that information should be collected 'primarily because government needs it for its own busines' (Government Statistical Services, 1981, p. 15) makes this point explicitly. The poverty of statistical information on homeworking production illustrates the extent to which governments have not seen the need for such data, and confirms the argument that in general 'the range of [official] statistics available is such as to give a picture of society in which some features are remarkably out of focus' (Miles and Irvine, 1979, p. 126).

Although the scope and volume of official statistical information has expanded rapidly in the two decades after 1960, virtually no headway was made in the area of homeworking. The reasons for this become very clear when one looks at the regular ways of collecting statistics on the size and composition of the labour force in relation to homeworking. The Annual Census of Employment, for instance, was begun in 1971 in order to provide data on a more frequent basis than the decennial Census of Population. It is based on information provided by employers. However, only firms employing in-workers are included, and they are required to supply information only on employees in one specified week and only on those who pay income tax. It therefore provides no information on those suppliers of homework who do not have inside employees, nor on those who supply work on an irregular or seasonal basis. Similarly, homeworkers employed by these firms and those whose work is irregular are excluded, as are those who earn too little to pay tax. Consequently, many, and possibly most, suppliers and homeworkers are unlikely to feature in the Annual Census returns.

Because the decennial Census of Population collects data on the entire population, it should be more comprehensive as far as the number of homeworkers is concerned. However, it raises several rather different problems. The Census collects information from households, but although compulsory for household heads, it is a self-completed questionnaire, with all the problems attendant on this method. For instance, the perceptions of those who must complete the census form for themselves and on behalf of other members or visitors in the household are crucial for any questions which allow, or require, the exercise of discretion in answering them. This applies to the questions on jobs and work. There is considerable evidence to suggest that homework is not seen as a job, or even as work, either by men (who in the majority of cases complete the form) or by women, who may or may not influence the returns made. In addition, there is, for a variety of reasons, a reluctance to admit that homework is being carried out. Moreover, the wording of the questions on jobs in most recent censuses does not enable homework to be recorded with any accuracy. Where only the main job is asked for, all those who do homework as a second job are excluded (Townsend, 1979; Pugh, 1984). Other problems arise because census returns do not make it possible to distinguish between the different categories of those working at home. They may record themselves and others in such a way that the self-employed, labour-only workers, those running small businesses, and freelance workers are not clearly differentiated. These are important differences and are discussed in more detail below. A further problem is that, like the Annual Census on Employment, information is required only on a specified period. On these counts, the population census provides no more than a very rough and possibly very misleading record of the size of the homeworking labour force. Most of these defects and omissions apply in the 10 per cent *Longitudinal Survey* sample which provides a more elaborate data base.

Other official calculations which are used to provide statistical information on the economically active population are similarly unable to provide information on homework. Those based on the insured population or the filling of vacancies through official agencies omit, by their very nature, all but a very small minority of homeworkers. The *Labour Force Survey* and the *General Household Survey*, which aim to provide data on employment and unemployment, have been subjected to some of the same criticisms as those applied to the Census. In addition, as Allin and Thomas argue, the Census, the *Labour Force Survey* and the *General Household Survey* have limited validity because they focus 'on the interaction between the individual and the organisation and they focus on what may be important for organisations . . . not on what is important for individual respondents' (Allin and Thomas, 1984, p. 5). Valid and reliable statistics, they maintain, can be produced by such surveys only where the subject matter is not of crucial importance for the respondent. This indicates that national estimates of the homework labour force based on these surveys should be treated with considerable circumspection.

It was against a background of mounting criticism of official statistics for their use of categories, definitions and classifications based on men's working lives, and therefore generally inappropriate or irrelevant to women's participation in the labour force and their experience of paid work (Oakley and Oakley, 1979) that attempts have been made to collect more adequate data on women's employment and paid work (Martin and Roberts, 1984). In addition, the realisation that the number of homeworkers was likely to be underestimated in, if not altogether absent from, national statistics – a criticism voiced with increasing frequency from the 1970s – led to efforts to provide more comprehensive and reliable data on them. Thus although there have been changes in and cutting back on data collection during the 1980s which have had adverse effects on the knowledge base in several areas (unemployment for instance), this has not been entirely the case with homeworking. In 1979 the Department of Employment initiated a programme of research on homeworking which included two attempts to provide estimates of its extent. The 1981 Survey of Homeworking provides national estimates of the homeworking labour force, based on supplementary interviews with a sample of those respondents in the 1981 *Labour Force Survey* who said that they were working at or from home. Secondly, data drawn from the 1980 *Workplace Industrial Survey* have been used to estimate the use of homeworking by firms, by including questions on the use of outworkers and homeworkers and other forms of contract labour in interviews with management representatives (Hakim, 1984a, 1984b, 1985). But as is shown below, these estimates are biased by various of the same inadequacies in relation to homeworking as the regularly collected information.

National estimates of the number of homeworkers

Table 2.1 summarises the available national estimates of the numbers of homeworkers and their division between manufacturing and service sectors (Hakim, 1984a; Pugh, 1984, Townsend, 1979). It also includes figures for home-based workers and freelance workers. The geographical coverage varies, and is indicated in each case. Where possible, the employment status is given. The earlier national estimates made by Townsend in his research on

Table 2.1 *Estimates of number of homeworkers*

	Women	Men	All
I. Townsend, 1968/9 – United Kingdom			
Working at home as employees:	280 000	150 000	430 000
– manual	—	—	(150 000)
– white collar/services	—	—	(300 000)
Working at home, self-employed:	330 000	390 000	720 000
Total	610 000	540 000	1 150 000
II. Census of Population			
Home-based Work:			
– 1971	342 320	476 700	819 020
– 1981	335 510	441 660	777 170
Total self-employed:			
– 1971			< 2 000 000
– 1981			> 2 000 000
III. Homeworking Survey 1981, England and Wales:			
Total home-based workers	294 590	363 660	628 250
– of whom working *at* home	177 860	73 190	251 050
– of whom in manufacturing homework	60 270	12 000	72 270
IV. Workplace Industrial Relations Survey 1980 – Great Britain (all establishments with 25 or more employees)			
Outworkers and homeworkers:			111 000
– of whom in manufacturing			52 000
– of whom in service sector			61 000
Freelance workers:			281 000
– of whom in manufacturing			91 000
– of whom in service sector			187 000

Note: As these are rounded estimates totals do not always tally.

poverty in the United Kingdom are presented because they were for many years the only estimates available and have been so frequently quoted. Their inclusion is not to be taken as an indication that they are being categorised as official statistics.

In both the official surveys (1980 and 1981) estimates are dependent upon the scope of the original investigations. From the point of view of estimating the numbers of homeworkers, there were several inadequacies, and it is necessary to bear these in mind if the estimates are used to support general statements about, for instance, the decline in homeworkers in manufacturing industry or the low proportion of women homeworkers involved in manufacturing compared with those in white-collar and service work. As national estimates they are the most comprehensive available, but as each is based on samples drawn for other purposes and on answers to questions put by interviewers working in an official capacity, the reliability of the coverage of homeworkers gives rise to some doubts. The WIRS survey included only those firms with 25 or more employees and so excluded any homeworkers working for those with less than 25 employees. In fact, some firms with a majority of outworkers but fewer than 25 in-workers refused to complete the questionnaire on the grounds that they were excluded by its terms of reference. The use of homeworkers by smaller firms and through a variety of sub-contracting arrangements indicated in various studies (see below, Chapter 4), suggest that Hakim's (1984b) 'guestimate' of double the number of homeworkers revealed by the 1980 survey probably underestimates the true figure considerably. In the Wages Council Industries, for instance, the direct employment of homeworkers is reported to be usually related to the size of the firms (Rubery and Wilkinson, 1980). Moreover, although the WIRS survey obtained some information from both management and worker representatives, information on the use of homeworkers, including the numbers employed, was obtained only from management representatives. As one in ten of the managers interviewed was unable to say how many homeworkers were used in any one month, and a quarter were unable to give the month of the lowest use, the quality of the estimates has to be judged in the context not only of incomplete and skewed coverage, but also of management's ignorance of or reluctance to admit to the number of the homeworkers who were supplied with work, whether they were self-employed or employees.

The 1981 Survey of Homeworking raises problems of a different kind. Rather less information has been given publicly about the collection of these data. But as the sample was drawn from among those who said that they were working at or from home, the reluctance of many working at home to recognise their paid work as a job, or to admit to official enquirers that they are doing paid work, needs to be taken into account. This is thought by some commentators to affect in particular the likely responses of those drawing supplementary or unemployment benefit, those whose legal status as residents may be in doubt, or those who fear it is illegal to do paid work with industrial machines in their council homes. If this is the case, the estimates of manufacturing homework may be dispropor-tionately affected by such factors.

National estimates of the number of suppliers

Estimates of the number of suppliers of homework are given in Table 2.2. As will be readily observed, these are more limited even than the data available on homeworkers. But because the WIRS survey estimates the numbers of suppliers, as well as the numbers of workers they supply, and is based on a sample of just over 2000 firms, it provides the most comprehensive coverage in geographical and industrial terms for many years. Manufacturing and service establishments are included, and it is argued that the exclusion of agriculture, fishing, forestry and coalmining (together with any establishment employing exclusively Armed Forces personnel) is not important because there is very little outwork in these industries (Hakim, 1985). This may be so, but agriculture and fishing have given rise directly to homeworking in the past and the provision of uniforms to the armed forces has been an indirect (sub-contracted) form of homework.

As pointed out above, however, the WIRS survey covers only establishments with 25 or more employees, while most homework suppliers are thought to have well below this number of employees. Among its other drawbacks were the time of year when it was carried out, which was recognised as a period in which the use of homeworkers is relatively low, and the problems arising from the lack of systematic distinctions between homeworkers/outworkers and freelance workers. None of these categories was defined in the questionnaire, and there is no way of knowing whether manage-ment representatives included both employees and self-employed categories in their returns. This leads to the possible exclusion of some homeworkers and in the case of freelance workers supplied by more than one firm, double counting. There is also the possibility that firms using middlemen or sub-contractors would not have recorded themselves as suppliers of homework and made no report of the numbers of homeworkers they used.

Table 2.2, which lists estimates of the number of suppliers, also lists previous official estimates based on industries covered under

Table 2.2 Estimates of suppliers of homework

| Industries surveyed/source | Number of firms in survey sample or sub sample | Number supplying homework | | | As (%) of total surveyed |
		Manufacturing Sector	Service Sector	Total	
Wages Councils: Clothing manufacture and retail (CIR, 1974)	120	39	—	39	30.00
Wages Councils: Button manufacture (ACAS, 1978a)	79	33	—	33	42.00
Wages Councils: Toy manufacture (ACAS, 1978b)	153	87	—	87	57.00
Ex-Wages Councils: Cutlery (Craig et al., 1980)	42	33	—	33	75.00
National estimate: Workplace Industrial Survey 1980 (Hakim, 1984a)	2040	102[a] (36)[c] 236[b] (24)[c]	58[a] 283[b]	160[a] 519[b]	7.80[a] 25.00[b]

[a] outwork and homework
[b] freelance
[c] clothing and textile

the Wages Council Act 1959 and the Factories Act 1961 (ACAS, 1978a, 1978b; Commission on Industrial Relations, 1974; Craig *et al.*, 1980; Hakim and Dennis, 1982; Rubery and Wilkinson, 1981). These estimates need to be judged in the context of the purposes of Wage Councils and the adequacy of their coverage of home-workers, and are discussed below.

Wages councils and other official records

In Britain, unlike the United States, legislation has sought to regulate homeworking rather than outlaw it. It has always been argued by lawyers, employers and others that apart from the problem of administering a law to abolish it, such a move would be arbitrary and oppressive. Instead, homeworkers were included in legislation covering sweated trades as a whole.

The legislative reforms in the late nineteenth and early twentieth centuries which arose in part from the widespread concern about conditions and pay in factories, workshops and among home-workers, attempted to deal with several aspects of the problem of sweated labour, including rates of pay, hours of work and insanitary conditions. One of the arguments for including homeworkers in legislation was that 'every improvement in the Factory Law or its administration tends to drive work out of the Factory into the home' (Hutchins, 1907, p. 5). This was not the only argument. It was, in part, the very low pay and appalling conditions of homeworkers themselves that spurred on the establishment of the first Trade Boards as a result of 'public agitation out of moral indignation' (Wootton, 1955, p. 100).

One of the objectives of the Trades Boards Act 1909 was to provide a 'living wage' for all workers not by establishing a national minimum wage enforceable by law, but by setting up Boards for industries in which 'sweated' labour was particularly dominant. Trades Boards which had existed for over a decade in the State of Victoria in Australia were taken as a model. Representatives of employers and trade unions, together with three independent members nominated by a government minister, composed each Board. The Board set a legally enforceable minimum wage in trades where prevailing rates were exceptionally low and the possibility of collective bargaining poor. The encouragement of collective bar-gaining was reinforced in 1918, when additional legislation permitted the establishment of new Boards in other industries where there was no adequate machinery for regulating wages.

In 1945 the Trades Boards became Wages Councils, and the only legal regulation of wages paid to homeworkers is in those industries covered by Wages Councils. But even within these trades their coverage of both in-workers and homeworkers is patchy, and has decreased over time. In 1962 there were some sixty Wages Councils, covering 3½ million workers. By 1983, following the abolition of some and the merger of others, there were twenty-six, covering some 2.7 million workers, of whom 90 per cent are in catering, clothing and retailing (Low Pay Unit, 1983, p. 7). In 1979 the Department of Employment estimated that there were some 29 000 homeworkers in Wages Councils Industries, leaving the vast majority of homeworkers outside their scope (Hakim and Dennis, 1982).

The rules setting out the operation of the Wages Councils and the inspection of the wages in the industries covered by them mean that large numbers of homeworkers never come to their knowledge. Under the Wages Councils Act (1959) the Wages Inspectorate and its regional divisions have the power to demand from employers in these trades the details of payment to both inworkers and outworkers and to investigate whether or not the firms are paying the wages set by the appropriate Wages Councils. The responsibility for building up lists of firms and keeping them up to date rests with the Wages Inspectorate, but as employers in these trades are not obliged to register with local authorities, the Wages Inspectorate relies on the lists of factory premises registered with the Factory Inspectorate under the 1961 Factories Act. There is no guarantee that the Inspectors in an area know of all the firms covered by Wages Orders, especially where there is a rapid turn-over of firms or where there are no in-factory employees (Winyard, 1976).

Under the provisions of the Factories Act 1961 a duty was also placed on a person giving out work in specified trades to send lists of homeworkers to the local authorities at six-monthly intervals, so that local authorities would become aware of possible health or safety hazards. However, these procedures are no longer operating. The Health and Safety Commission noted in 1979 that 'Existing arrangements for the notification of homework . . . are no longer, appropriate and have, in fact, largely fallen into abeyance' (Health and Safety Commission, 1979).

Our own investigation of homeworking in West Yorkshire suggests that a good deal of scepticism about the coverage of homeworkers by the enforcing authorities is justified. When we approached the official agencies in West Yorkshire in the initial stages of our research, we found that they were unable to supply reliable figures either on suppliers or homeworkers. The following replies illustrate the lack of information among those who had the statutory duty to compile it. From Environmental Health Offices it was reported that:

Reminders are no longer sent out, so returns are lower; After nearly six years it is appreciated that the list must be somewhat out of date . . ... Thought is being given to arrangements for up-dating the list of employers; Responsibility for enforcing the provision of the Health and Safety at Work Act 1974 lies with the Health and Safety Executive . . ... Accordingly my staff are not involved in the routine inspection of outworkers premises, except perhaps in the event of unwholesome premises which in practice rarely occurs.

The Factory Inspectorate kept lists of factories giving outwork but did not know what the local authorities did with them and did not inspect 'homes where outwork is carried on'. The Wages Inspectorate dealt only with homeworkers in Wages Council trades and recognised difficulties with enforcement, but still assumed that there was 'no great problem in trades where there is a long tradition of Wages Councils'. Evidence from other areas of the country forcibly underlines the non-implementation of the regulations on record-keeping. The records of local authorities are scanty, if they exist at all. The first local authority to employ a Homeworking Officer, the London Borough of Hackney, had 68 employers registered in August 1981, yet it was estimated that 10 per cent of clothing production alone was carried out by homeworkers. Bath City Council is reported to have registered six to eight homeworkers and the North Wiltshire District Council only nine (Beale, 1978). In Dundee the registration of homeworkers is reported to have completely ceased (Dundee, 1984).

Given the poor coverage of homeworkers by the enforcing authorities, the estimates of the numbers of suppliers in the Wages Councils studies shown in Table 2.2 are undoubtedly underestimates, as are the estimates of the number of homeworkers provided by these and other surveys of homework in Wages Councils industries (see Table 2.3). In the survey of Toy Manufacturing, for instance, ACAS found that the lists of firms were not up-to-date, and since only part of the industry fell within the scope of the Wages Council an unknown number of both suppliers and homeworkers were excluded. Of the 421 firms within the Wages Council sector, only 153 replied to the postal questionnaire (ACAS, 1978b). Similarly, in button manufacture, it was reported,

> Much the larger part of the industry is excluded from the scope of the Council mainly because the scale or nature of the processes involved on work other than buttons is such as to identify the firms concerned more properly with other industries, notably the metal small ware industry and the clothing and trimming trades. (ACAS, 1978a, p. 9)

Moreover, those employers who are unaware that homeworkers fall within the scope of the Wages Councils may exclude them when returning figures to the Councils. In one study 22 out of 35 employers interviewed lacked, or claimed to lack, this awareness (CIR, 1974).

The Health and Safety Commission put forward proposals in 1976, and in an amended form in 1979, which would have gone some way towards remedying the lack of records. In accordance with the new regulations it proposed, a person putting out homework would

Table 2.3　*Estimates of the numbers of homeworkers in particular industries*

Source	Number	Industry
NBPI 1968/9	15 000	Clothing manufacture
CIR 1974	19 300	Clothing, manufacture and retail
	(18 500)	(Manufacture)
	(800)	(Retail)
CIR 1973	760	Pin, hook and eye and snap fasteners
ACAS 1978(a)	380	Button manufacturing
ACAS 1978(b)	2 679	Toy manufacturing
	(1748–3385 seasonal variation)	

be required to supply to the enforcing authority, at six-monthly intervals, the address from which homework is provided, the name and address of the person providing it and the name and address of any third party through whom the homeworker is in contact with the provider, the nature of the homework; the number of home-workers supplied during the previous six months and, if required by the enforcing authority in writing, the names and addresses of all or any specified group of homeworkers. Although it was stated in 1979 that 'the Commission intends to submit proposals to the Secretary of State with a view to the making of regulations as soon as possible' (Health and Safety Commission, 1979), further action is still awaited.

The number of suppliers and homeworkers could be more accurately estimated if all those giving out work to be done at home were required to register with the legally designated authority, and realistic fines introduced for those who failed to comply. Evasion of such a law, it is argued, would be widespread. Until serious attempts are made to introduce and implement it there can be no way of testing such a proposition.

In view of the poor coverage of homeworkers by the regulatory agencies, and the inadequacies in official statistics, as discussed above, the estimates from the 1981 Homeworkers Survey and 1980 survey remain the only ones which can claim to be national official figures. But for the reasons already discussed, as well as additional ones considered below, they are far from adequate as a representation of homeworking within the economy.

Non-official estimates

The gap in official records about the incidence of homeworking both nationally and locally is not easily remedied by research lacking the resources, in terms of the personnel, privileged access to official records and the command of statistical and data processing services, available to central or local government departments. The Greater London Council Industry and Employment Unit included questions on the use of homeworking labour in a survey of employment among the top 100 firms which supplied it with goods and services. The results of this survey are not available at the time of writing, but it at least indicates that more information on the extent of homeworking can be acquired when those with authority insist that it be included. Independent researchers do not have the power to require employers to report the number of homeworkers they employ.

Several studies of homeworking have been conducted by independent researchers (groups and individuals) since the early 1970s. These have mainly concentrated on contacting individual homeworkers and recording (through interviews or questionnaires) their pay and conditions, and have provided much valuable data. In fact, it was through such efforts that homeworking emerged on to the political agenda out of the obscurity of several decades (Beale, 1978; Bolton, 1975; Brown, 1974; Crine, 1979a; Evans, 1975; Field, 1976; Hope *et al.*, 1976; Jordan, 1978; Thomas, 1978). Pressures of all kinds from the Low Pay Unit, the Trades Union Congress and a variety of local groups, notably The Leicester Outwork Campaign, resulted in the setting up in 1978 of a Special Homeworking Unit in the Wages Inspectorate to oversee the wages of homeworkers in Wages Councils, but it is not known whether or not it still functions (Ewing, 1982; GLC, 1983). The work of the Unit was to be monitored by a tripartite Homeworking Advisory Committee composed of employers, trade unionists and government officials. This, as far as is known, has not met since 1979. (See Chapter 6 for a fuller discussion.)

What such studies cannot do is compile national representative statistical data on the extent of homeworking, in terms of the size of the labour force, the number of suppliers, or the exact spread throughout different industries. What they can and have done is point to some of the ways in which more reliable statistical data could be collected and analysed by those with the resources and the legal power to do so.

A variety of methods have been used to establish contact with homeworkers and suppliers. For homeworkers these have included appeals through national and local media and advertisements in shops, and on occasions offers of payment for information have been made. Other researchers have relied on personal introductions by public and social services personnel, or community representatives. Some have used a snowball technique, in which one homeworker is asked to introduce others, who in turn provide yet more contacts (Beale, 1978; Brown, 1974; Hope *et al.*, 1976; Shah, 1975). All these methods have helped to reach some homeworkers and to provide information on their conditions of work. But it has been argued that biases of various kinds are inevitably introduced by such methods, which make the findings difficult to assess or compare.

In the West Yorkshire study we rejected both media appeals and payment for information. Having drawn a virtual blank on official sources of information on homeworking we initially used personal introductions. These were successful in obtaining some interviews, and we continued to rely on this method to obtain interviews with Pakistani homeworkers. But we concluded that only a sample based on a door-to-door survey could provide more realistic estimates of the size of the homeworking labour force within specific areas and sufficient interviews to assess the kinds of work being carried out.

In order to reduce the likelihood that homeworking would be denied or interviews refused we did not use anyone holding an official position or coming from outside the West Yorkshire area. For the most part women, with local backgrounds (and local accents), knocked on every door within a specified area. More homeworkers were found than could possibly be interviewed within our resources and little resistance was encountered in the city or small towns in either public or private housing areas. More difficulties arose in a mining village, where men on shift work answered the door more frequently and refused information. In all, 4190 households were surveyed, in 48 per cent of which someone was at home. One hundred and fifteen homeworkers and 177 homework contacts were found by this method, and 71 of them interviewed.

These data indicate a much higher density of homeworking households than that suggested by the National Survey of Homeworking. As regards the city area (Metropolitan District of Bradford) the number of homeworkers found was 1.2 per cent of the total number of households and 2.6 per cent of those where someone was at home at the time of the survey. If these figures are taken as proportionate, then the number of homeworkers can be estimated as between 1.06 and 2.6 per cent of those officially recorded as economically active. The latter figure is almost identical to the 2.8 per cent cited by the National Survey of Homeworking, but that was based on the much broader definition of home-based workers so that its estimate of homeworkers is much less than ours (Hakim, 1984a).

The major difficulty with a door-to-door survey is its cost, but it is arguable that it would be more cost effective in producing the necessary information than the methods adopted in official surveys. Applied systematically on a national sample it would provide information on the size of the homeworking labour force and the work being carried out which has so far proved elusive. It is possibly the only method which would reveal the amount of disguised waged labour being carried out, and it could also be used to elicit and categorise information on the many other forms of work carried out in the home.

Compared with collecting information on the number of homeworkers, obtaining data on the suppliers has presented even more difficulties, as the inadequacies of the 1980 WIRS survey and those on Wages Councils industries show. In the West Yorkshire study a number of methods were used to identify suppliers of homework and the types of work supplied (Allen, 1981a).

We carried out a content analysis of newspaper advertisements in eighteen local newspapers and monitored Job Centre advertisements. Further information was obtained from homeworkers and ex-homeworkers about who supplied their work. In the door-to-door survey in the Bradford area, some twenty-eight firms (nineteen identified by name) were discovered. Interviews were also carried out with agents, middlemen, employees and ex-employees of firms supplying homework and with trade union officials. In all, over eighty-eight firms were identified, over seventy located in the region and twelve outside it (see Table 2.4). This finding in a small-scale study compares very interestingly with the number of firms identified in the WIRS survey (see Table 2.2), which found only double this number in a national sample of over 2000 firms.

It is not possible to estimate how far the number of suppliers we identified falls short of the total in the region. A complete coverage of the area would be likely to reveal numbers far in excess of those we were able to identify. The methods we used indicate the possibilities of uncovering the volume of suppliers of homework more realistically than has so far proved possible in official surveys.

Definition of homework: who is a homeworker?

So far in the discussion of the extent of homeworking we have not considered the different definitions of homework which have been

Table 2.4 *Suppliers of homework, 1980[a]*

Industries (SIC classification)	Number of firms using homeworkers[b]		
	West Yorks	Bradford	Total
Food, drink, tobacco	1	1	2
Chemical & allied industries	4	3	7
Textiles	4	4	8
Clothing & footwear	12	9	21
Paper, printing & publishing	5	5	10
Other manufacturing industries	7	6	13
Distributive trades	7	4	11
Insurance, banking & finance	1	1	2
Professional & scientific services	1	1	2
Total	42	34	76

[a] Named firms only
[b] Twelve firms identified were based outside the West Yorkshire and MDC area.

adopted. These differences affect estimates of homeworking labour, of the number of suppliers and the trades and industries involved. While some differences in definition involve fairly easily resolved questions of clarity or syntax, others reflect a range of conceptual approaches and political and policy concerns, as well as the legal complexities surrounding self-employment and employment.

Many people work at or from home for payment of some kind. Townsend estimated that well over a million people, including those working on their own account in business or in occupations adjoining their homes, were doing so at the time of his survey in 1968/9 (Townsend, 1979). They included people working under a wide range of employment conditions, including general practitioners, farmers, publicans and shopkeepers, as well as 300 000 employees providing services at or from their homes such as clothing club agents, childminders and nurses.

Given the increasing recognition of paid work done *at* or *from* home and the wide range of possible contractual arrangements (Hakim, 1985; Leighton, 1982, 1983a, 1983b, 1984; Purcell *et al.*, 1986; Scase and Goffee, 1982, 1983), it is imperative that a definition of homework specifies the relationship between those performing the work and those who supply it, in order to differentiate it from other forms of home-based work. Such relationships have very practical outcomes.

An example from India illustrates the result for several thousands of workers of changing the definition of the relationship. After the Supreme Court in 1974 declared The Beedi and Cigar Workers (Conditions of Employment) Act 1966 constitutional in all states of India, attempts through the courts to nullify its wide provisions – including hours, pay, maternity benefits, and holidays – became more difficult. (*Beedi* workers roll cigarettes from leaf and tobacco.) Not only were increased amounts of the work formerly done by in-workers then put out from factories to homeworkers, but homeworkers were then redefined as self-employed traders.

> Even the extremely wide definitions of the terms 'employer' and 'employee' were circumvented. The 'seths' introduce intermediaries who are neither contractors nor sub-contractors of independent contractors. There is 'someone' to whom they sell the raw materials; the sale is a paper transaction . . .. That 'someone' then sells back to the seths the finished product. In Gujarat, an even more explicit practice is developed. The raw materials – the leaf, the tobacco, the thread – are 'purchased' by the beedi workers. At some other point of time, the finished products are 'sold' to the seth. No question of the employer–employee relationship emerges here for the law to regulate. The phenomenal form of the entire transaction is the 'contract', with both parties engaging in market transactions with a free will. (Baxi, 1985, p. 8)

The same work was being carried out but without the protection of the law, devised to improve among other things the wages and conditions of homeworkers.

As will be discussed below, many – perhaps the majority – homeworkers in Britain are treated by their suppliers as self-employed, but regard themselves as employees (Chapter 5). It has been argued that 'the label and nature of an employment relationship have become increasingly important . . . because the "floor of employee" rights established in employment legislation . . . almost invariably excludes the self-employed' (Leighton, 1983b, p. 197). It was for this reason among others that the Homeworkers (Protection) Bill 1979 attempted to provide a definition which would distinguish homeworkers from others who worked *at* or *from* home under different sets of relationships. It defined a homeworker as

> an individual who contracts with a person not being a professional client of his for the purpose of that person's business, for the execution of any work (other than the production or creation of any literary, dramatic, artistic or musical work) to be done in domestic premises not under the control or management of the person with whom he contracts, and who does not normally make use of the services of more than two individuals in the carrying out of that work. (HMSO, 1979)

This definition arose out of discussions among some researchers and others concerned to improve homeworkers' legal status, in order to improve their conditions, and has been adopted by many of those who have done research on homeworking (Allen and Graham, 1981; Crine, 1981; Dundee, 1984; Greater London Council, 1983; Leeds TUCRIC, 1984; Pugh, 1984). It differs from several earlier definitions, some more restrictive and others more general. For instance, in identifying those to be termed homeworkers, Townsend and others used the definition adopted by the Committee on Industrial Relations (CIR), the predecessor to ACAS (ACAS, 1978a and 1978b; Brown, 1974; CIR 1973 and 1974; Townsend, 1979). The CIR definition includes only those who receive work and payment directly from a manufacturing establishment *and* who work in their own homes. Though convenient, it excludes those homeworkers who are supplied with work by middlemen, agents or sub-contractors, by retail establishments and service industries, and those working in other people's homes. A broader definition was used by the TUC – 'Work done in the home for another person for sale to another person' (TUC, 1978). This includes workers involved in literary, dramatic, artistic and musical work, who are normally regarded as freelance or self-employed, as well as childminders. As such it covers a much wider range of contractual relationships and would produce substantially higher figures of homeworkers.

In contrast, the Homeworkers Bill definition sets out certain conditions which specify the nature of the contract between the homeworker and the supplier of work. The main types of workers which it excludes are as follows:

1. Childminders, who, though a numerically large group, provide a personal service to another individual (the parent) in their own home, rather than 'for the purpose of that person's business'. The nature and importance of their work for childcare is not thereby in doubt, but regulation of the contractual relationships requires a different approach (Jackson, 1976; Jackson and Jackson, 1979).
2. Those working in their own home where the premises are owned and/or managed by the employer, such as publicans and resident domestic servants. They are excluded because the control of the work done and the financial or other rewards received are contractually different.
3. Those working on their own account who produce literary, dramatic or artistic work. Though frequently home-based, such people have greater control over the nature of the product and the marketing of their skills. This is not typical of the home-worker. Those excluded are, for instance, freelance journalists, artists and crafts people of many kinds. To these could be added large numbers of people who run small businesses from their own premises, such as painters and decorators, builders and landscape gardeners.
4. Those working *from* home, including mini-cab operators and insurance agents and those involved in sales promotion, agency selling, party-plan schemes, or market research. Their conditions of work vary widely and need to be seen in the context of the organisation of commission selling, freelance work, self-employment and entrepreneurial activity. All these may warrant attention by researchers, policy-makers, government departments and politicians. They should not, however, be confused with those who carry out paid work at home under the relationship and conditions defined in the 1979 Bill.

The debate on definitions of homework continues and results in substantial disagreement about the extent, nature and conditions of homeworking in Britain. While many independent studies adopted the 1979 definition of homework, most of the studies sponsored by or carried out by the Department of Employment have focused on either Wages Councils industries (Hakim and Dennis, 1982), outwork (Leighton, 1982, 1983a and 1983b), or on the very broad category designated as home-based work, including the self-employed as well as employees, and those who work *from* as well as *at* home (Hakim, 1984a, 1984b, 1985). While the term 'home-based work' is interesting in itself for those concerned with the patterns of work and the possible range of contractual relations, it does little to identify and specify the nature and extent of homeworking production. It leads to quite serious confusions about the issues which those who in the 1970s had made homework a visible phenomenon were concerned to see remedied.

It is incumbent on social scientists among others to attempt to arrive at a definition which distinguishes between different sets of social relations. The adoption of the category of home-based work is a step backward in analytical terms. While it is true that many (and perhaps an increasing number of people) work at or from home, they do so under different conditions and their relation with the market, clients or suppliers are not commensurate. By using the notion of home-based work official records and estimates blur the differences between petty commodity producers, small-scale entrepreneurs and self-employed artisans and waged workers. This results not only in confusion about the kinds of work which homeworkers do, but much more significantly, by rejecting an analysis in terms of the relations of production, makes it impossible to analyse the different sets of conditions under which people work.

Lumping together the plastic bag packer with the redundant executive, or the tax consultant with the addresser of envelopes, because they all work *at* home does an immense disservice to homeworkers, who are piece-rate workers, as well as to those who attempt to understand the social relations of work and production in the 1980s. Research using the broad definitions adopted by the Department of Employment inevitably comes to the conclusion that home-based work is characterised by diverse contractual relations and a wide range in levels of pay or remuneration. It conflates so many different employment conditions and includes people with such different positions in the labour market that it is impossible to identify the particular problems homeworkers encounter or to frame legislation to ameliorate them.

Some societies have not found such difficulties in identifying homeworkers and legislating to regulate their pay and conditions of work. These include Austria, Switzerland and Norway, and Germany legislated in the First World War and in 1951 and again in 1974 to regulate homework (Bajohr, 1979; M. Owen, 1984; TUC, 1978). The International Labour Office has latterly recognised the problems of homeworkers and has sponsored reports to enable it to draw up regulatory instruments (M. Owen, 1985). Studies from many parts of the world are regularly presented at international conferences which indicate a clear recognition of the distinctions between those who work at home at piece-rates of pay and those who are running small businesses, or carrying out work for clients for a fee *at* or *from* home, or performing services for clients in their homes. (Abidi, 1985; Bhatty, 1985; Dube, 1985; Hussain, 1985; Hvidtfeldt *et al.* 1982; Mohiuddin, 1985; Sulaiman, 1985; Hoyzer and Young n.d.). These studies increasingly view the specific forms of disguised wage labour carried out at home as an integral part of capitalist production, rather than as constituting a separate sector of the economy.

The occupations of homeworkers

As well as questions about how much homeworking there is or how it is most adequately defined, there is also a question about the kinds of work that homeworkers do. In Britain two images of this co-exist. One, re-emerging in the 1970s, characterised it as a feature of declining industries or traditional sectors at the margins of industrial production. A good deal of attention has been given to homework in the garment industry, where seasonal markets, rapid fashion changes and competitive conditions, it is argued, force entrepreneurs with small profit margins to use homeworking labour. A corollary of this is the stereotype of immigrant communities engaged in this production, both as suppliers of work and as workers, the latter often assumed to be female kin. This form of organisation exists (Anthias, 1983; Mitter, 1986; Saifullah Khan, 1979), but homework is by no means confined to or largely undertaken by immigrant entrepreneurs or their kinship networks (see Chapter 3).

The second, contrasting image, portrays homework as increasingly concentrated in 'new technology' industries, where many kinds of work, including clerical and secretarial tasks, computer programming and systems analysis can be decentralised to the worker's home. Claims are made that these workers and others in the service sector outnumber homeworkers in traditional industries (Hakim, 1984a).

Overviews of homeworking occupations based on official records suggest that they are fairly highly concentrated in particular sectors. For instance, Pugh's review of the *Longitudinal Survey* data, which are drawn from the decennial census, found that 84 per cent of homeworkers were in the clothing and textile industries or in clerical work (Pugh, 1984). In contrast, small-scale and local studies have uncovered a much broader range of occupations. Many of the basic necessities and luxuries of our lives are produced wholly or in part by homeworking production. Clothes, food, toys, leisure goods, household furnishings, cleaning materials, incontinence pants, greetings cards, boxes for chocolates and perfume, swimming pool cleansers, brushes, industrial transmission belts, fireworks, and shoes are but a few of the examples. Assembling and packaging of a wide range of products – windscreen wipers, car tax discs, coil winding, plastic bags, tights, electrical equipment and fishing nets – are only some of the many activities of homeworkers (Allen, 1981a, 1983b; Beale, 1978; Brown, 1974). The goods and services are at every level of quality, incorporated by firms into their final products or marketed by retail outlets through exclusive 'high class' shops, high street chain stores, mail order and market traders. Homeworkers work for restaurants, preserving and pickling plants, local government services and regional health authorities, as well as firms of accountants and building societies, and central government departments are also involved.

Homeworking is not tied to specific traditional or marginal products or services. We classified the range found in West Yorkshire and other studies according to the processes undertaken. These may involve the production of whole articles from raw materials to the finished product, by one or a combination of homeworkers. These articles are typically hand-crafted, knitted garments, hand-sewn clothing and hand-made household and leisure goods. Their value lies in the materials used, the skill of the worker and/or in their handmade quality, which are used as a selling-point and can be highly profitable to the retailer.

Other products involve main line production by in-workers, with the hand-crafted processes put out to homeworkers. These include both quality goods for quality markets, and industrial goods – such as hand-sewn transmission belts for washing machines and burling and mending in textile production. Homeworkers in West York-shire were making decorations by hand for greeting cards, or assembling them and fixing them to the cards. Others were involved in the skilled pleating, stitching and glueing of linings and decora-tions for boxes of chocolates (Easter egg 'nests', for example) and perfume.

There is a wide range of other products in which part of the process is carried out by in-workers and the rest put out to homeworkers. Much of the machine sewing done by homeworkers in the clothing and footwear industries fits this category. The homeworker may make through the whole garment from pre-cut pieces or carry out only one process, such as the sewing of cuffs, hemming or buttoning. Coats, dresses, blouses, suits, all traditional clothing for men, women and children, sportswear, overalls, medical underwear, curtains and cushion covers, as well as the world-famous thermal clothing, together with the machining of horse-riding gear and accessories (reins, leg bandages, head collars, rugs for night and day, and summer and winter use) all featured in homeworking in West Yorkshire. Alterations to newly bought or renovated clothing and household goods, such as curtains, were put out to homeworkers by retail outlets.

Yet other homeworkers were engaged in assembling parts previously hand-worked or machine-produced by in-workers or other homeworkers – for example, putting together nuts and bolts, covering fireworks, and assembling display boxes or sample cards. Packing and packaging included a variety of related processes, such as washing, sorting, trimming, collating, bagging, stapling, labell-ing, sealing, and so on. The products being packed spanned a very wide range, and included greeting cards, car tax discs, plastic bags, plastic liners and pants, tights, envelopes and vegetables.

In addition, as evidence from other surveys has shown, a wide range of white-collar occupations are to be found among home-workers. These include clerical work, accounts, typing, checking invoices, envelope addressing, indexing and proof-reading. As Pugh points out, clerical homeworkers were in the majority of those officially recorded in 1971, so do not constitute a new phenomenon (Pugh, 1984). To these have been added a number of occupations linked to 'new technology'. Ursula Huws has indicated that compared with traditional-style homeworking 'when it comes to new-technology-related homeworking there is even less evidence, and the researcher must turn to the speculations of futurologists and equipment manufacturers, the experience of individual employers, and the results of overseas experiments in long-distance working' (Huws, 1984a, p. 13). In her own research the majority of the seventy-eight homeworkers who completed questionnaires were computer professionals, with 9 per cent 'engaged in work of a clerical nature such as word processor operation' (ibid., p. 17).

Some preliminary research has revealed the beginning of the 'global' or 'offshore' office as, for instance, where firms in North America put out work to the Caribbean (Posthuma, n.d.). This 'distance-working' is made possible through new technology, but it is argued that 'the danger is real that offshore sites could result in fast-paced work, low pay and little or no regard for health hazards'. Data processing homework is similar to traditional forms: 'These girls are behind computers, but they could just as easily be behind a sewing machine.'

The importance of new technology in altering the kinds of work which are or will be carried out at home rather than in an office is already recognised. It is, however, premature to assume that such work will numerically displace the older kinds of clerical and manufacturing work, or that the work relationship between the computer operator and the supplier of various forms of data processing, for example, will differ significantly from that associated with older forms of technology. Those personnel in 'new technology' industries who earn relatively high wages or enjoy comparatively favourable terms of employment are those who currently command scarce skills, but this situation cannot be expected to last indefinitely. It is as well to remember that 'new' technology has always been a part of homeworking production. The sewing machine and the type-writer, the knitting machine and the griswold (invented 1850) for knitting socks were once new technologies (Wix, 1984, p. 116). Their adoption did not lead to new relations of production between supplier and worker, or employer and employee.

The woman working 9 hours a day, 6 days a week, processing medical insurance claims on a terminal in the basement of her New York home has no job security and no fringe benefits such as overtime, holiday pay, sick pay or maternity leave. While she may be able to earn $80 a day, $8 a day is paid to lease the terminal and she bears all the costs of her work-place (Keller, 1984). The companies maintain that such new technology work is 'a potential boon to workers because it will give them perfect mobility to sell their services to the highest bidders'. But at the same time they are exploring ways in which medical insurance claims, can, with the aid of more technology, be printed directly by hospital doctors – which will dispense with the homeworker. There is nothing new about these relations between new technology workers and suppliers. They are as old as the beginnings of the industrial revolution.

It is of little importance whether or not, as is claimed by some, that at least half the homeworking labour force is now engaged in white-collar jobs or in service industries (Hakim, 1984b). The figures from the WIRS national survey of firms indicate this to be the case. But as Pugh suggests, such a claim may well rest on a false premise, since 'particular types of homeworking and many home-workers' are left out of official surveys (Pugh, 1984). Moreover, new technology by itself, even if its full potential is realised in shifting work from factory and office to the home, is no guarantee that there will be a change in the social relations between those who work with the new technology and those who control and own it.

Conclusions

This chapter has presented the information on the numbers of homeworkers and suppliers of homework and the kinds of work and processes involved. It has outlined the main limitations of official estimates, together with the problems associated with making visible a form of waged work which is still not recorded systemati-cally in national, regional or industrial statistics.

It has been argued that the manner in which measures of labour force activity and production are compiled makes it virtually impossible for official statistical accounts to include reliable esti-mates of homework. This means that existing estimates must be treated with great care, and their use in drawing conclusions about who does homeworking, who supplies it, what sort of work is involved, the conditions under which it is carried out as well as whether or not it is increasing in volume or spreading to a wider range of work, remains highly problematic.

The existence of homeworking in many societies can no longer be disputed, as is evident from studies in Western Europe, Scandinavia, Hungary, Bulgaria, Latin America, India, the United States and Canada as well as Britain. The argument that it is a relic from an earlier form of production located at the periphery of highly industrialised production has been confounded by the growing evidence of its association with new forms of technology. Similarly, the argument that it is the precursor of new working patterns and signals the future organisation of work leaves out both its continuous existence throughout industrialisation and its integration into the power relations within households and the wider economy.

It has become obvious that the model which assumes the separation of home and work and adopts able-bodied adult male working patterns as the norm has produced a distorted picture of economic activity. Paid work carried out at home is in fact integral both to household economies and to the economy more generally. The approach which has been dominant in social science, as well as in official accounts at national and local government levels during the twentieth century, is still very much in evidence. Its inadequacies have been pointed out by many feminist scholars and researchers (for example, Gamarnikow *et al.* 1983; Llewelyn Davis, 1977; McNally, 1979; Phizacklea (ed.), 1983; West, 1982). However, increasing levels of unemployment, new forms of technology, the discovery or re-discovery of the 'informal' sector, and the recognition of the variety of contractual obligations necessitate in an acute form not an amalgamation of all kinds of home-based work in the 1980s, conflating waged workers, the self-employed and small business entrepreneurs, but a sharper clarification of the distinctions between such categories of relationships.

For instance, it has been argued by Child (1986), Littek (1986) and Cockburn (1986) that the initial degree of autonomy and status of work groups is a more accurate indicator of the effect of new technology than any intrinsic characteristics of technical innovation. This observation is relevant to all forms of home-based work but, in particular, to homeworkers. The nature of existing power relations between suppliers of homework and homeworkers, together with power relations within households, suggest that the ideological and material subordination of women homeworkers will continue to be a major issue for both 'traditional' and 'new' homeworkers. The adequacy of estimates of their numbers and the contribution of their work to the wider economy and to the household is crucial to efforts to alter their pay and conditions of work.

The following chapters discuss the ways in which homeworking production operates and the attempts being made to struggle for minimal conditions.

3

Who does homeworking and why?

Images of homeworkers and homeworking are constantly shifting. No sooner is evidence produced to discredit one stereotype than it is succeeded by another, often a revised version of those popular at an earlier date. The creation of apparently contradictory images of homeworkers is one way in which the issues raised by homeworking are evaded. Because so many accounts of homeworking portray homeworkers as having characteristics unusual or atypical of those considered to be real workers, it is presented as a minor problem, confined to the periphery of labour force activity – whereas, in fact, it involves major questions about the sexual division of labour.

The widely accepted assumptions about the characteristics of homeworkers have come to be seen as an explanation of homeworking itself. It is all too easy to move from possible explanations of why individuals are constrained to work at home to using these to explain why homeworking is so extensive. By so doing the belief is fostered that homeworking is a function of the needs or preferences of its work-force, a burden they have brought upon themselves, or a choice they have made freely, rather than a form of production in which they participate. For these reasons the images of homeworkers which have been given widespread currency and the assumptions on which they rest, require close examination.

In the 1970s the homeworker was increasingly being portrayed as pitiable and degraded. The results of work by the Low Pay Unit and others (Bolton, 1975; Brown, 1974; Crine, 1979a, 1979b; Jordan, 1978), which had revealed exploitation and poor working conditions among homeworkers, were picked up and used by the press in a highly salacious manner. Articles, for instance, featured many examples of homeworkers' appalling low pay: Mrs Eliot, who earned £2.50 for a 40-hour week binding and covering games boards, Mrs Hill, who made soft toys for 4½p an hour, Mrs Lewis, who is paid £3.50 for painting 1000 tiny toy footballers (Forester, 1975). But their main focus was the dire circumstances which force women into homeworking. Termed 'these unfortunate people' (*Telegraph and Argus*, 1978) homeworkers were described as suffering from a 'handicap' (*Guardian*, 3 August 1976), and assumed to be at home with small children but forced nevertheless by desperate economic circumstances to do paid work. When the plight of individual homeworkers was mentioned, they were nearly always women whose husbands were out of work, or the mothers of large families of five or even seven children. Other homeworkers forming part of this 'captive labour force' were thought to be 'immigrant' women kept at home by language difficulties or cultural restrictions (*Guardian*, 3 September 1976; *New Equals*, 1978) or restricted by their illegal immigrant status (Campbell, 1978) from seeking employment in the formal sector.

As a corrective to the neglect and invisibility of homeworking that was then dominant, articles like those quoted above represented a necessary and long overdue intervention. The stress on homeworking 'as a last resort, never from choice' (*Guardian*, 3 August 1976) was particularly important in countering the notion of homeworking, when it was recognised to exist, as a leisure time activity done for 'pin money'. This picture of homeworking, highlighted in advertisements for home-working labour ('Earn extra cash in your spare time') continues to have a wide currency. Indeed, alongside the new emphasis on homeworkers' desperation, descriptions of homeworkers as housewives using their initiative to 'turn a hobby into cash' continued to appear. One article described a mother as hating to sit at home with nothing to do, and the author even adds coyly that in her paid work she had the help of her sixteen-month-old baby (*Halifax Evening Courier*, 8 November 1979). Articles like this show that the evidence collected by the Low Pay Unit, on child labour in homeworking, for instance, or an awareness of the time women put into unpaid labour in the home, has never been seriously integrated into much of the media's perspective on homeworking.

Other reports during this period quoted from employers of homeworkers, thereby giving space to their constructions of homeworkers and their explanations of the low wages they paid. These employers stressed that homeworkers did not work as hard as ordinary workers. 'The average homeworker only works at half the normal speed,' reported one employer. 'The majority fiddle and mess about, so they only earn half what they should do' (*Woman*, 1979). Another explained that for homeworkers the level of pay was unimportant: 'Homeworkers work for love and a little pocket money. We are not interested in those who do it only for the money' (*Woman*, 1979).

In this context the publicity given to homeworkers' financial circumstances, appalling wages and conditions could only be welcomed. But headlines like 'The Scandal of Kitchen Workshops', 'Untouchables of the Labour Market' or 'Sitting Room Slaves' conjured up the exotic, in exceptionally desperate circumstances, rather than what are in reality common predicaments faced by ordinary women workers. While picturing homeworkers as 'housewives' earning pin money in their spare time clearly marginalises homeworkers, the image of homeworkers as members of exceptionally deprived social categories continues to portray them as outside the main body of the labour force.

The notion that homeworkers comprise a separate, identifiable group, distinguishable from ordinary workers, was and continues to be an important component in the image of homeworkers propagated in official circles. In testimony before the Parliamentary inquiry into homeworking in 1981, for instance, it was argued that

> Very often the homeworking is done by people who would not otherwise be in the ordinary labour force and therefore are not going in any way to be directly affected by the unemployment rate of an area. To some extent it is a different labour market. (House of Commons, 24 February, 1981b, para. 47)

As in the press, discussion in official circles concentrates on the characteristics or needs of homeworkers which place them in a special category. A study commissioned by the Department of Employment, for instance, looked at fifty homeworkers, and reported that 'Dependent children were overwhelmingly regarded as the main reason for working at home', with ill-health, language and cultural reasons as additional factors (Cragg and Dawson, 1981, pp. 6–8). The reasons for working were the twin needs of money and fulfilment, with the first being 'collectively paramount' (ibid., p. 4). Homeworking is also associated with those whose employment is restricted by physical disability or other commitments, such as students, and who therefore seek or require only casual employment. Compare, for instance, these two excerpts from testimony before a Parliamentary Select Committee:

> We also have evidence of many people who like to do various jobs. They like the opportunity, for instance in the summer months to go off and dig potatoes or tread grapes in France or what have you and they do not like the idea of being tied down to a particular type of job that is involved with the type of factory disciplines . . . that would be created if we were talking about a fully employed situation for these people.   (House of Commons, 1981a, para. 151)

> The Wages Council Inspectorate suggested . . . that the performance of many homeworkers was below average and in consequence they might meet difficulties in seeking factory employment.   (House of Commons, 1981b: 14 April, para. 21)

Official and media stereotypes of this kind persist in using a picture of normal employment and ordinary workers which is out of touch with the actual character of much of the paid labour force. The normal employment to which homeworking is implicitly or explicitly compared, regular, full-time factory or office employment, does not apply and has never applied to a substantial proportion of the waged labour force, including many women workers. Part-time work or casualised employment conditions and the family responsibilities of most ordinary women workers are not taken into account. The assumptions about employment which underlie these accounts ignore women's participation in the labour force more generally, and the context in which it takes place. Consequently homeworking is seen as a marginal social phenomenon, and the characteristics of much of the work, low-paid, irregular and unskilled, attributed to supposed characteristics of the work force.

A separate reconstruction of homeworking exists within the discussions on 'the future of work' which typically includes reference to the increasing role which working at home is expected to play in British households (Clutterbuck and Hill, 1981; Gershuny and Pahl, 1979/80; Handy, 1984; R. E. Pahl, 1984; Toffler, 1980).

The potential of new technology for work at home is one factor, while rising unemployment and its insupportable costs to the state are seen as indicators of the need for people to support themselves or add to their state benefits through a portfolio of 'bits and pieces' of paid work in their homes. These developments are seen as offering more flexible and autonomous conditions of work. We are offered pictures of young women combining child-care with high wage work as systems analysts (Toynbee, 1985) or of men's independent backyard repair shops or agricultural small-holdings (Postgate, 1984). The seminars and conferences being organised to press for the relaxation of planning regulations in residential areas, or the adaption of domestic housing for home-based production, seem a transparent effort to present an image of homeworking as an acceptable alternative.

In later chapters we shall look in detail at the working conditions in homeworking, and at the social relations between homeworkers and the suppliers of work. We shall also examine explanations of homeworking which go beyond the attributes of individual workers. In this chapter, however, we want to consider how far the common images and explanations fit with the lives of the ninety West Yorkshire homeworkers we interviewed. We concentrate in our analysis on locating homeworking labour within the more general constraints in which women's paid work is conducted. This demonstrates that in many respects the constraints homeworkers face are very similar to those affecting other women workers.

The economic constraints

The facts of women's participation in the labour force are increasingly recognised, at least as far as employment is concerned. Most women now engage in waged work for most of their adult lives. Marriage in itself does not affect whether or not a woman is in paid work, and even the presence of pre-school children is not a reliable indicator of whether or not a woman is in or seeking employment (Martin and Roberts, 1984). Over half the mothers of dependent children are economically active, and this includes 30 per cent of mothers with children under five years of age (*General Household Survey, 1981*, p. 94). Were it not for married women's earnings, four times as many people would fall below the Supplementary Benefit level (MacLennan, *et al.*, 1983).

It is also being recognised that most households in Britain are not composed of a married couple and their dependent children. Households of this kind comprise only about 30 per cent of British households (GHS, 1982). Less than half of the married couples have dependent children living with them, while increasing numbers of children live with and are financially supported by a lone parent, and an increasing number of adults live on their own and manage their households on their own earnings. Homeworkers' family circumstances and their need to earn a livelihood are part and parcel of this larger situation.

Yet despite all statistical evidence, the notion that women are economically dependent housewives supported by a male bread-winner continues to dominate the perception of employment patterns, including homeworking. This is due partly to part-time work patterns, particularly among married mothers, and partly to the fact that women earn less than men. Although the increase in part-time working can be explained, at least in part, by the advantages to employers of a part-time, flexible labour force, and women's low pay by their concentration in low-paid industries and occupations, these facts are more usually cited as evidence for the conventional view of women as economically dependent wives and mothers who are at best secondary earners. In this way all women are marginalised as workers.

Accounts which perceive an association between women's involvement in homeworking and its casual character fit in with and replicate the conventional view of women's paid work as of only secondary importance. They take little or no account of homeworkers' actual attachment to the labour market, which can be demonstrated in a number of ways. In our survey we looked at a number of dimensions of homeworkers' households and employment histories. These data demonstrate that homeworkers' contribution to household earnings is similar to the contribution made by women working outside the home, and just as vital to the support of their families. Moreover, homeworkers' employment histories and preferences show that, like other women workers, they consider their paid work to be essential.

Socio-economic status

The classification of homeworkers' households in terms of socio-economic status presents some of the problems which have been widely discussed during the past decade in relation to the issue of how the class position of adult women is best determined and by what measures household or 'family' units should be classified (Armstrong, 1982; Dale *et al.*, 1985; Delphy, 1981; Dex, 1985; Goldthorpe, 1983; Middleton, 1974; Stanworth, 1984). Objections to the usual classification of a woman according to her husband's or father's occupation, however valid, face those who depart from this method with a range of problems in making comparisons with official statistical material. We analysed our survey findings in terms of the homeworker's occupation(s) and that of her husband or male partner. In addition we looked at all adults with jobs outside the home and those households without anyone employed, for homeworkers live in a range of households, not only in ones where a couple with their dependent children are found.

If we classify the homework being carried out, then all but three of the ninety women in the survey were doing manual work. This differs from the assumption that 50 per cent of homeworking is white-collar (Hakim, 1980). The three in white-collar work were involved in typing and auditing accounts, calculating VAT and typing records, and calculating and typing stock sheets. All worked directly for firms and two were married to men in non-manual occupations, one was a self-employed builder and one a telephone salesman. The third was married to a welder.

Sixteen of the homeworkers also held part-time jobs outside the home. Apart from two, who did secretarial work and would be classed as non-manual, the rest were in service work, cleaning, catering, serving in bars or shops, with only one working in manufacturing as a machinist. The two with non-manual outside jobs were also white-collar homeworkers (one married to a non-manual and the other to a manual worker). The remaining fourteen were all manual homeworkers, thirteen of whom were married to manual workers, six of whom were in skilled or supervisory positions. The other was a single parent, who did two part-time jobs and childminding in addition to homeworking.

In sixty-nine households there was a male partner or husband in full-time work outside the home and in a further three other male relatives, father, brother-in-law and son respectively, were working full-time outside. If we use the scale developed by Goldthorpe and Hope, then we find that forty-nine of the households are working-class, twenty-one are intermediate and two are service (Goldthorpe and Hope, 1974). The more usual division between manual and non-manual would give sixteen non-manual households and fifty-six manual. The households with no one in full-time work outside the home, eighteen in all, included four where the husband was unemployed and four where he was on sick pay. All were (or had been) manual workers. The remaining ten were either retired married couples, or lone mothers, living alone with their children or, in one case, with retired parents, or single-person households.

All classifications are open to criticism, but using several different labour market indicators it is clear that well over three-quarters of the households fall into the manual/working-class bracket. Not surprisingly, however, if the homeworkers' job histories were taken into account many more of them had had white-collar experience before the birth of their first child. In this sense they were downwardly mobile on becoming mothers and having to seek work to do at home. Some remarked that this then affected their confidence when looking for work on a part-time basis.

This is also underlined by the fact that of the sixteen home-workers married to men in non-manual occupations, fourteen were doing manual homeworking. Some examples might illustrate the homework carried out in these largely lower middle-class, but also middle-class (measured by the man's occupation) households. These include men with their own businesses whose wives assembled rollers for woolcombing or were machinists of clothing and industrial belts; a store manager and a production manager whose wives relabelled and packaged plastic bags and bin-liners; and an insurance clerk, a teacher and a coach operator who were the husbands of women sorting and packaging greetings cards; a police officer and computer officer whose wives made satin linings for chocolate and perfume boxes. These women were not short-term homeworkers: many of them had been homeworkers ever since they became mothers. Some had undertaken different kinds of manual homework, moving between different kinds of seasonal work or switching to packing or assembly work, for instance, when brush-making slumped. Others had moved from pyramid and party plan selling into homework.

There is much anecdotal evidence of middle-class women under-taking homeworking, such as packing chemical cleansing kits for swimming pools or packaging electric bulbs and painting glassware. We were not able to check this with the women themselves. The evidence from our survey indicates that wives of non-manual workers do manual homeworking but how widespread this is remains unknown. With some forms of new technology, the potential exists for the spread of homeworking, both for manual and white-collar/middle-class occupations, not least because of its cost-cutting aspects. As yet, there is no firm evidence to show that homeworking is a major or even a common feature of middle-class work experience.

It is also necessary to be cautious in defining white-collar work carried out by homeworkers in middle-class terms. An example brought to our notice illustrates this point. An agency supplying typing and clerical work operates a system whereby women are required to report to the office at 9 am to be allocated the work available. A second allocation is made at 1.30 pm and those not given work, together with those who have completed their 9 am allocation, are expected to attend again to pick up any further work. In terms of employment conditions such a system is closely akin to that practised formerly in the docks and contemporarily for construction workers. It is a casualisation of labour, heavily criticised in the past and finally abolished in the case of dockers. It bears no relation to middle-class occupational conditions. At least the dockers, unlike the non-manual women, did not have to take their children along with them when seeking work.

Household earnings

Estimating homeworkers' household income from all sources presented several problems. The number of different contributors to the household income could be ascertained fairly easily. But it was not always possible to know how much of their earnings were actually contributed to household expenses. These problems arose not only in the case of teenage and adult children, or when husbands were contributing to the support of a household formed through an earlier marriage, but also because the relation between the husband/male partner's income and the amount of this made available for household use is by no means axiomatic (J. Pahl, 1983). For these reasons the income available for household expenditure may have been somewhat lower than figures for household earnings indicate.

None the less, it is possible to present an overall picture of homeworkers' family circumstances. This indicates the existence, within the framework of manual working-class wage levels, of a fairly wide distribution in the level of household earnings. However, homeworkers contribution to household expenses was substantial at all income levels and in all types of household.

Seventy-two of the ninety homeworker households had at least one person working outside the home, usually but not always the homeworker's husband or male partner. The homeworker's contribution varied between 2 and 76 per cent of total household earnings. As Table 3.1 demonstrates, the highest proportionate contributions are concentrated at the lowest end of the income scale. But many homeworkers whose husbands earn comparatively good pay, as a computer operator or skilled metal worker, for instance, expect to make a sizeable contribution to household earnings. The importance of homeworking earnings is not confined to the very poor.

Many homeworker households earned very close to or below the level of low pay, as defined by the Low Pay Unit. Over one-quarter of the 72 homeworker households fell below the Low Pay Unit definition of low pay for 1980, £74 a week (Pond, 1981). For our sample this is calculated on the basis of average weekly earnings per person employed outside the home, as shown in Table 3.2. When these low-paid households are added to those with no one in outside employment, it can be seen that the economic situation of many

Table 3.1 *Homework earnings: contribution to household earnings*
(n=72)

Income group outside earnings weekly (£)	Homework earnings as (%) of outside earnings	Contribution to each household weekly (£)
60 to < 70	24	16
70 to < 80	26	20
80 to < 90	18	15
90 to < 100	18	16
100 to < 110	16	16
110 to < 120	18	20
120 to < 130	9	11
130 to < 140	13	17
150 to < 200	6	11
200+	8	19

Table 3.2 Homeworkers' households[a]: weekly earnings 1979–80, excluding homework (n=72)

Income group outside earnings only (£)[b]	No. of households in each group	Average weekly earnings (£)	Average no. of persons in household	Average no. of employed persons per household[c]	Average weekly earnings per employed person	Ratio of employed to dependents
60 to <70	5	66	5.2	1.0	66	1:4.2
70 to <80	7	75	4.1	1.0	75	1:3.1
80 to <90	11	82	4.5	1.0	82	1:3.5
90 to <100	6	94	4.3	1.0	94	1:3.3
100 to <110	7	103	4.1	1.0	103	1:3.1
110 to <120	8	113	3.9	1.25	90.4	1:2.1
120 to <130	13	123	4.6	1.46	84.2	1:2.2
130 to <140	9	133	4.8	1.88	70.7	1:1.6
150 to <200	4	176	5.5	2.0	88.0	1:1.8
200+	2	240	6.0	3.5	68.6	1:0.7

a With at least one member in full-time outside employment
b Including women's earnings
c Homeworkers not included as employed

homeworker households is very tight, and would have been far worse without homeworking earnings.

Another way of demonstrating the importance of homeworking earnings is by asking whether they are spent on 'extras' or comprise an essential part of the weekly budget. Homeworkers in West Yorkshire said that their pay was used on essential budgetary items, such as food, heating, lighting, rent or mortgage repayments, rates and shoes and clothes for children. Only three homeworkers said that their pay was used primarily for items which they defined as 'extras' or 'luxuries': Christmas presents, holidays, cosmetics, cigarettes, and husband's car expenses. The expenditure pattern of homeworkers' pay clearly indicates that it is not used as pin money, but as a contribution to regular expenses. Without this there would be financial hardship.

Homework and outside jobs

Homeworkers' employment histories and preferences indicate that homeworking is sought in order to meet the same requirements as work outside the home. All except eight of the ninety homeworkers had been previously employed outside the home, and most would have preferred work outside the home to homework. Twenty-four had actively sought outside employment and turned to homework only when unsuccessful. In hours of work, also, their participation in paid work was identical to women going out to work. The majority of homeworkers were working the same hours as women with part-time jobs outside the home, 11 to 30 hours a week, and twelve were working over forty hours a week.

Homeworking is not undertaken for short periods, to cover family emergencies or exceptional circumstances. Half the sample had been homeworking for two or more years, and nearly a fifth for over five. Six had been homeworking for over ten years. This clearly demonstrates that homeworkers look to homeworking as a continuing source of employment, although in practice they find it wanting. Their jobs offer little security and any reduction in the supplier's own orders means less work and even lower earnings. For example, the homeworker in our sample with the longest record of homeworking, over 40 years, had started when she was 19, and when interviewed was almost 60. She had always done the same work, burling and mending, a skilled job she learned in the factory after leaving school. Over the whole period she had worked for three firms, the last for 20 years. She began homeworking when she was married, and had worked as a burler and mender in a factory and at home for a few months at a time after her first child was born. After the birth of two more children she became responsible for her house-bound mother, in addition to her husband and three children, and her paid work was confined homeworking. All three firms treated her as self-employed, and despite the length of service she had never in 40 years had any holiday pay or any other form of employee benefit. Her only breaks occurred when the firms had no work to give her. She had no contract of employment, and no guarantees on the supply of work. The amount of work she was allocated varied from 4 to 5 or 8 to 9 hours a day. In some weeks she was given none.

As this example shows, the homeworkers' reasons for undertaking homework clearly derive from their need to earn a livelihood. In addition, like other workers they see their earnings as a source of social identity and independence. The subsistence factor was often intertwined with a desire for some modicum of independence, either from a male partner or from the state. 'He has all the say when there is only his wage', summarises the attitude of many homeworkers. Women without a male partner described the humiliation and harassment they had experienced at the hands of state officials, and their desire to avoid the stigma associated with accepting state money. One homeworker supported herself and her two children only by taking on homeworking in addition to two part-time jobs outside, and earned £69 for a total of 55 hours work a week. As her situation demonstrates, homeworking earnings are not adequately conceptualised as a supplement to other household income: they are necessary to bring women's wages up to a level by which they can fulfil their obligations as supporters of families.

This woman's combination of homeworking, with two outside jobs and childminding was unusual. But the most telling indication of the importance of homeworking to women's earnings is that of the women in the sample who were doing homework in addition to an outside job. Sixteen of the homeworkers had taken on homework in addition to jobs outside the home, and several others were doing child-minding as well as homework. Many of the others were actually looking for outside work on a part-time basis. Pay levels in women's occupations, whether in homework or part-time jobs, take no account of the contribution women need to make to the support of their households (Hurstfield, 1980). This applies to married women as well as those who are the sole earners in their households. For example, one woman added 15 hours' homeworking, which brought in £8 to an already fragmented work day. She was working split shifts as a school cleaner, 17½ hours a week, for which she earned £18. In combination with the £50 to £59 a week her husband earned they barely survived. Such women workers, whose earnings are characterised as secondary, at a level appropriate to supposedly dependent housewives, take on more than one job, particularly where the supposed main breadwinner is low paid. These women, who combine homework with a part-time job outside the home and/ or childmining within it, demonstrate the lengths that they have to go to in order to contribute to the financial survival of the household. In the literature relating to the Third World they would be designated as the working poor. In the First World, including Britain, despite the contribution they make as workers and providers, their concentration in part-time jobs and homeworking puts them outside the definition of workers adopted in dominant constructions of the labour force, and the vital economic contribution which they make to their households is ignored.

The social constraints: dependent children and homeworking

The fact that women ordinarily engage in paid employment does not explain why some women work at home rather than outside employment. As we pointed out above, the most common explanation for this is women's responsibility for the daily care and supervision of young children. This has been interpreted in terms of either constraint or choice. In the studies conducted by the Low Pay Unit homeworkers are portrayed as 'trapped in the home' by young children, and therefore highly vulnerable to exploitation by the suppliers of homework. But others have argued that because many homeworkers prefer to be at home while their children are small, they make a positive choice to forgo the higher wages to be earned in outside employment (Hakim, 1980). Whether this latter assumption can be supported is highly debatable. Our own and other surveys have found a number of homeworkers who work at home in order to 'fit in' with their children's needs. This appears as an expression of the only practical alternative. As sociologists have long recognised, choice may be little more than the expression of internalised constraint. If there were adequate public child-care facilities, or more jobs outside the home to suit those responsible for dependents homeworkers' 'choice' of work might be very different.

This question of choice versus constraint is so important to more general debates on the acceptability of homeworking that it has received a great deal of attention. Yet, oddly enough, the emphasis on homeworkers' responsibility for children is rarely questioned. It seems to follow from the assumption that the mothers of young children are needed or are expected to be at home. Yet as the statistics already cited demonstrate, many women with children work outside the home, full-time or, more usually, part-time. They include many women who believe that women should remain at home with young children. Martin and Roberts' survey of women and employment found that nearly one-quarter of women with a child under the age of 5 who were going out to work felt that women with pre-school children should stay at home (1984, p. 191). The presence of dependent children in the family, and the belief that a mother should stay at home with them, are, like other *ad hoc* explanations of homeworking in terms of homeworkers' characteristics, also applicable to women in the formal labour market. Like women's need to contribute to household earnings, child-care responsibilities are obviously relevant to an understanding of homeworking, but they do not distinguish sharply between homeworkers and other women workers.

Once it is recognised that children do not preclude women's participation in the labour force, the picture begins to look far more complex than if 'dependent children' is accepted as an adequate explanation. This explanation of involvement in homeworking assumes, quite correctly, that the mother, not the father, is expected to care for children, and sensibly thus highlights one of the ideological constraints which shapes women's paid employment. But this emphasis also obscures women's other family responsibilities, making it appear as if limitations on women's waged labour are confined to a single stage in the life cycle, which they clearly are not. Moreover, this explanation focuses exclusively on women as wives and mothers, relegating their place as workers, and the options open to them as workers, to the background. The existence of homeworking labour force cannot be understood without reference to women's position in the labour-market. For instance, differences in the relative amount and kinds of training received by women and men, the over-concentration of women's work opportunities within a very narrow range of low-paid, often part-time, jobs, and the differential impact of unemployment are also part of the explanation. The sexually segregated labour-market is both a reflection of women's unpaid work on behalf of the family as well as a cause of the limited options open to them. In considering homeworkers' circumstances we are concerned to show that the presence of dependent children is only one factor among many.

In analysing our survey data we assessed the link between the presence of dependent children and homeworking in several ways. One was to compare the age distribution of the homeworking sample with that of women in West Yorkshire generally. This demonstrates that homeworking is concentrated among women in their child-rearing years. As compared with women in the general population, the age groups between 25 and 34 were over-represented, with a marked concentration in the 25 to 29 age group (see Figure 3.1 and Table 3.3). While women of 15 to 19 who had not yet had children, and of 40 to 47, whose children were likely to be older, were under-represented in the sample, in fact nearly a quarter of the sample were under 20 or over 40. Their circumstances

Table 3.3   *Age distribution: females in West Yorkshire and homeworkers'*
sample 15–74 years

Age group (years)	West Yorkshire females (%)	Homeworkers sample (%)
15–19	11.0	2.0
20–24	9.0	9.0
25–29	9.0	33.0
30–34	10.0	19.0
35–39	8.0	18.0
40–44	7.5	7.0
45–49	7.5	3.5
50–54	8.0	1.0
55–59	8.5	4.5
60–64	7.0	2.0
65–69	7.5	—
70 and over	7.0	1.0

Figure 3.1 *Age distribution of homeworkers*

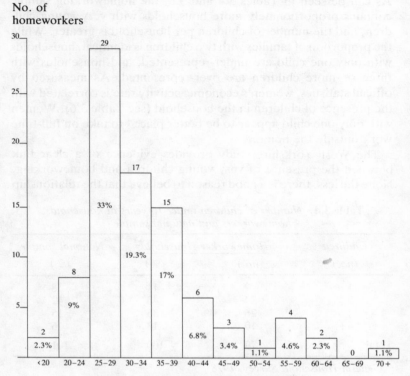

No. of
homeworkers

Ages of homeworkers: proportion shown
(n = 88; no information on age of 2 respondents)

are crucial to understanding the complex relationship between homeworking and family life.

Age at entry to homeworking, as compared with age when interviewed, also shows that while the care of dependent children is a factor in entering homework, it is far from the only one. Twenty-five women became homeworkers for the first time in their late thirties and forties, when the care of young children was not the main reason. In addition, some of the older homeworkers, who had entered when their children were very young, continued homeworking long after young children furnished a reason.

Another way of measuring the relationship between homeworking and dependent children is to compare households with children in the homeworking sample with those in the general population. As can be seen in Tables 3.4 and 3.5, the homeworking sample contains proportionately more households with very young children, and the number of children per household is greater. While the proportion of families with two children is identical, households with only one child are under-represented, and households with three or more children are over-represented. As measured by official statistics, women's economic activity rate is correlated with the presence of children in the household (see Table 3.6). Women with only one child appear to be better placed to take on full-time work outside the home.

The West Yorkshire study provides evidence of a clear link between the presence of very young children and homeworking. None the less, there is a good reason to believe that the relationship

Table 3.4   *Number of children under 16 years in households: homeworkers and national sample*

Children	Homeworker Households		National sample[a]
(no.)	(no.)	(%)	(%)
1	9	11	38
2	34	43	42
3	26	33	15
4+	10	13	6
Total	79	100	101

[a] *General Household Survey, 1978*

Table 3.5   *Households by age of youngest child: homeworkers and national samples*

Age of Youngest child[b]	Homeworker households		National sample[a]
	(no.)	(%)	(%)
0–4	46[c]	54	36
5–9	26	31	30
10–15	7	8	30
16+	6	7	4
Total	85	100	100

[a] *General Household Survey, 1978*
[b] Children living at home
[c] 32 with at least 1 child 2 years of age or less

Table 3.6 *Women in all working age groups*[a]

Economically active No. of Children	Full-time (%)	(%)	Part-time (%)
1	54	21	33
2	53	14	39
3+	45	13	32

[a] *General Household Survey, 1978*

between them is not so easily explained as might be assumed. For our data also provide evidence that often homeworking is not undertaken as an alternative to outside work but in addition to it. As has already been mentioned, a number of homeworkers combine homeworking with an outside job. They tend to have more dependent children than the others and their household income also tends to be lower. The situation of these women, who combine multiple jobs with the labour of looking after their families on a tight budget, forcibly demonstrates that having young children does not preclude going out to work. Rather, with greater financial pressure and young children the options become tighter, and undertaking a variety of waged work more likely. Involvement in homeworking is better understood in terms of the constraints young children impose on the work options of women than by accepting the ideological definition of them as mothers and housewives.

Moreover, among the mothers of young children who said that they could not seek outside employment were many who offered additional reasons for needing to be at home. Many were affected by the husband's job demands, including those whose husbands' employment required them to be away from home for long periods. One was required to be at home to answer telephone enquiries for her husband's own business (see Finch, 1983). Homeworkers' difficulty in getting out to work is thus affected not only by the care of their children, but the need to fit in with looking after the husband. The decision to remain at home was also influenced by the husband's preferences regarding child-care arrangements. How having young children affects women's work options can only be fully understood in the context of husbands' implicit or explicit preferences, as well as the structuring of male work patterns (Phillips, 1983). These constraints on women's paid labour are discussed more fully in Chapter 5.

The fact that homeworkers have to consider their husbands' needs, as well as their children's, serves as a useful reminder that the family responsibilities which limit women's work options are not confined to the care of young children. In fact, in the population as a whole the number of women at home looking after elderly or handicapped dependents is greater than those looking after 'normal' children (Oliver, 1983). This puts women's responsibility for young children in its proper perspective, as only one among many domestic obligations.

Women's other obligations are clearly illustrated by the circumstances of the older homeworkers in the West Yorkshire sample. Although the age distribution of homeworkers in the sample shows it to be more typical of women of child-rearing age, it also demonstrates its prevalence among women of all ages, except the very elderly. Over a quarter of the sample were above normal child-bearing age. The situation of these women highlights the never-ending character of women's family responsibilities, as well as the importance of ill-health, redundancy and other factors. Of the 26 per cent of the sample who were above normal child-bearing age, three were over 60 and had retired from outside work. They did homework to supplement their pensions, and combined it with caring for grandchildren after school and in the school holidays. Another had left her outside job when her daughter was divorced, in order to keep house for her and her children. Still others had teenage children who did not mind her working 'as long as they get their meals'. The world of these women is one in which they are expected to maintain a wide range of service activities for other members of the household, including teenage and adult children.

Of the other homeworkers who were over normal child-rearing age, nine were in poor health themselves, or had to care for sick or elderly relatives. In contrast with the usual expectation, many had worked outside the home, full-time or part-time, when their children were young and had resorted to homeworking when they were too ill to work outside but too poor to leave the paid labour force. For example, one homeworker in her fifties, whose husband was in full-time employment, had worked all her life outside the home since leaving school. As a homeworker she commented that, 'My money goes to pay for prescriptions. I have a bad heart and need drugs. They are too much if I don't work. My husband's wage is not enough.' Another homeworker had left outside work at 53, in order to care for her husband when he had a stroke. After he died she began homeworking as a hand-knitter, earning 19p an hour for knitting garments sold in exclusive shops for £20 each. She pointed out that she liked to knit, and without the homeworking could not afford the wool, but added that 'the bit I earn helps me to exist'.

These women clearly identified themselves as workers. Although they recognised that at 50-plus their chances of obtaining outside employment were slim, many hoped to return to outside work once they were able. A homeworker who sewed blankets and other articles for horses was well aware of the price and markets in which these products were sold. For sewing and binding a horse blanket sold for £20 to customers she received 75p. Despite the risk to her job she was willing to testify before the Parliamentary Committee on homeworking and commented afterwards:

> I was made redundant three times. I've always worked and now I'm quite disabled. My daughter is on short-time and my husband has to have an operation. We can't manage but anyhow if I did not earn I'd be a nobody.

Even those homeworkers without young children who were neither in poor health nor had elderly or sick relatives depended on homeworking as a source of income. Two of them had part-time jobs in addition to homeworking. One pointed out that she would prefer outside work, but could not risk losing her homeworking by looking for an outside job.

In other words, the explanatory emphasis put on the care of young children obscures what is a life-long experience of women, namely that of servicing others on an unwaged basis, until they become too old or too ill themselves to carry on. It also neglects the fact that mothers of young children, like all women, are hampered in their work options by the character of the labour-market. Existing data do not make it possible to know whether the health and family responsibilities of homeworkers differ in any significant way from those of women who work outside the home. The increasing literature on women and waged work leads one to believe that domestic obligations are fairly similar for all women (see for instance Cavendish, 1981; Coyle, 1984; Westwood, 1984). At present all we can say with any certainty is that for women with dependent children or other family responsibilities, such as the care of the elderly and handicapped together with those in poor health, or redundant one possibility of earning is homeworking.

Homeworkers as members of minority ethnic groups

Some other explanations of homeworking labour are open to the same kinds of objections as those already raised with respect to 'dependent children'. These rely on assumptions regarding the needs or capacities of particular social categories, and ignore the participation of women with the same social characteristics in work outside the home. Presenting homeworking as an exclusive minority group activity obscures the common experiences of women workers in the labour market. These explanations risk dividing homeworkers from each other and from other women workers, rather than laying the basis for mutual support.

An example is the importance given to homeworkers' ethnicity as an explanation of homeworking labour. Those who have looked at homeworking among black women and women belonging to other minority groups have illuminated many of the problems they face as homeworkers (Anthias, 1983; Hackney–Islington Partnership, 1980; Hope *et al.*, 1976; Mitter, 1986; Saifullah Khan, 1979; Shah, 1975). All of these have concentrated on homeworkers in the clothing industry, however, and most have focused on homeworkers from one or two ethnic communities. They thus have the important advantages of making it possible to explore links between homeworking and the economic conditions prevailing in a particular industry, marketing strategies and technology, or investment costs and practices. They highlight the racism endemic in British society. Bringing these issues together in this way can, sometimes unwittingly, foster the belief that homeworking is negligible or marginal for other groups. Given the present state of knowledge about the use of homeworking labour in a wide range of disparate manufacturing and clerical tasks, in which, as we showed in Chapter 2, it is impossible to enumerate accurately the total number of homeworkers and suppliers in our society, this implication is not warranted.

Problems arise not only as regards the incidence of homeworking among ethnic groups but the kinds of explanations offered. Homeworking by women identified with particular minority communities has been variously explained by the prejudice these women face on the labour-market or by their lack of English or work experience and skills, and particularly by the persistence of cultural norms regarding women's work which are believed to differ significantly from those affecting indigenous white women.

Other explanations have focused on the ethnic identity of those who supply homework. In the popular press, for instance, suppliers who are identified as members of ethnic groups are blamed for bringing 'slave' conditions to Britain (see examples cited by Shah, 1975). More serious investigations have concentrated on a combination of factors – high unemployment rates among men belonging to minority communities, experience in the clothing trade, and the comparatively low setting-up costs involved in employing homeworkers – which may lead or force members of minority groups to establish themselves as subcontractors employing homeworkers from their own communities.

Arguments like these are quite different in character, and open to emphases which have many implications for explaining homeworking labour. Explanations which focus on unemployment rates among black women or women from other minority communities, for instance, are references to discrimination in the labour-market, and need to be carefully distinguished from the easy assumption that women from certain communities are precluded by the cultural norms of their communities from working outside the home. The latter explanation completely ignores the extensive participation of women from these same communities in the labour force, not only in Britain but in their country of origin (Allen, 1982c). Moreover, while some authors couch their discussion within the framework of those common features which constrain the work options of all women (see especially Saifullah Kahn, 1979), others have drawn a *contrast* between white women, who are assumed to be affected by 'life cycle' factors and women from ethnic minority groups, who are constrained by cultural norms peculiar to their communities (Shah, 1975). The absurdities of this contrast are readily apparent when one realises that the same ethnic community is placed in the first category by one author (Shah, 1975), and in the second by another (Anthias, 1983). It ought to be possible to do justice to the diversity of women's experience without ignoring the shared constraints and difficulties women face.

Our sample of homeworkers in West Yorkshire included a small number from one minority community and suggested that their reasons for forming part of the labour supply in homeworking overlapped considerably with those of other homeworkers in the sample. With the exception of one young unmarried woman, whose parents did not allow her to take up outside employment for religious reasons, the ten Pakistani homeworkers cited material and ideological constraints similar to those faced by the other homeworkers. Like white homeworkers, the Pakistani homeworkers usually mentioned the need to care for children. All worked out of economic need and, like other homeworkers, contributed a substantial amount to household earnings. White homeworkers were more likely to say that their husbands 'preferred' them to work at home, while Pakistani homeworkers were likely to say that their husbands would not 'allow' or 'permit' them to take outside employment. This may reflect comparatively minor differences in language use, or it may indicate that patriarchal controls are more overtly acknowledged in Pakistani households. In any case, the effect of the husband's wishes with respect to women's work options was identical. Psychological factors were also mentioned by a few women in both groups. Three Pakistani homeworkers said that homeworking helped to take their minds off the anxiety they had experienced since coming to Britain, while a few white women mentioned, in addition to other reasons for doing homework, that it helped to relieve the boredom of the domestic routine. Moreover, although three Pakistani women cited their lack of knowledge of English or fear of outside work as reasons for undertaking homework, others had worked outside the home before beginning homework. The determination of their work options was clearly more complex than popular myths regarding the housebound 'Asian' woman imply.

Other findings from this small number are relevant to some of the arguments regarding those who supply homework to women from minority communities. While one should be wary of drawing conclusions from so few, none the less our findings were so different from some of the usual expectations that they are worth pointing out. None of the Pakistani homeworkers were employed by their own relatives, and over half were employed by enterprises owned or managed by whites, not members of their own community. One homeworker machined disposable paper garments for the local health authority, for instance, and another worked directly for a locally-based international company. While these homeworkers relied upon family and friends to find out where homework was available, family connections between the homeworker and supplier, and all that connotes about particular forms of the control of labour, were absent. So far as we could judge, relations with the supplier were conducted on the same employer–employee basis as among other homeworkers. At least in our survey, then, homeworking was not strongly associated with the factors which might lead or force men from minority groups to establish small enterprises relying on homeworking labour. One of our highest paid homeworkers, a white woman, did work for an Indian employer and several other white women worked for a London-based white-owned business which used two Pakistani men as their agents. If evidence is thought to be needed, our data does not provide any support for the view that suppliers from minority communities are responsible for the poor employment conditions experienced by homeworkers.

The association of homeworking with ethnic minorities is becoming increasingly widely accepted, so much so that many people hearing about our research on homeworking in West Yorkshire have assumed that the project focused on the problems of 'Asian women'. While many women involved in homeworking are members of minority groups, and some face special problems, the ready identification of homeworking with minority groups suggests that little thought is being given to the restricted work opportunities of and family constraints on women more generally.

Homeworkers and the labour market

Some of the arguments about the participation in homeworking of women from minority groups, or those with dependent children, are not so much fallacious as inadequate, and need to be carefully distinguished from assumptions about homeworkers which have no basis whatsoever. Arguments about homeworkers' low performance as workers fall into this latter category. The argument that homeworkers perform below the standards of other workers, and for this reason are unable to obtain or are unsuitable for outside employment is frequently raised by the suppliers of homework. It is also cited by Wages Councils as a reason for setting homeworkers' wage rates below the rates set for in-workers doing precisely the same work, or for allowing employers to set a lower rate for particular individuals (ACAS 1978a and 1978b; Hakim and Dennis, 1982). We could find no evidence for homeworkers' lesser capacity as workers, however, and would argue that this argument draws attention away from crucial characteristics of the market for women's labour.

It needs emphasising, in the first place, that not all homeworking is unskilled. Many of the tasks involved, like machining garments, are defined as low-skilled, but this is as much a reflection of the way women's skills are defined as the actual character of the work (Armstrong, 1982; Phillips and Taylor, 1980). Moreover, many of the skills homeworkers use are not defined as 'trades', although the value added is considerable. The rosettes and other decorations made by homeworkers and attached by them to greeting cards triples the price at which the cards are sold.

More importantly, even if much homeworking is unskilled or low paid, it does not follow that the homeworkers themselves are unskilled, inexperienced or inefficient workers. Almost all the homeworkers in the West Yorkshire survey had previously worked outside the home, and two out of three had received some training in their previous jobs. Some of them were able to use this training as homeworkers, those working as burlers and menders or overlockers, for instance. In some cases these had earnings somewhat above the average for homeworkers. But most were forced to accept whatever homework was available and were unable to capitalise on their skills. They include homeworkers who had previously worked in white-collar occupations as punch card operators or telephonists.

Homeworkers' inability to use previously acquired skills does not differentiate them from other women workers. Women forced to accept part-time work after child-bearing or redundancy only rarely return to jobs with the same status, pay or skills as those they left (see also Ballard, 1984; Coyle, 1984). Women acquire the skills obtained through long apprenticeships much more rarely than men, and they face a labour-market which is highly segmented by age as well as gender. The part-time jobs held by homeworkers who also work outside the home are indicative of this. Apart for the two in secretarial work, two had jobs as cooks and one was a VDU operator, but the others were in the relatively unskilled jobs typical of the part-time sector: morning and evening cleaning, bar work, school meals assistant, sales assistant and factory evening shift work. Their hourly rates were higher than those they earned from homeworking, but still indicative of the narrow job options offered to women as part-time work.

Conclusions

Much of the discussion about homeworking has polarised around two contrasting interpretations of homeworkers' position as 'housewives'. Either they are assumed to need to earn only a bit 'extra', as pin money, or they are thought to be so exceptionally desperate that they are forced to accept very low wages for their work. The first explanation has no validity whatsoever. But even the second is not fully adequate. By any definition of the labour force which includes women as ordinary workers, homeworkers are not exceptional or atypical in their requirements or circumstances. According to official Department of Employment figures, one out of four workers is low paid, and the Low Pay Unit reckons the true figure is closer to one out of three (Pond and Winyard, n.d.). Homeworking is a particularly appalling example of women's position in the labour-market, not a contrast to it.

Homeworkers frequently have young children, or are responsible for the care of elderly or disabled relatives, but so do many women working outside the home. Ill-health appears as a particular problem. Even so, we know little about the health of women in the formal labour market, and cannot presume that many are not forced to continue in jobs outside the home despite ill-health. The factors which lead women into homeworking may well include the traditions of their communities, and in this case must be seen to include a tradition of paid homeworking among indigenous white women in particular trades and regions, not only the cultural norms of particular minority groups. But although individuals may experience a combination of circumstances which influence their entry into homeworking, the key features of their responsibility as economic contributors and for unpaid labour within households are similar to those of other women.

In looking at homeworking labour, therefore, one is not seeing the position of a marginal few but the effects of pervasive ideological and material constraints which limit the work options of a large proportion of the labour force. The sexual division of labour is not a division between male breadwinners and economically dependent housewives, but a division between women's need to fit paid work into the laborious, caring unpaid work of looking after their households and men's relative freedom in this respect. The importance of the notion of homeworkers as housewives is not its empirical validity but the ideological force which it carries. The construction of homeworkers as housewives/mothers provides a neat rationale for homeworking, but bears little relation to their actual needs or experience.

4

Homeworking as a method of production

Homeworking and its allied forms of outworking are very old forms of production which have been ignored in analyses of industrial production over a very long period. Their demise has long been predicted, and their persistence within industrial production is rarely investigated. Yet as Samuel (1977) so vividly demonstrates, along with other 'outmoded' forms of production, outwork persisted well into the nineteenth century and its expansion was fostered by the industrial revolution. In the nineteenth century rising demand for industrial and consumer goods was met by a proliferation of manual trades, small producers and outworkers. Productivity was transformed not only by steam power and machinery but by the intensification of work through outwork and sweating. Similarly, in the economies of Third World countries today, a large proportion of the demand for consumer goods and services and for industrial components continues to be met by unregulated production often based in domestic premises. Although this portion of Third World production was for a long time ignored by development planners and financial backers, its existence is increasingly being recognised and its potential for increasing employment and capital accumulation is the subject of extensive debate. Yet in the discussion of homeworking in Britain, particularly in official circles and publications, these debates and their implications for conditions of work in homeworking are noticeably absent.

In this chapter we want to look more closely at the role of homeworking in the modern economy. An understanding of homeworking as a method of production and the place of this form of production in the economy requires an analysis of the advantages and disadvantages homeworking offers. The identification and explanation of these has so far been approached in an extremely one-sided fashion. The distinctive gender composition of the homeworking labour force in Britain has led investigators to explain homeworking in terms of its advantages to 'housewives' who are constrained from accepting other forms of employment. This emphasis on the characteristics of the labour supply as a sufficient explanation is typical of accounts of women's work more generally and in part derives from them. As Alexander (1980) points out, most explanations of women's position in the labour-market invoke women's 'dual role' as an explanation of women's segregation in low-paid jobs and the expansion of part-time employment for women. Cultural expectations regarding women's roles are seen as the most significant influence on the character of women's paid work, although reference may be made to practical constraints as well as ideological influences. In contrast, comparatively little attention is devoted to the organisation of women's paid labour by employers to suit their own priorities.

Examples of explaining homework in terms of constraints on the women who undertake homework or their preference for working at home are numerous. In Chapter 3 we noted the frequency with which official reports trace homeworking to the preferences of homeworkers themselves. The distinctly ideological character of this emphasis can be seen in the conclusion that homeworking is mutually advantageous to both homeworkers and the suppliers of work (House of Commons, 1981a). This point of view follows from theoretical frameworks which attempt to derive the characteristics of labour-markets from the preferences and attributes of workers themselves. However, this emphasis on the needs of homeworkers is shared by other parties to the debate on homework whose political perspectives differ in other respects. The first *TUC Statement on Homeworking* (1978), for instance, begins a section entitled 'Why does homeworking continue to exist?' with a discussion of the characteristics of homeworkers themselves. Other examples are to be found among local authority projects which seek to organise homeworkers and to improve their employment prospects (National Homeworking Conference, 1984). These projects have tended to interpret homeworking as primarily a 'women's issue' and have seen improvements in homeworkers' pay and conditions of work primarily in terms of an attack on the sexual division of labour which confines women to the home. Among academic research projects too, many research designs have assumed that the best way of understanding homeworking is through obtaining information about homeworkers themselves through interviews or surveys.

Our material on homeworking in West Yorkshire convinced us that the identification of the characteristics of the labour supply cannot provide a sufficient explanation of the place of homeworking in the production of goods and services, nor serve as an adequate guide to the complexity of this method of organising production. Our material was collected by a number of different methods. One of the most fruitful was that of following up information given by homeworkers and ex-homeworkers. Information gathered in this way included data on firms supplying homework, how the supply of work was organised and where and for how much goods were sold. We also carried out a content analysis of advertisements for homeworkers appearing in local newspapers. Further information was obtained from interviews with agents and middlemen, employees and ex-employees of firms supplying homework, and from interviews with local trades unionists. We also found some of the existing literature on the role of subcontracting (especially Friedman, 1977) and on domestic production in other countries useful in thinking through some of the distinctive features of homeworking in Britain.

Homeworking as a method of production

Recent research on employment in Third World economies has given domestic production an important place in its analysis of forms of production. By the early 1970s development planners had become aware that a large number of persons who did not have secure, waged employment were not actually economically inactive, but engaged in a range of income-earning activities. They conceived of Third World urban workers as divided into two sectors, a 'formal sector' consisting of secure, comparatively well-paid waged employees recorded in official accounting, and a larger 'informal sector' dominated by self-employed workers engaged in marginal, unproductive or illegal economic activities (Hart, 1973;

International Labour Office, 1972; see also Moser, 1978 for related uses of these concepts). Since then, critics have argued that the conventional division between waged and self employment does not accurately distinguish those workers who enjoy a moderate degree of stable, secure employment from those who do not. Bromley and Gerry (1979), for instance, suggest the term 'casual workers' for the latter category, and include those involved in:

1. short-term wage work, paid and contracted for by the day, week, month or season or for fixed tasks or terms;
2. disguised wage-work, including workers who because they do not work at the employer's premises are not legally considered employees, but whose earnings are derived from piece-work payments or from commissions from one or more related firms;
3. dependent work, in which the worker is wholly dependent upon one or more larger enterprises for credit, the rental of premises or equipment, raw materials and an outlet for the product; and
4. true self-employment, in which the producer owns the means of production and has a considerable degree of real freedom in choice of supplier and outlets. In this last case the producer's livelihood is precarious, but depends upon general market conditions, not specific firms.

If the critical issues are level of income, security of employment and potential for capital accumulation, they argue, 'casual workers' include workers whose work is subject to a variety of modes of appropriation and legal relations to the individuals or firms who appropriate their labour.

Others have suggested that these issues are more effectively analysed by shifting the focus of analysis from the individual worker to the type of enterprise or mode of production. The term petty commodity production has been adopted to characterise production which takes place in small-scale enterprises in which the direct producer owns the means of production but has little autonomy over the production process (MacEwan Scott, 1979). The term, derived from Marx, has come to be associated with a school of thought which stresses the subordination of nominally independent small-scale commodity production to large-scale capitalist enterprises (Moser, 1978). Illegal or unproductive services are now recognised as comprising a very small proportion of the economic activity undertaken under this mode of production.

Homeworking in Britain is not petty commodity production. For although most homeworkers in Britain own or rent the means of production and the premises in which they work, they do not operate enterprises, dependent or otherwise, nor buy and sell on the market. Most would be included in the category Bromley and Gerry term 'disguised wage-work'. They are not subcontractors but waged workers. Most have worked outside the home as part of the waged labour force before entering homeworking. In West Yorkshire some had previously worked in factories owned by the same firm which later supplied them with homework (see also Hakim, 1980), thereby *casualising* their employment conditions.

Nor are there clear-cut differences between the types of enterprise which supply homework and those which do not. Many homeworkers are employed by subcontractors or agents who organise homeworking as the intermediaries of large enterprises, but others are directly employed by national and international firms. For this reason it is not appropriate to define homeworking in Britain as part of a mode of production characterised by small-scale commodity production. It is better described as a *method* of production, one adopted by large and small-scale capitalist enterprises in a wide variety of circumstances.

The adoption of homeworking

A range of circumstances which are most likely to lead firms in industrial societies to adopt homeworking as a method of production have been identified (Hakim, 1984b; Mitter, 1986; Murray, 1983; Rainnie, 1984; Rubery *et al.*, 1984; Rubery and Wilkinson, 1981; Wray, 1985). Technical feasibility is an obvious consideration. Homeworking is most easily adopted when the production process is already highly fragmented, or where considerable handiwork is required as part of the production process. But homework is also feasible in many other circumstances, as the production process only rarely presents insuperable barriers. Mechanisation and homework are not antithetical. Indeed, mechanisation can increase the supply of homework if the mechanisation of one stage of production generates more labour-intensive work at later stages. In the Victorian period, for instance, sugar was refined in factories but manufactured into sweets in back street kitchens, while in Sheffield thirty or forty rolling mills supplied steel for the cutlery trade organised by outworking journeymen (Samuel, 1977). Today technological developments can open or re-open opportunities for the vertical disintegration of production through the development of independently operated tools. Typesetting is a recent and important example of a production process which is said to have moved out of the factory into the 'garage' (*Printing World*, 1984). Even when production is necessarily highly centralised, as in batch flow processes, homeworking may be adopted for ancillary processes like packing, packaging, maintenance and cleaning.

As important as technical considerations are the economic and organisational advantages of homeworking. Some studies have suggested that firms which use homeworkers and other forms of casualised labour are characterised by better financial performance than firms which do not (Hakim, 1985). This is partly because the capital/output ratio is low, due to the absence of fixed capital costs. Profitability is also enhanced because homeworkers are used as a buffer against market fluctuations. This is particularly important to firms dealing in a product market in which competition is particularly intense or in which the market is highly unpredictable. Conditions like these are typical of firms in declining sectors, in which either the market is shrinking or international competition undercuts sales. But homeworking is also adopted by expanding firms. In the latter case, the development of new markets accompanies the production of new products, and homeworkers may be employed while it becomes clear whether or not markets justify capital investment (Rubery and Wilkinson, 1981).

Sub-contracting

The use of homeworking appears to be particularly pronounced when subcontractors are forced to compete among themselves to reduce prices as a condition of obtaining orders. The best known example of the use of homeworking in conditions of this kind is the clothing industry. Seasonality of sales and frequent fashion changes which lead to short production runs are two reasons for the prevalence of homeworking in clothing manufacturing. However, its use is also derived from the structure of ownership and control of the retail market, particularly the increasing domination of the market by High Street retail chains and mail order houses (Mitter,

1986; Rainnie, 1984). These firms, which used to manufacture many of the goods they sold, have now withdrawn from direct production and farm out the work on a contract basis to small firms who themselves put out work to agents and homeworkers. Competition between retail chains makes them resistant to passing price increases on to the consumer, while their monopolisation of the retail trade enables them to pass costs and risks of production 'backwards' on to their suppliers. This distribution of costs and risks is typical of subcontracting arrangements and of course is one of the main reasons why the larger firm adopts them (Friedman, 1977). They force the supplier at the end of the chain to seek ever-cheaper sources of labour and to avoid assuming obligations which, with the possible loss of later contracts, would prove highly costly. In this situation the use of a homeworking labour force is a practicable and advantageous solution for any individual supplier, and competition between suppliers forces others to adopt a similar solution.

The relation between the homeworker and the supplier of her work is directly analogous to the relation between firms at different levels. In order to obtain work homeworkers are forced to compete among themselves to increase their output, to accept lower wages if necessary and to assume costs of production as part of their domestic economy. The advantages of homeworking to the supplier (and the disadvantages to the homeworker) are spelled out in more detail below.

Benefits to the supplier

In documenting the expansion of labour-intensive production which formed a major part of the industrial growth of nineteenth-century Britain, Samuel (1977) points to a number of advantages which labour-intensive technologies, including outwork, had over mechanisation. First and foremost he includes the existence of an abundant labour supply, both skilled and unskilled, which encouraged the perpetuation of capital-saving rather than labour-saving technologies. He also points to a number of ways in which labour-intensive production could be used to increase productivity or to keep costs down. The intensity of work, or productivity, in labour-intensive technologies is capable of being easily enhanced through the pushing down of piece-work rates, or 'sweating' and through an intensification of the division of labour. The use of labour-intensive technologies also made possible extensive savings in raw materials, as machinery tended to be wasteful of raw materials and often required raw materials of a better standard (and therefore more expensive) for efficient running. 'Putting out' or domestic production saved the employer fixed costs of production which enables the enterprise to cope with market uncertainties. Finally, some consumer preferences, especially in the luxury market, could only be satisfied through handicrafts.

Analysts concerned with Third World economies have identified similar reasons for the persistence in them of small-scale commodity production. They have been concerned to understand why international and national capital does not enter into production of the identical goods and services and drive out the small-scale producer through the use of economies of scale. They point to a number of advantages of small-scale production. In the case of Third World economies an abundant supply of labour, the use of unpaid family labour, and the undervaluation of the labour of the self-employed often makes goods produced in domestic premises even cheaper than could be achieved through capital-intensive methods.

This list of benefits domestic production has offered in two quite different contexts indicates that the availability of low-cost labour is an important consideration in any explanation of homeworking. It also indicates that the availability of labour is only one of a number of possible considerations, however, and that the availability of labour with certain qualities is constituted historically through diverse processes. The contribution made by unpaid family labour to the low cost of domestic production in the Third World, for instance, derives partly from patriarchal forms of control of labour, while the creation of a surplus labour force in Victorian Britain was influenced by capital, in the form of changing capitalist relations and techniques of production in agriculture, and guaranteed by the state through reforms of the Poor Law.

In contrast, the extent to which the homeworking labour force in Britain today is constructed not only through the ideology of appropriate work for women, but also through state policies and through the recruitment preferences and production practices of management has been almost ignored. In a wide-ranging discussion of the construction of different categories of female labour power, Pearson (1986) points out that different production processes and industrial branches require different kinds of labour power, supplied by different sub-sectors of the female labour force. To achieve a highly productive and flexible labour force managements actively manipulate differences between women in age, class and cultural attributes. In existing accounts of homeworking, however, so little attention has been given to firm-level employment strategies that we know very little about their selection practices. We do not even know whether the preponderance of homeworkers who are married women with young children reflects the recruitment practices of suppliers rather than constraints on the employment of these women outside the home (Smith, 1976).

The construction of homeworkers as a cheap and flexible labour force through the production practices of suppliers is another area which has received little attention. Some of the benefits homeworking offers the supplier, and the ways they are achieved, are not easily identified. The home has been separated from the factory/ office both conceptually and ideologically and consequently the criteria applied to the costing of in-firm production are not usually applied to the home.

From our research it is clear that there are many ways in which homeworking as a method of production cheapens labour and other costs of production, or creates other organisational advantages for the supplier and for the ultimate seller of goods. Some of these are discussed below.

The reduction of fixed capital, overheads and running costs

The advantages of homeworking to the supplier derive in part from savings in capital and running costs. It is important to remember that with homeworking overheads do not disappear but are borne by the worker as a condition of taking on work at home.

A reckoning of the costs borne by homeworkers includes various forms of overhead and working capital and their associated costs, including workspace, work benches and warehousing, lighting, heating, cleaning and maintenance, equipment, machinery (including repairs and replacement of parts), and insurance (both personal and for the machinery, materials and products). The level of costs varies with the type of product, the organisation of the supply and collection of work, and the provision of machinery and materials.

Some savings to suppliers of homework carry risks for the

homeworker which go beyond quantifiable economic costs. These derive from the absence of safety and health regulations in homeworking and non-enforcement of those which exist. Many homeworkers are required to store and use glue which gives off dangerous fumes, while for others the storage of large quantities of material creates serious fire hazards. As individuals homeworkers are not in a position to provide the safeguards used in factories, like complex and expensive ventilation or fire protection systems, and often are not warned of the need for special containers and dispensers for glue (Greenwich Homeworkers Project, 1984b). They therefore bear these costs as increased risks of accident, fire and ill-health rather than out-of-pocket capital costs.

Other costs merge into household expenses and are therefore ignored or under-estimated not only by some of the homeworkers but by those commenting upon or analysing homework data. Nearly half the homeworkers in West Yorkshire mentioned only the cost of electricity for their machines, although a higher proportion admitted to other costs when specifically asked about them. Because it is assumed that heating and lighting will be used in the home anyway, these are usually discounted. Actually this ignores the cost of the extra heat and lighting used, for instance, when working late at night, for a workroom not usually heated, or to provide adequate heating and lighting to maintain good working conditions for close sedentary work. Other expenses which merge into the domestic economy include the depreciation of domestic furniture and fittings and the cost of telephone calls to arrange for the delivery and collection of work or to report faulty machines.

The majority of homeworkers are not reimbursed for these expenses either by the supplier or through the tax system. Only 17 per cent of the West Yorkshire homeworkers reported some contribution to expenses by the supplier, and nearly half of these were working for the same firm. The contribution did not in any case cover even the homeworker's additional electricity. Some firms pay expenses to some homeworkers but not others. The reason for this was not clear, but accords with the pattern of paying different rates to homeworkers doing the same work.

A good example of the difficulties homeworkers face in claiming expenses for tax purposes comes from one homeworker's testimony before the Select Committee in 1981. Many homeworkers earn below the tax threshold, and are therefore unable to reclaim expenses in the form of tax rebates. In her case, however, the firm which supplied her work withdrew tax, but she did not reclaim the extra £3.50 a week on her electricity bill. Nor had she been able to obtain adequate advice from tax officials about her other expenses. At the end of her testimony she came back with a question:

> As far as tax rebates are concerned for certain things, do they [the tax inspectors] have the right at different offices to turn round and say: 'Look, that's your choice, that's your problem', because I do not say I would claim for carpets but I go through a carpet a year . . . . So I have to pay out money to buy that once a year. I shampoo and shampoo it till it is threadbare [to get rid of the industrial waste] but there are other things you have to consider – the fact you are using electricity. I have to buy tools. I have to have my scissors sharpened and my scissors in particular are very expensive. I pay £4 a pair for good scissors which you have to have.   (House of Commons, 1981b, 28 April)

The chairman of the session could offer no sensible source of advice. Whereas academics and other professionals and self-employed businessmen can recoup such expenses and in factory-organised production they are included in accounting, home-workers carry them as an additional burden.

Savings in variable capital or labour costs

In addition to the supplier's savings in capital investment and overheads, there can be no question but that the employment of homeworkers reduces average labour costs. As a method of production it cheapens the price of labour and carries organisational advantages which reduce total labour costs per unit of output. We shall now consider in more detail why this is the case.

The employment of a homeworking labour force makes it possible for the supplier to purchase labour only as and when required. This flexibility is acquired at no cost to the supplier. Payment is for output only. Homeworkers are paid piece-rates, with no basic wage component or guaranteed weekly earnings when work is slack. There are no paid holidays, no overtime pay for evening, night or weekend work, and no redundancy pay. Home-workers set up and clear away work in their own time. They are forced to bear the costs of fluctuations in the flow of work which arise out of the production process. These include not only seasonal fluctuations in demand, but also poor management of the flow of work, management mistakes in forecasting demand, and changes in the product. In fact the presence of homeworkers in the labour force makes it possible for employers to remove from the factory work which disrupts the smooth flow of factory production, thereby increasing the efficiency of more highly paid in-firm labour.

The construction of homeworkers as a cheap and flexible labour force is easily misconstrued. The characteristics of homeworking as a method of production are often confused with the characteristics of homeworkers themselves, whose domestic responsibilities are seen as preventing them from working on a regular basis. Nothing could be further from the actual situation. As we demonstrate in Chapter 5, to meet their orders suppliers call on homeworkers' labour without notice or regard for their circumstances and shed labour when orders fall off. Rather, it is the absence of trade union and legislative protection which enables the employer to treat homeworkers' labour as a completely variable factor. The highly mystifying designation of homeworkers as 'self-employed' removes them from protective legislation for employees, including health and safety regulations, and leaves them without the benefits of paid maternity or sick leave and pensions in addition to those mentioned above. As they are not protected by so-called 'restrictive practices', they can be asked to take on any work within a broadly agreed range of products. The absence of a guaranteed weekly wage or a training premium means that they themselves bear the costs of their lower output while learning new work. Suppliers' savings of employers' National Insurance contributions therefore represent but a very small portion of the actual savings involved.

Wages

In addition to acquiring flexibility without incurring the costs which would be involved with other forms of labour, the use of a homeworking labour force appears to make it possible for the employer/supplier to purchase labour at a lower price than is the case for in-plant production. The lower rates of pay prevailing in homeworking have been explained in a number of ways: first in terms of homeworkers' lower productivity, level of skill, irregular working patterns, and freedom from industrial constraint; and secondly as a consequence of homeworkers' weak bargaining position and unregulated employment status. These explanations have serious implications for the possibility of improving homeworkers' earnings, and have to be considered with this in mind.

The comparability of homeworkers' and in-workers' rates of pay is most easily ascertained in industries governed by Wages Councils orders. In toy manufacturing it was found that 82 per cent of homeworkers earned less than the Statutory Minimum Rate (ACAS, 1978b), and a survey of wages in the clothing industry found eight times as many homeworkers as in-workers (16 per cent of the homeworkers surveyed) earning below the minimum rate (Hakim and Dennis, 1982). Although outside the Wages Councils comparisons are more difficult to make, generally homeworkers earn considerably less than in-workers doing the same work (Cragg and Dawson, 1981; TUC, 1985). Even highly-trained white-collar homeworkers who do not fall into the category of low paid, like programme analysts, earn considerably less than in-workers doing the same work (*Guardian Women*, 1985; Huws, 1984b).

Surveys of homeworkers in manufacturing and routine clerical work almost invariably uncover very low rates of pay (Beale, 1978; Brown, 1974; Crine, 1979a, 1979b; Jordan, 1978). The wage rates of homeworkers in West Yorkshire were no different. We compared them with the various indices of low pay for 1979–80. when the survey was conducted. For 1979 the official figure, derived from Supplementary Benefit entitlement for a family of four, was £60 for a 40 hour week, or £1.50 an hour (Crine, 1980b). By 1980 the equivalent figure was £74.03, or £1.85 an hour, which for 1980 was very similar to indices of low pay used by the Low Pay Unit, which are based on either the lowest decile of full-time male workers or two-thirds the mean level of male earnings (Pond, 1981). Most homeworkers' earnings were below either of these figures, some very much below. Ninety-two per cent of the West Yorkshire homeworkers earned less than £1.50 an hour, bringing the homeworker into the low pay bracket, and 40 per cent earned 50p an hour or less. Twenty-two of the ninety homeworkers worked in industries governed by the Wages Councils, but sixteen of these were earning below the rate set by their Wages Council, some grossly below.

The wage rate and productivity

The lower rates paid to homeworkers are taken as given in official circles and seen as a fair reflection of the relative amounts of skill and effort involved. This view is illustrated by two reports on homeworking in Wages Councils industries. The Council governing wages in button manufacturing sets a rate for homeworkers which is only 60 per cent of the rate set for in-workers. This is presented as a mechanism through which the Wages Council seeks to link the wage levels of homeworkers and in-workers and thereby prevent home-workers' wages from sinking even lower (ACAS, 1978a). In a second survey ACAS recommends instituting this kind of differen-tial in toy manufacturing, where previously it did not exist (ACAS, 1978b). The arguments put forward by employers and the trade unions for differential rates are couched in terms of the productivity differential between homeworkers and in-workers, differences in their aptitude and skill, and differences in their work situation, in which industrial discipline is exercised in one, while in the other it is absent and the demands of domestic life are presumed to interrupt the homework. Arguments of this kind are used to support the inference that it is more expensive to employ homeworkers than in-workers and/or that in-workers can justifiably claim a higher rate of pay as recompense for their discipline and superior skills.

These conclusions and the assumptions on which they are based are open to question. Although homework is often associated with unskilled labour, this is by no means always the case (Rubery and Wilkinson, 1981). Productivity is determined by many factors other than the skill and effort of the work, such as the level of capital investment, the degree and quality of mechanisation, the organisa-tion of work and the proficiency or otherwise of management. The argument that homeworkers are more expensive to employ rests on measures of productivity and their relation to profitability which are not applicable to homeworking. Productivity is conventionally measured as output per unit of time worked, such as an hour's work or a week's work. But since homeworkers are paid only for the output, the time taken and the manner in which goods are produced does not affect the employer's costs so long as orders are met. The kinds of factors cited by ACAS and others are not relevant to the production costs of the employer of homeworkers. Homeworkers bear many of the costs of production which in in-plant production are met by the employer, and their labour is cheap even when they are paid the same rate as in-workers.

Since homeworker's lower rates cannot be explained on grounds of lower productivity, or high costs of homework production, other aspects of their position must be considered. Their weak position in the labour market is often attributed, for example, to competition for the work available, to homeworkers' isolation from other workers, to their ignorance of prevailing wage rates and the market value of the products they make or services they provide. A further argument adduced is that homeworkers undermine their position by their willingness or capacity to accept lower rates. All these arguments, apart from the first, put the onus of the explanation for low pay on to the homeworkers themselves. They are similar to the arguments discussed in Chapter 3 which seek to explain the existence of homeworking in terms of the supposed characteristics of homeworkers and they exhibit the same analytical shortcomings.

In West Yorkshire we found, however, that many of the women who made items which were sold in retail stores or local markets, advertised in specialist or quality journals, or included in mail order catalogues, were very well aware of the prices charged. They told us of the difference between what they were paid and the sale price of the goods. Several of them knew of in-workers doing the same work as they did and the differences in the rates paid. In addition, the isolation of homeworkers which is usually assumed rather than demonstrated proved in many cases to be a wrong assumption. Apart from the co-operative working practices mentioned in Chapter 6, women working for the same supplier or agent shared, through the van driver, details not only of pay, but who was being given what sort of work. The 'isolated' homeworker has, in fact, a store of information, through a variety of networks and her experience. Her problem is not a lack of information, but a lack of effective means to change the highly individualised relationship in which the supplier of work operates in a totally unregulated manner. He/she was recognised as holding all the cards, giving out the work, setting the rates and the deadlines. The explanation lies not with the homeworkers but with the casualised nature of homeworking.

Another explanation for their low pay is that they have lower income needs (Rubery and Wilkinson, 1980, 1981; and above, Chapter 3). This construction of homeworkers as economically dependent leaves out of account the major contribution they make to household budgets. The secondary earner/family wage argument assumes that male breadwinners are paid at a level according to family or household needs. It also assumes state benefit is adequate for bringing up a family. Such assumptions are obviously false. They remain, however, very popular.

The reproduction of labour in terms of day-to-day costs is met in part by women undertaking homework, combining this in some instances with paid work outside the home. Some households are entirely dependent on homework (Mitter, 1986) frequently including the labour of children. In West Yorkshire the majority of homeworkers were found to be in households with at least one member employed outside the home, but without the homeworkers' contribution the households would have been financially unviable (see Chapter 3). Those who justify lower rates of pay for homeworkers by labelling them as secondary earners with lower income needs, are able to do so only by ignoring the economic and social realities of their households.

The over-supply of homeworking labour and the competition between women to get such work is not explained by describing the situation in which women, particularly those with young children or with elderly or handicapped dependents, search for work. The ideological and material constraints on all adult women place them in a weak market situation. The conditions under which women engage in waged labour, inside or outside the home, were discussed in Chapter 3. The payment women receive for their work varies, but for homeworkers, it is essential to focus on the organisation of homework production and the legal parameters in which it takes place.

Homework is set within an organisation of sub-contracting and tendering. Firms, of national and international standing, put out work for tender or sub-contract whole or part-processes. Middlemen and agents are engaged in recruiting workers and supplying firms. At each level these activities are hidden. For example, one of the largest national firms selling babies' and childrens' wear, clothing, prams, cots and all manner of goods relies in part on a system of tendering. Few of the customers are aware that there are homeworkers employed by sub-contractors who earn less than 75p an hour, to produce some of the goods. These final distributors do not take responsibility for the wages paid by those to whom they sub-contract. Neither the final distributor of the goods, nor the agent or sub-contractor, is bound by any minimum rates of pay or required to include a fair wages clause in any tender put out.

By abolishing the Fair Wages Clause, and encouraging a squeeze on wage rates, the issue of fair competition is raised in the most acute form (Low Pay Unit, 1983). In the case of piece-rates in homeworking there is no effective regulation and a total abdication of responsibility by all those involved.

The present rates paid to homeworkers bear no relation to the needs of their households, or to their skill or productivity. Piece-work rates fall to the lowest levels at which labour is available. In the very short term this economic logic has its attractions. Whether or not considerations which exercised those at the end of the nineteenth century and in the first decade of the twentieth century should be revived is a question of both moral and economic concern. Such concerns have been raised by the Low Pay Unit and hinted at by the TUC, but in general they are ignored by politicians and by those in power. The firms which use homeworking labour refuse to recognise it and fail to speak up against the conditions in which it is employed. Homeworking, far from being a damper on a firm's profitability or possible expansion, is being used increasingly for short-term profits with no regard to longer-term economic and social costs.

The devolution of management functions

In addition to the savings outlined so far, the supplier derives considerable benefits from the way in which the management of labour is exercised. The problems of organising homeworking labour is dealt with in many cases by the use of agents and middlemen, who assume some of the costs of management. They in turn devolve the economic costs and organisational tasks on to homeworkers.

From our research in West Yorkshire it appears that there are a number of quite different arrangements for managing home-workers. Overall supervision may be organised by the personnel department of a small firm in a comparatively sophisticated formal fashion, or by individuals whose status and function differ considerably. For example, a firm which supplied decorative linings to a box-making factory (which was in turn supplying a national company which produces chocolates) recruited homeworkers through newspaper advertisements, and used written instructions to communicate with them. In another case middlemen working on their own account, without fixed premises, delivered and collected work in Bradford for a London-based sub-contractor in the clothing industry. They recruited and trained individual homeworkers, supervised the quality of work and set piece-rates each time a new dress style was distributed. They were not normally paid for spoiled work until it was passed back to homeworkers to be made good.

Savings to the ultimate supplier through using sub-contractors or agents can be considerable. For example, a businesswoman who was an ex-homeworker undertook all the essential management tasks. She recruited homeworkers, supplied and organised the work, calculated and paid their wages, costed and bought in materials, and designed the product. These were supplied to firms using homeworkers to decorate greeting cards both in West Yorkshire and in the Midlands. Her costing did not include the expense of using her own home as an office or her time on management tasks. Her level of reward was much lower than the manufacturers would have had to pay a manager doing the same work. It derived from her ability to recruit and pay her home-workers a rate of sufficiently low to provide her with a profit margin which she found acceptable, which kept orders coming in.

Recruitment, training and quality control

Although sub-contractors (or occasionally 'one of the partners') maintain overall control of production, many management functions become the responsibility of the homeworker. The examples from three areas of management, recruitment, training, and production, indicate that homeworkers frequently assume management responsibilities as a condition of being supplied with work themselves.

Homeworkers are involved in the recruitment of other workers. As our data show, nearly half the homeworkers were recruited by a neighbour or friend. This is actively encouraged by the supplier. For example, one homeworker recruited another fourteen workers after being told that 'it is not worth sending a truck for one woman'. In many other cases where homeworkers are unable to cope with the level of work they recruit help from neighbours, relatives or friends, who then begin homeworking on a regular basis. The new workers continue to be given work by the first worker, or she may organise for them to receive work directly from the supplier. But in every case, the recruitment of workers is carried out by the homeworkers themselves, often as a condition of receiving work.

In training homeworkers, savings in management costs are additional to savings in homeworkers' pay rates. Homeworkers receive only a modicum of in-service training for their homeworking tasks. Suppliers exploit skills homeworkers have acquired before entering homework, as, for example, those of machinists or overlockers. In these cases as well as in even the most repetitive assembly work, a learning period is required before speed and accuracy are built up. This period is financed directly by the very low earnings homeworkers can make. There is usually no initial training rate, regardless of productivity. Homeworkers are left to get on as best they can, and until their speed is built up earnings are especially low compared with the time they spend.

The meeting of target dates, quality control and supervisory functions, all of which carry costs under in-plant accounting, are left to homeworkers. The intensity of work is adequately controlled through the incentive of piece-work rates, through the threat of no more work if the homeworker fails to complete orders, or to get others to do so, and through the spacing of the delivery and collection of work.

The main way of controlling quality of work is the refusal to pay for any work not up to standard. Corrections have to be made in the homeworker's own time. Moreover, since homeworkers are paid only for work completed satisfactorily, firms can afford to be careless of homeworkers' time. One agent told us that the instructions homeworkers are given are usually less adequate than in factory production. In other cases homeworkers have to correct mistakes made in earlier stages of production before getting on with their own work, but their piece-rate are not necessarily adjusted accordingly. Because it is the homeworker who bears the cost of making good any mistakes, the supplier has no incentive to improve methods of production by giving proper instructions or training. For example, the women making decorations for cards are linked with the women fixing on these decorations. Those who are required to sort and box the cards pass back any inadequacies. So between them groups of workers at their own expense, often geographically separated, supervise the work of each other, providing the sub-contractor/supplier with goods of a quality he can guarantee to his 'firm'.

Conclusions

As a method of production, homeworking is as old as capitalism itself. It has never gone out of existence, but has rarely been visible. Understanding why it persists and the conditions under which it is carried out are crucial to any understanding of the modern economy. For an understanding of the advantages that homeworking offers and the conditions under which it is likely to be adopted requires a grasp of who benefits by it. Where many women are unable to find work outside the home firms gain far more from this situation, for numerous reasons than the women workers do. By using the labour of women to work in their own homes considerable savings are made in fixed costs, overheads, management and labour costs. The flexible use of labour is a primary element in profitability. Risks and costs of production which the employer would bear in factories or offices are passed on to the homeworker. These include not only the overhead costs, but also those of recruitment and supervision.

Trade unionists have recognised the threat this poses in their struggles to achieve negotiated agreements, on, for instance, hours, the length of the working week, guaranteed basic wage rates and over-time. The locus of this struggle has been outside the home. By default a method of production has been allowed to go largely unchallenged which incorporates every source of exploitation they have sought to combat. Cynical observers might say that this has happened because it was only women who did this work. Others might argue that collective action for those at home is impossible. For whatever reason, the method of production in homeworking has produced a situation in which very low pay and no employee rights exist.

There are many lessons to be learned from this. The relation between the supplier of work and the homeworker has many parallels with the relation between large firms and their subcontractors and is in fact deeply enmeshed in it. Homeworking is an extreme form of what can be called the peripheralisation of production (Friedman, 1977). The national or international firm which sub-contracts a portion of its production obtains alternative sources of supply and benefits from the lower rates commanded by workers in small firms as compared with those in large organised plants. Its employees' jobs are, it may be argued, to some extent protected by those sub-contractors and workers who are forced to bear the burden of risk.

Rather than firing its direct employees and leaving capital equipment idle, which was once the case but perhaps no longer, the large firm facing fluctuating or declining sales fails to renew its contracts. It does not bear any responsibility for the costs of redundancy of the sub-contractor's labour force, nor, because they are defined as self-employed, for any homeworkers it supplies with work, directly or indirectly.

The contribution of homeworking to the viability of the sub-contractor, or agent or middlemen is clear. It represents a way of passing on the risks and costs of production to the homeworker, a way of preparing for and dealing with uncertain demand, and surviving under conditions in which access to the market is dominated by the interests of the larger firm. However, the long-term advantages of homeworking are less clear, especially as regards the long-term profitability of large firms and the employment prospects of their workers. As in the case of the clothing industry, homeworking may lead employers to dispense with in-plant production entirely, and unfair competition for short-term advantage may substitute for capital investment, product innovation and market development and so override viable competition in the long-run. There is also the distinct possibility that homeworking and other kinds of unfair competition will intensify rather than resolve the particular economic problems to which they are in part a response. There is an important international dimension to the class and sexual division of labour, and while the expansion of homeworking in Britain is in part a response to competition from abroad, so long as their wages are lower Third World homeworkers can in turn undercut those in Britain. Moreover, strategies which depend on obtaining competitive advantage through pushing down wages or passing on costs need to be judged in relation to the level of effective demand. While homeworking production can, by enabling firms to lower their prices, help to increase the size of the market, the various forms of sweating can also push wages so low that effective demand is reduced, forcing firms to lower their wage costs still further in the hope of capturing a share of a still further declining market. The wider implications of the casualisation of labour for sustained economic growth mean that the problems it poses extend far beyond its effects on the low-paid workers and their families.

5
The mechanisms of control: the myth of autonomy

One of the attractions of homeworking is thought to be the autonomy the homeworker has in deciding when and for how long she will work and at what pace. The time and effort control exercised over the assembly line worker and all those who clock in and out of work is contrasted with a person working in her own home, with no supervisor or timekeeper. In the abstract such a contrast appears to give the homeworker a freedom and flexibility denied the factory or office worker. It is a critical component of positive evaluations of remunerated work at home, and a major reason why homeworking is assumed to be a boon for women who need to adjust their paid work around family responsibilities. But this picture is quite misleading.

Working at home presents problems which beset many kinds of workers. The resident railway crossing keepers employed by British Rail, for instance, do not work continuously all day, but they must be available to open crossing gates for up to 16 hours a day, a working week of some 85 to 90 hours. For these workers and their families meals, sleep and leisure are punctuated by so many interruptions that normal life is impossible. Nor are they entitled to the overtime pay which most British Rail workers can take for granted (T. Owen, 1980). In their case the 'free time' which presumably is supposed to make up for their low pay and long hours is totally illusory.

Accurately ascertaining the character of work obligations is particularly important in the case of homeworkers because assumptions about their conditions of work are frequently used to justify their exclusion from rights and benefits conferred on employees under the law. Along with other workers who have no formal contract or whose employment status is ambiguous, homeworkers who wish to claim benefits are permitted to apply as individuals for a ruling on their employment status to an Industrial Tribunal or, on appeal, to an Employment Appeal Tribunal (EAT). This is an option which is taken up by very few homeworkers, but tribunal cases have come to form an important arena in which homeworkers' employment status has been debated. The arguments and the decisions reached provide illuminating examples of the different conceptions of homeworkers' actual obligations to the supplier as well as of the very narrow definitions of normal employment.

In deciding homeworkers' employment status, tribunals have to determine whether homeworkers' obligations to the supplier and the supplier's obligations to the homeworker are of a contractual character (see Baxi, 1985). The narrow interpretation favoured by some judges, including the dissenting judge in a Court of Appeal case (*Nethermere (St. Neots) Ltd.* v. *Taverna and Another*, 3 May 1984; *The Times*, 1984) has been to allow only a 'legally binding contract' as evidence of contractual mutual obligations. But tribunals may also consider whether or not the homeworker's conditions of employment, including control and supervision of their work, entitle them to employment status. This has led the Inland Revenue, for instance, to argue that homeworkers are not employees because they

> are not bound by the conditions of normal employment. They work for any number of principals, do the work when they like, and for such hours as they want. No notice is legally required from either party of termination [of contract].   (*D'Ambrogio* v. *Hyman Jacobs* (1978) IRLR 236, quoted in Townshend-Smith, 1979, p. 1022)

In this and several other cases which have come before Industrial Tribunals, EATs and the courts, the Inland Revenue classification of homeworkers has been successfully challenged. In *D'Ambrogio* v. *Hyman Jacobs* (1978) IRLR 236 the tribunal concluded that 'it cannot follow merely from the fact that a person works at home that they can work when and for how long they wish'. The EAT in the case of *Airfix Footwear* v. *Cope* (1978) ICR 1210 made a similar ruling. It accepted the reasoning of the industrial tribunal that, had a homeworker been unwilling to work, the relationship (with her employers) would have been rapidly terminated, and argued that

> the non-provision of work does not prevent the coming into existence of a long-term contract of employment in the case of a worker who works at the employer's premises, so equally there is no reason why this should not be the case as regards an employee who works at home.

The EAT also set out useful guidelines for judging the character of the relation between the supplier of work and the homeworker, that is, whether or not the company determined 'the thing to be done, the manner of performance, and in reality the time and place of performance'. In the 1984 Court of Appeal case, too, the majority opinion followed *Airfix* v. *Cope* in finding that a 'lengthy course of dealing' between homeworker and supplier could be construed as an 'umbrella contract', a concept rejected by the dissenting judge.

In the decisions taken in these cases, a critical factor has been evidence regarding the length of time the homeworkers worked for the same supplier. Either they worked continuously over a longer period or the homeworkers have been able to point to the supplier's provision of machinery as evidence of the supplier's intention to continue to provide work. The fact that many homeworkers are not given work continuously or supply their own machinery means that they would not necessarily qualify as employees under such rulings. In any case any ruling applies only to the individual homeworker appealing to the tribunal. The cases highlight the need for more careful scrutiny of homeworkers' conditions of work. In this chapter we consider the evidence collected in the West Yorkshire study on the extent of the control exercised in homeworking. The nature of this control supports the case for the inclusion of homeworkers in legislation providing employee rights, since their conditions of work are basically similar.

Our discussion is not confined to homeworkers' relation to the supplier of work. For the question of the homeworkers' choice and autonomy in deciding how and when they work is not simply one of the employer's control. The restrictions and obligations under which women work are not confined to those imposed as part of the wage labour contract. The notion of homeworkers' autonomy is part of the powerful contrast between the home, privacy, and freedom, and the work constraints imposed 'by the rude, commercial, aggressive world' (Barker and Allen, 1976, p. 1). In order to appreciate homeworkers' actual position within the labour process, we need to understand what the domestic sphere means for women and, in particular, the work obligations which women experience within it. It is only through confronting the diverse work obligations which women carry that we can comprehend their waged work at home and relate this to the lives of working women more generally.

Systems of control in homeworking

To turn labour into labour for profit requires a system of control (Paul Thompson, 1983). To discipline and reward the work force, and to supervise and evaluate its performance, entails authority over it. The attempt to exercise this authority may be more or less direct or hidden, more or less subtle, more or less successful. Control of the pace and intensity of work and the quality of output is in many cases exercised directly, through close supervision; or technically, through the design of machinery and work processes which demand a certain way of working and which leave the actual producers with little discretion over how they perform their jobs. This applies to both in-workers and homeworkers.

The attempt to exercise control over labour appears to reach its extreme in assembly line production, in which the pace of work is set by the tempo of the line and the worker is to a greater or lesser extent subordinated to the machine. It is this kind of control to which most investigation has been directed, and which has come to symbolise the subordination of the work force and its lack of autonomy at work (Braverman, 1974). Mechanisms through which labour is controlled directly or technically are often thought to account for the growth of factory production over 'putting out' in the rise of industrial capitalism. In addition the development of 'scientific management' techniques in the twentieth century, and the increasing utilisation of computer technology in the past decade are portrayed in the same way. All other modes through which labour is set to work have come to appear as inefficient survivals, in which workers are assumed to be free to set their own hours of work, to choose the pace and intensity of work, and to exercise control antithetical to high profits.

An example of control through the use of computers is the way in which the productivity of many office workers is tracked by computers in keystrokes per hour. As the General Manager of an American-owned offshore data processing firm describes their system,

> When a worker turns on a machine, she must sign on with her identification number . . . If she goes for a break, she must turn off the machine.

Nor can operators leave their machines running when they go to the toilet, the manager says:

> Yes, some think they are being smart and fooling us by leaving the machine on when they go to the bathroom, but we can tell when they do this, because their recorded productivity level drops since they've been gone from their terminal.   (Posthuma, n.d.)

But control is not limited to direct supervision or to subordinating the worker to the machine. In homework, as in the factory or office, it is not the worker who organises and exercises control but the supplier. Employers have available, depending on the context, a range of mechanisms through which to control performance and output. Although production in the factory has come to appear as the dominant form by which labour is controlled, a substantial proportion of the labour force is subject to controls of other kinds. The mechanisms which determine the homeworker's pace and quality of work are comparatively indirect. Consequently homework can take on an appearance of autonomy which is more apparent than real.

The work task

As we demonstrated in Chapter 4, homeworkers are not independent contractors trading on their own account. The supplier provides the materials and sells the product. The homeworker does not design or choose her work tasks. Much homeworking is in fact characterised by a division of labour in which production is subdivided into discrete, standardised tasks using standardised components, leaving the homeworker with discretion over only the most trivial aspects of the work process. In the production of greeting card decorations, for instance, we found that one set of homeworkers makes the decorations, another group of homeworkers attaches them to the cards, and yet another is employed to box the finished cards. The last homeworker acts as the quality controller who can refuse payment to the others. The homeworker who stitches together the ends of fan belts has no control over her work tasks. Any possibility or originality or discretion has been organised out of the work of the majority of homeworkers. However, some homeworkers do complete the whole product and rely on craft skills. Hand-knitters are one of the best examples. They are skilled workers who knit whole garments and before they are accepted as homeworkers they must prove their skill. Once they become homeworkers, they work with materials supplied to a design and size specified by those giving out the work. Those hand-knitters whose task did not include stitching together the pieces of the garments complained that they missed the satisfaction of seeing the finished product. Machinists who complete whole products, making through dresses, blouses, trousers, leisure wear and so on, do so from cut-out pieces supplied by the supplier and according to his instructions. For this reason, contrary to the view expressed by Campbell, machinists are unable to make extra money for themselves by making and selling extra garments out of the materials supplied (Campbell, 1978).

Output

Like the design and performance of work tasks, output is also effectively under the supplier's control. The homeworker only rarely has a meaningful choice in how much work she takes on. Although many homeworkers pointed to some degree of flexibility in their work, it was clear from our data that this operated within severely constrained limits.

The chief mechanism through which the supplier controls output is the payment system typical of homeworking. Homework is almost invariably piece-work, and usually so not only in manufacturing but among clerical workers (Brown, 1974; Cragg and Dawson, 1981; Crine, 1979a; Hakim 1980, 1984a; Jordan 1978). Computer programmers are sometimes paid hourly wages (Huws, 1984a, 1984b), but their employers have both the financial resources and the technology to monitor the pace of their work with extreme accuracy. In the West Yorkshire survey all the homeworkers were paid at piece-work rates and their hours and intensity of work were determined by it (Allen 1981a, 1981b, 1983b).

Because payment by results establishes an immediate connection between payment and pieces produced it is one of the main mechanisms through which suppliers attempt to maintain or increase the intensity of work. In some kinds of employment these attempts are not always successful. Factory employees evolve methods of work which enable them to establish norms of piece-rates (Marriot, 1957; Roy, 1952). In most cases for in-workers piece-rates operate on top of basic hourly, daily or weekly wage rates. In the case of Wages Council industries the flat rates are based on an hourly wage rate. In times of full employment rate-setting has led to frequent annual disputes, so that its cost to employers in time 'lost' over changes in piece-rates have out-weighed its other benefits to the employers (Baldamus, 1961; Bowey *et al.*, 1982).

In homeworking, however, piece-work operates much more successfully from the employer's point of view. In the situation known as 'sweating', piece-rates can be pushed down almost indefinitely, making it necessary for homeworkers to require the help of family labour to make up their earnings or to meet deadlines. Not only is there no basic rate in the homeworker's wages, but the absence of a standard working day or week means that employers do not need to establish a national hourly or daily or weekly wage from which to calculate piece-rates. Moreover, employers have no need to consider collective action from their workers when the labour force is employed under casualised conditions and largely unorganised.

Under such conditions piece-work earnings can appear to be the result of individual effort and the worker 'a willing accomplice to his or her exploitation' (Braverman, 1974; p. 62). The homeworker is discouraged from seeing herself as a regular worker, earning a regular wage, and her earnings come to appear as deriving from the additional tasks she takes on by choice. It is because homeworkers are characterised as housewives and irregular earners, supported by a male wage, that the obvious constraints posed by piece-work can be ignored so consistently in depictions of the homeworker's autonomy or flexible workload.

The ideological force of piece-work, as a system of payment, is reflected in conflicting assessments by homeworkers themselves. For example, one homeworker with two children under five packed greeting cards for 3 hours a night, 7 days a week. Her earnings were so low that even though her husband helped her most nights, they earned only £15 to £20 a week between them for 42 hours' work. Not surprisingly, she said that she was 'permanently tired', but went on to say that 'this is my own fault, I needn't take all the work I do'. In fact when the greeting cards work 'finished', she had to take another homeworking job packing rubbish bags for even less pay.

But homeworkers also recognise that the low piece-rates make long hours essential. 'To earn anything worthwhile,' one home-worker comments, 'you'd have to chain yourself to the envelopes.' Many recognise the peculiar meaning of 'choice' in this context. As one homeworker put it,

> It was up to the worker to say how many boxes she wanted delivered to her in any week so I suppose there was an average order – but often I'd order ten boxes and only complete seven. Nobody complained – it was up to me just what amount of work I'd do. But then the less I did the less I got paid, so the incentive was there to do more.

They also recognise the severe limits on the extent to which piece-work enables them to control their own earnings by taking on more work, for they rarely have any choice between differently rated products. Piece-work earnings depend on being able to build up speed and accuracy with a consistent product. But homeworkers are asked to do anything within a broadly agreed range of products and level of skill. They may experience changes in the product from week to week, but the rates are not adjusted to reflect the difficulties and time necessary to complete different products. The supplier's control over earnings through the allocation of work is shown by the commonly recognised practice of rewarding more experienced homeworkers with work carrying higher piece-rates. Homeworkers' earnings depend on the type of work they are given as well as the hours they are prepared to put in.

The homeworker's dependence on the employer for the type of work, regardless of the effect on earnings, is evident in the following comments from homeworkers in West Yorkshire:

Earned £5 a week on average – occasionally I had thicker wool and earned about £6 a week.   (Hand-knitter; average hours 30 per week)

Pay varied between £5 and £5.50 depending on the difficulty of the pattern, i.e. whether it is part or all Fair Isle.   (Hand-knitter; average hours 28 per week)

The extra money was for a better paid job that could be done more easily – splitting packs that hadn't sold well and repacking them in different combinations.   (Card-packer; average hours 17½ per week)

Earned £9.25 last week, usually £7–£8 week. If I get all the higher paid overalls I can earn £10 a week.   (Machinist; average hours 16½ per week)

Earned £11.80 last week. Varies between £8–£11 depending on the amount of work done. Some cards take longer to do than others, e.g. larger, stiffer cardboard.   (Card-packer; average hours 13 per week)

While suppliers are free to allocate work of different kinds as and when it suits them, the homeworker is obliged to accept the work provided and to complete it on time. Despite weekly or seasonal variations in the amount supplied, the homeworker expects to complete the work, filling rush and seasonal orders as necessary and going without her income when no work is supplied. Fifty-eight per cent of the sample stated that there had been times when they had been wanting to work but no work was available, and half said that there had been times when there had been more work than they could comfortably manage.

Apart from the piece-work system and the control over the type of work assigned, the provision of machinery by the supplier is one of the more obvious modes through which the supplier ensures that homeworkers meet production targets. This is recognised by those industrial tribunals who have accepted suppliers' provision of machinery as evidence that the homeworker's work obligations are those of an employee. The clearest example we found of a supplier explicitly controlling output was the homeworker who stated: 'He will provide £20 of work [weekly]. If you drop below this he will take the machine away.' In this case the obligation was one-sided. This homeworker had been without work for three or four weeks on a number of occasions. Clearly the expectation was that she would take a set amount of work when the employer made it available or risk losing her job. The non-provision of work by her employer did not offset or reduce this obligation.

Equally important is that the supplier sets the times for the delivery of materials and the collection of finished work. Homeworkers therefore frequently work to tight deadlines, leaving little scope for adjusting their hours to suit themselves. For 90 per cent of those in the West Yorkshire survey, work was delivered and collected by the supplier, in some cases with such frequency that the management of the work-flow is reminiscent of factory employment. Weekly collection and payment was most common, but in at least fourteen cases work was delivered/collected more than once a week and in two cases more than once a day. One supplier even made two deliveries on Fridays, so that the homeworker would have 'enough' work over the weekend. It is clear that these homeworkers had to adjust to the flow of work which suited the supplier.

Quality of work

Employers' control over labour also includes the control of the quality of work. In much factory employment this is exercised through direct supervision. Where direct supervision is impractical, as in homeworking, or in highly skilled occupations where some degree of work autonomy is expected, other mechanisms are brought into play. The recruitment and training of workers can provide familiarity with the standard of work required and instil company loyalty and discipline as alternatives to direct supervision.

A significant minority of the West Yorkshire homeworkers were working for firms where they had previously been employed as in-workers (see also Hakim, 1980). In several cases the approach had been made by the employer and some employers were said to take on as homeworkers only those who had been previously in-working employees. In addition some referred to some test or trial period, either in the factory or at home, where they had to demonstrate their ability to complete a sample of work according to the employer's instructions, and five referred to employers' demonstrating how the work was to be done. When asked specifically, twenty-five of the ninety homeworkers said they had done some training at the firm.

Those employers who do not exercise this kind of control, which they are less likely to do if the work is unskilled, operate control on the quality of work through the piece-work system. If work is found to be faulty, either payment is refused or work has to be made good before payment is made. In fact, very few homeworkers referred to not being able to complete their work satisfactorily, for if they find that they cannot do the work at a rapid pace to the standard required they earn almost nothing and look for other homework.

The organisation of consent

Many methods for controlling output and retaining a loyal workforce rely upon apparently consensual co-operation between homeworker and supplier. The self-discipline required of the homeworker by the supplier of work indicates the extent to which suppliers prefer to engineer what appears to be voluntary compliance rather than to exercise direct control. Because meeting production targets is made the responsibility of homeworkers as individuals it provides considerable scope for the supplier to present himself or herself as an 'understanding employer' (Freeman, 1982) willing to make allowances on occasions for the homeworkers' other commitments. This kind of interaction between supplier and homeworker ensures that production requirements are met, while at the same time fostering the illusion that homeworking permits an unusual degree of autonomy.

Existing research on homeworking reveals some difference between suppliers in their expectations regarding aceptable variations in the individual homeworker's output from time to time (Crine, 1979a; Saifullah Khan, 1979). Of the homeworkers interviewed in West Yorkshire, one-half mentioned times when they had refused work or had been unable to complete work on time. Some had been told they would lose their job if it happened again. Other suppliers were reported to be more sympathetic to workers whose other commitments make it difficult for them to manage an identical allocation of work each week. They let it be known that they will allow some latitude in meeting obligations. 'If you can't manage the work in a particular week', says one West Yorkshire homeworker, 'you just tell the driver not to put you down for work.'

Although in the abstract this appears a wholly reasonable approach, it legitimises the homeworker's low pay and lack of employment security by confirming the primacy of her family responsibilities and the supposedly secondary importance of her paid employment.

Variations in output are of course not unique to homeworking. All employers allow for workers' holidays and illness in scheduling work, and few expect to meet their production targets all the time. But homeworkers are led to perceive commonly provided employee benefits as privileges. For homeworkers holidays or sick leave, for which in-workers are usually paid, are unpaid and granted as a special favour. Although many homeworkers saw the supplier's willingness to accept occasional refusals of work as an indication of the flexibility of the work, it is quite clear that homeworkers refuse work very rarely, and only on those occasions when in-workers expect paid leave. When asked if they had ever refused work, homeworkers replied with comments like the following:

Once when going on holiday.

Twice when ill, nothing happened.

Another time I cut my finger and had to go to hospital. The firm didn't mind that the orders were not completed in time.

Twice a year when I needed a break.

They were so grateful for the work and fearful of losing it that some felt the supplier to be sympathetic even when very little more time was given to complete the work:

Nothing much happened when I told them that I hadn't done the work. They said we will come next morning, have it ready as it has to be sent off for delivery.

Oh, they don't care you know. I just tell them that this or that has happened. Like last week this girl next door died, so we had to go there . . .. So I had to leave it and then I finished it after. I'd 400 left, so I did 200 last night and have 200 still to do.

Women employers and sub-contractors, or women employed as agents by the suppliers of homework, may be particularly likely to adopt the role of the 'understanding employer'. The relationship between the female supplier of work and the homeworker is mainly that of employer–employee, but it is coloured by the supplier's own experience and expectations. One woman sub-contractor we interviewed, an ex-homeworker who managed her business from home, sympathised with the stresses of the job, like sore fingers and frustration with detailed work, and said she was understanding if family problems interrupted work or her employees needed a break – without pay. She distributed bottles of sherry as a Christmas bonus. Her identification with the problems facing women working at home was no doubt sincere, but was clearly functional to keeping a loyal, hard-working force at no cost to herself in real employee benefits.

Another business which has sought a favourable reputation for its understanding of the difficulties of women workers is F International, a computer software contractor. It is headed by a woman and employs women programme analysts as homeworkers. One *Guardian* report readily accepted the claim that F International workers are well-paid and able to combine looking after their children with work at home 'in hours to suit the individual' (Toynbee, 1985). But others have pointed out that in practice F International homeworkers are required to spend part of the week in a firm's premises. They are paid much less than in-firm employees with the same training, and less than the employees of other software sub-contractors (*Guardian Women*, Letters 1985).

Suppliers also encourage homeworkers to identify with their employer's interests. Homeworkers recognise that the supply of work is contingent on their employers' obtaining contracts for further work, and this can be strategically emphasised by the supplier. We found that instructions to homeworkers could be accompanied by direct hints that further contracts depended upon the homeworkers' quality and speed of work. One firm which supplied fancy packaging to chocolate and perfume manufacturers mentioned this specifically in its written instructions to homeworkers.

In fact, the mechanism of control used to obtain the compliance of a homeworking labour force vary enormously. It has been suggested, for instance, that in homeworking quality of work depends upon forms of 'non-economic coercion', especially the mobilisation of kinship ties between supplier and worker (Young, 1981). Kinship ties between supplier and worker have been found in the production of lace in South India (Mies, 1982), carpets in Morocco (Maher, 1981) and clothing by Cypriot and Bangladeshi homeworkers in London and the West Midlands (Anthias, 1983; Mitter, 1986). Although in these cases the husband or male relative controls production partly through the same mechanisms as other suppliers, through – for instance – the timing of the delivery and collection of work, his authority is patriarchal in character.

In contrast, the West Yorkshire survey found no homeworkers employed by their husbands or other kin, and very few cases in which the husband mediated between the homeworker and the supplier. This suggests that kinship links are not essential to control of the quality of work, and where they exist stem from somewhat different aspects of the organisation of homeworking production. Or they may be important only when homeworkers are new entrants to the waged labour force, and consequently unfamiliar with factory discipline. This was not the case in West Yorkshire, as nearly all the workers had previous experience of paid employment outside the home. In Britain most suppliers can rely upon a labour force which is already fully habituated to the demands of waged employment. The West Yorkshire homeworkers took pride in being seen as 'responsible' or 'reliable' workers turning out good work. Although their presentation of this image no doubt emerges partly as a strategic response to the limited and uncertain supply of homework, it reflects also widespread cultural values regarding the 'fair day's work' owed an employer.

Non-wage obligations

So far we have been concerned to challenge those aspects of the myth of homeworkers' autonomy which derive from a confusion between the position of homeworkers and the self-employed. In view of the immediate benefits homeworkers would gain from legal recognition of their status as employees, this emphasis is not misplaced. But it must be stressed that this represents a very partial, and for that reason misleading, picture. Constraints associated with the wage labour contract are only one form through which control over labour is organised. When women's work is examined, we also have to consider other limitations on women's autonomy in setting their hours and pace or work.

These are limitations imposed by the sexual division of labour. The ability to realise those advantages which men often seek in self-employment, like the capacity to set one's own hours and pace of work, or to exchange time spent on leisure or family life for a higher income or more rewarding work (Scase and Goffee, 1982) rests in part on men's position as men. Homeworkers share with other women controls on their use of their own labour which men experience much more rarely.

The working day

Even when homeworkers are acknowledged to be employees, the freedom to set one's own hours 'to suit oneself', to fit the work around housework and child-care, is believed to distinguish home-work from other kinds of paid employment. In the course of discussing homework with academics, trade unionists, neighbours and friends we have come across the extreme tenacity of this image. People retain an image of the homeworker popping out to do the shopping in a 'convenient moment' or stopping work to run a load of washing, to get the children's tea, or to comfort a crying baby, and then picking up work where she left off. Or the homeworker is thought to get down to work when the family is busy with other things.

Close attention to the real conditions of women's work, paid and unpaid, suggests that this image must represent a very partial picture of the homeworker's working day. This whole scenario, with its assumption of convenient moments and orderly routine is misleading, and smacks more of some imagined domestic idyll than the harassed coping strategies with which most women are familiar. Since homeworkers work the same number of hours, paid and unpaid, as women going out to work, they face most of the same problems. Added difficulties, distinctive to doing paid work at home, compound the problems.

Some studies of homeworking have repeated the conventional wisdom, arguing that it allows 'a more flexible, even easy-going day' than going out to work (Cragg and Dawson, 1981). Some home-workers do perceive their work in this way. In West Yorkshire nine homeworkers cited working at their own pace or without super-vision as a reason for enjoying homework, and twenty-one specifi-cally mentioned that working to one's own pace or to fit in with one's own routine was an advantage homeworking offered or a reason for recommending it to others. However, the rest of the ninety homeworkers either saw no advantages in homeworking or mentioned other aspects. Some had begun homeworking with the idea that it would give them control over their hours of work, but as experienced homeworkers had come to see the situation differently. As one commented, 'It starts off okay but then you get a lot of pressure put on you'. Another tried to hold on to the view that homeworking offered advantages but recognised that in her own case they had become illusory. She saw the advantages of homeworking as being able to 'work when you feel like it' and to 'fit it in' with household and children, but in practice found that she frequently worked 'until two in the morning' and had come to 'resent the pressure my boss is putting on me'. Since the actual workload is set by the supplier it does not offer much scope for the worker to fit it in at her convenience. When homeworkers in West Yorkshire were asked to explain the reasons why their hours of work varied, more cited the supply of work than all other reasons combined.

Homeworkers' own accounts provide striking evidence that the working day is tightly structured by the constant demands of paid work and unpaid domestic labour. This is true, not simply exceptionally, as when children are ill (Cragg and Dawson, 1981), but as the normal condition of work. As the following reports demonstrate, the combination of homeworking, housekeeping, child-care, and in some cases other paid work, mean that every moment is accounted for:

> I get the kids off to school, then do the washing and clean round for 10 o'clock when the work is delivered. I work through until lunchtime, stop for a sandwich, and continue until 4 in the afternoon. About 6, after tea and clearing it up, I work another hour, get the youngest off to bed, start again about 8 and work until 11 at night. Sometimes I stop work at about 9 and get up early the following morning so it will be ready at 10 in the morning, when the delivery comes. My day varies according to what crops up – some days the youngest goes to the speech therapist – and how fast I can do a certain job. I am faster at each job as I go along. But it always has to be done by 10 am the next day.

I get up and give the family breakfast and tidy the house. I try to start work about 9.30 am and work until 3.30 in the afternoon with a break for lunch. Sometimes I work in the evenings if I have not been able to get enough done during the day due to the children needing attention.

At 5.30 in the morning I clean an office at the bottom of the road. Then I get home, get breakfast and see the kids to school. I sew until lunchtime, and then get back to sewing . . .. I am also childminding for two other children.

Accounts like these show that despite the claims of some suppliers (Rubery and Wilkinson, 1981) homework is not done casually, in front of the TV, nor picked up and put down in odd moments. While there may be a few opportunities for day-to-day adjustment in the particular hours homework is done, this is limited by the employer's control of the amount of work and has to be seen within the context of an extremely long working week. In the West Yorkshire study the majority of the women did homework for 11 to 30 hours a week, and twelve worked over 40 hours a week. Over a third worked in the evenings, as well as during the day, and nearly as many worked at the weekend. This is added to the time put into unpaid domestic labour. The real situation is that homeworking permits the worker to go on working until she drops. It allows her to extend the working day into unsocial hours, evening and night work, and the working week into a full seven days.

Indeed, in many respects homeworking is more onerous than going out to work. This is partly because there is no spatial separation between paid and unpaid work. Homeworking is 'always on your mind, always there'. As homeworkers recognise, 'You do not come home from work and leave it behind you.' Moreover, while those going out to work at least are allocated tea breaks, the homeworker's day is so dominated by simultaneous demands on her labour that a break in one kind of work is used to get on with another. The use of domestic space means that this way of organising work is not even convenient. Few homeworkers have a separate place to work, and they are therefore unable to leave their work set up. Three-quarters of those in West Yorkshire worked in the kitchen or living room, and had to clear work away to prepare meals or to make room for children to play, and then set it up again, all in their 'own' time.

Further difficulties arise from the character of domestic responsibilities. Unlike work governed by commercial transactions, the time required by housework and child-care is not calculable or easily rationalised. Standards of work are established quite differently. Studies demonstrate that the domestic labour of women going out to work is rarely reduced or shared with other household members (Hartmann, 1981; Hunt, 1980; Meissner *et al.*, 1975), but household routines may be adjusted to some extent. Meals may be served earlier or later, or consist of different foods, or the house may be left untidy and cleaned in long hours put in at the weekend. In contrast the homeworker's family still expect the services of a full-time housewife, including, for instance, the preparation of a cooked dinner in the middle of the day:

> I get up at 7.30, give the kids breakfast and take them to school. Then I do the washing and clean the house and put my youngest to sleep. I set to work for about two hours from 9 to 11. I stop to prepare a cooked lunch, my husband comes home for this. When he leaves about 1, I wash up, and then work until 3 when the kids come from school. I cook dinner for 7. After I've put the kids to bed I work from 8 to 10, and then to bed.

Nor is homework as readily combined with the care of young children as is sometimes supposed. It is true that homeworking enables mothers to be at home with children young enough to require the presence of an adult, but this is simply a caretaker role. Homeworkers recognise that despite being at home they are still unable to give their children their full attention, and have the same worries as women working outside the home:

> It took attention away from the three-year-old if I did only 250 boxes a week. Five hundred, and I neglected home, children, husband.

> I have to work very hard to earn a worthwhile wage, and can't look after my children properly.

> The house is neglected and the children play out long hours.

> Can't pay attention to the children, care for their clothes, cleaning.

Considerations like these make it evident that there is little about homeworking which is convenient for the worker. The homeworker adapts herself to the amount of work, and makes time for it through a lengthening of her working day. Her position is a particularly vivid example of the situation of women with dependents more generally. Part-time work outside the home is also portrayed as fitting into the other responsibilities of women workers. In practice, however, employers hire part-time workers to cover periods of high customer demand or to keep machinery running during breaks in the work of full-time employees (Robinson and Wallace, 1984). For part-time workers also, other responsibilities must be fitted around the hours set by the employer, however inconvenient they may be (Coyle, 1984).

Family expectations: the husband's control

> My husband says *I should* be here for the kids if they're ill etc., and *I have* to take them to and from school in case of accidents. Also he doesn't want me to meet other men or women who'd put ideas in my head [italics added].

Who defines and enforces the sexual division of labour within conjugal households? In addition to the more general ideological and practical constraints on the working day, homeworkers may be subject to more personalised controls over the terms under which they sell their labour. Husbands exercise considerable control over homeworkers' conditions of work.

In West Yorkshire the husbands did not directly exploit or appropriate women's labour as homeworkers. As we have already mentioned, none were employed by their husbands and only a few gave their wages to the husband. Two homeworkers had husbands and one a father-in-law who were employed or who previously had been employed by the firm which supplied the homework. These men brought the work home and returned it to the factory, but their role did not extend beyond this. For our respondents homeworking was clearly waged employment, not unpaid family labour controlled or supervised by male family members.

However, the decision to do homework rather than go out to work is frequently influenced by the husband. Fifty homeworkers said that their families expected them to stay at home rather than go out to work. In a large number of these cases the husband's opinion was seen to be crucial. Homeworkers were aware that their husbands had definite preferences either in favour of or against their wives' working outside the home.

Husbands' views were justified in terms of a number of rationales. In some cases the husband's view was that it was 'a woman's place' to be in the home, and his to be the breadwinner:

> My husband feels he should support the family financially.

> He likes me to stay at home. My husband is willing to work longer hours to discourage me going out to work.

More usually, however, the husband's preference for a wife at home was expressed in terms of the wife's obligations to their children:

> My husband objects to me not looking after our child.

> He would not like the idea of a childminder.

Husbands also made references to their own needs. The nature of these varied but each showed a high expectation that the wife should fit in with the husband's routine:

> My husband is away a lot so he wants me to be at home on the days he has off.

> My husband prefers it – because sometimes he finishes work at 3.00 pm and expects me to be in when he comes home.

> He likes me at home although he wouldn't force me to. He likes me to be at home when he gets in from work. He doesn't like coming in to an empty house.

> My youngest child has asthma and I'm expected to be here in case he's ill. My husband likes meals ready when he gets home also.

The overriding impression is that many husbands expected their wives to fit in with their definition of satisfactory family life or acceptable standards of housekeeping. With some exceptions both husband and wife accepted the husband's right to determine the use of the wife's labour. Even those husbands who were said to have no preference were given this right:

> My husband does not prevent me going out to work. I have to think of the children – so I decided.

> My husband lets me please myself.

Several homeworkers whose opinion differed from the husband's still gave way to his views, feeling this to be part of their marital bargain:

> He thinks that women should be in the home. He is a male chauvinist pig, but I let him get away with a lot because he treats me well.

Husbands who preferred a wife to go out to work did not express concern for the children's situation but left it to the wife to sort out. Consideration of the children's welfare was treated as the wife's responsibility:

> My husband would like me to go out and earn – I cannot because of the children.

Particularly significant is that where husbands preferred their wives to be at home, the couple sometimes saw housekeeping and child-care as a full-time job which left no room for paid employment:

> I have a full-time job at home. I don't want to go out to work, as there is enough to do at home. My husband likes us to relax at night, he doesn't like to see me ironing.

In this situation, in which the wife is perceived as *already* doing a full-time job, then the homework becomes invisible as work and as a source of income. When homeworkers collude in this definition, homework becomes the wife's 'choice' in the use of her free time, rather than an extension of the working day. The importance of her earnings to family living standards is only half-acknowledged, at least by the husband:

> My husband insists that we don't need my homework money, but he's glad of the extra really.

The strength of the conventional view of women as wives and

mothers is obvious in these cases. Some husbands object only to their wives work outside the home, and to compensate for the loss of these earnings are willing to help with homework ('He helped to get more done, he wanted a little extra money and hated my outside cleaning job'). But in other cases even homeworking was resented. It is in this context that some of the family tensions mentioned by homeworkers should be situated. Twelve referred to problems between themselves and their husbands arising out of their homework. Our general impression was that these often reflected the husband's irritation at his wife being occupied in this way while he was there:

> There are no serious problems, but all the knitting got on my husband's nerves.

> Some tension but slight. It gets on my husband's nerves sometimes.

Sometimes the dissatisfaction was expressed in terms of mess or inconvenience, but even then it could reflect other underlying tensions. An example is the homeworker whose husband complained about her 'neglect of the children' and 'the mess in the house from all the fluff'. However, she also mentioned that 'my husband has all the say if his wage is the only income'. It is not unlikely that her wish 'for a bit of economic independence' contributed to their arguments. She concluded that homework was 'too badly paid to be worth the upset to the family'.

Of course note needs to be taken of those husbands who condemned the fact that suppliers were getting away with paying wages so far below average (see also Sharpe, 1984). But in a few cases their comments about this aspect of homework were somewhat ambiguous. One homeworker reported that:

> Sometimes my husband gets annoyed because I regularly work at knitting until two in the morning. He complains about the poor pay and thinks I'm a fool 'cos I'm frightened to ask for more.

Another said that she and her married daughter had not told their husbands how little they earned, for fear the men would have 'thrown the sewing machines out of the window'.

Of course we have no reason to believe that homeworkers were working at home primarily because of their husbands' overt demands. Many husbands expect a wife at home as an integral part of married life, others do not care so long as their own needs are met. But in general husbands do not *need* to express their opinion directly. Forty-one of the ninety homeworkers said without comment that their families did not expect them to stay at home. But none of the husbands appeared to have contemplated the kind of shift in the household division of labour which would have made wives' work outside the home more practicable. Taken-for-granted ideological expectations of the division of labour are so effective that overt control need never emerge. It is these that are the most successful in controlling women.

Hidden labour

The interplay of controls on the homeworker's labour is most starkly apparent in the extent of the hidden labour of other members of the household, friends and neighbours. Low piece-work rates, and the need to have work ready for collection despite the other demands on their time, mean that homeworkers' require the help of others. The labour of other family members was mentioned by thirty-nine of the homeworkers in West Yorkshire. The husband's contribution was most often mentioned (24 cases), followed by the homeworkers' young children (9 cases) and adult relations (sons, daughters, mothers, mothers-in-law, and sisters being the most common).

Husbands and other adult relatives usually did the same work as the homeworker, although husbands sometimes did only part of the process. They worked in the evenings, or, if they were unemployed or off sick, for part of the day. Children worked after school or in the evening. Much of the child labour was packaging. For example, one homeworker paid each of her four children, aged between five and eleven, ½p for every teddy bear they turned to the right side after she had machined the parts together. The children also helped package them. She received 9p per teddy bear and earned 90p an hour. The stuffing of the bears was done by other homeworkers. In another family an 8-year-old, the eldest of four children, stacked greeting cards for 3 hours every night. His mother earned 38p an hour and gave him 50p for several nights' work.

The unrecorded labour of family members means that hourly wage rates in homeworking are even lower than total earnings at first sight suggest. For instance, one homeworker appeared to be earning £2.19 an hour, one of the highest wages recorded. This was her eighth job in five or six years of homeworking. She lived with her husband, a mechanic, and their four children and looked after two other children after school and during the holidays. She was able to begin work only in the evenings, 4 hours a night, 20 hours a week. She assembled Easter egg boxes, pleating the silk linings and attaching them to the boxes. Her husband worked with her every evening, sticking double-sided tape to the inside of the boxes. When his labour is included, their hourly wage rate works out at only £1.09 an hour.

In organising the help of other members of the family, these homeworkers are forced to discipline their children's work and monitor their husband's, saving the supplier the costs of this supervision but adding still greater tension and fatigue to their working day. Over half of these homeworkers paid other family members for their help. Although mothers and sisters were said to be willing to 'help out', female adult relatives were normally paid for their work, and usually worked on a regular basis. These woman were apparently sharing among themselves the few available jobs and their meagre rewards (see also Wallace and Pahl, 1986). Many of the children were paid, usually in the form of pocket money but sometimes, as in the cases cited above, on something like a piece or time rate.

The terms under which husbands contribute to homework offer insight into a wife's perceived right to call upon a husband's labour as compared with his rights to her unpaid domestic services. A husband's labour had to be bought or carefully negotiated. Four husbands were paid for their time, and another four worked the same hours as their wives and shared the pay equally. Fifteen husbands were not actually paid, but the homeworkers indicated that the husband helped his wife 'to get more done' because all the earnings were being used for household expenses. Even so, homeworkers avoided direct requests for help:

The homework sometimes created tension at home between my husband and me, if I wanted to get down to the work and he didn't feel like it.

He didn't mind helping as long as he felt he didn't have to.

In discussing husbands' perceptions of homework, it was apparent that many interpret it as a leisure time activity, and prefer to ignore the reasons why women are forced to accept such low-paid work. However, the contribution made by some husbands suggests that others are well aware of the competing demands on their wives' labour and the importance of meeting these demands to the functioning of the household. But while these husbands benefit materially from and contribute to homeworker earnings, they are still able to enjoy the status traditionally associated with being able to keep a wife at home.

Conclusions

Working 'in one's own home' conjures up a picture of work autonomy which is quite misleading. Homeworkers are thought to set their own hours of work, and combine homeworking with all their other obligations within the home and outside it. It is true that they do not have to clock in and do not have a supervisor leaning over their shoulder. In practice, however, their obligations to the supplier are those of an employee, and they are, if anything, more constrained than those who go out to work. The supplier establishes the hours of work through the times set for the delivery and collection of work and payment by the piece, and their earnings are limited, not by their willingness to work, but by the availability of work and the allocation of work with different piece-rates. Home-workers are not paid for work until it meets the supplier's specifications. Hours, pace and quality of work are so effectively controlled by the supplier that direct physical supervision is not required.

The disadvantages of paid work at home also reflect the many other demands of women's labour. Many of the assumptions regarding working at home are couched within a male perspective. These imply that waged work outside the home and bureaucratically-imposed controls are the main constraints on personal autonomy. People are assumed to be free of the demands of the workplace, once they return home. But for women, of course, this is far from the case. The domestic sphere incorporates other work obligations enforced by the explicit demands and implicit expectations of other family members. The woman who goes out to work returns to another set of demands on her labour. Calls on the labour of the homeworker are even more extensive, for with no spatial separation between her paid and unpaid labour family members do not lower or adjust their expectations. Husbands, children and elderly relatives are free to interrupt her paid work, and this may account for the preference by families that the women work at home. Popular images of working at home – flexible working hours, more time to spend with one's children, a reduction of work pressure, a less stressful day – have nothing to do with the experience of homeworking. The women experience the two sets of constraints simultaneously on a day-to-day basis. Homeworking is very far from being a boon to women, for instead of liberating them from or reducing the burden of the 'double day', it intensifies the pressures of both waged work and unpaid domestic labour.

Those who argue that homework represents the future 'life-style' and will replace going out to work in 'proper jobs' are either unaware of, or ignore, the evidence on present patterns of homeworking. As much evidence shows, the unemployed lack the resources to participate, either in the formal or informal sectors of the economy, as self-employed (McKee and Bell, 1986, Miles, 1983), but homeworking in the manufacturing sector may be an available form of paid work for them (Wallace and Pahl, 1986). This cannot be interpreted as a viable 'life-style' or a freely chosen option given the data analysed here.

6
Organising for change

The 1970s saw a mounting campaign to recognise the existence of homeworking and to press for reforms for what was seen as a vulnerable and exploited work force. Many arguments were put forward to support legal changes which would enable homeworkers to enjoy the same rights and benefits as employees in factories or offices. In the 1980s the existence of homeworking was not only acknowledged more widely, but its growth predicted.

This acknowledgement was put forward in a context of radical changes, where the rights of employees were being reduced, unemployment was rising, the employers' 'rights to manage' was advocated and the reduction in state expenditure and control of wages became primary aims in the name of reducing inflation. This context, in which privatisation and market forces are seen as the way forward to a more competitive and therefore a 'healthier' economy, requires deregulation (the removal of existing legal safeguards) and the selective reduction of state intervention in the economy. These, it is argued, have adversely effected the level of employment through, for instance, restricting the rights of employers to offer and the workers to accept lower wages and poorer conditions.

The predicted growth in home-based work (including homework) associated with new technology is portrayed as part of the restructuring of work and as different from 'traditional' forms of homeworking. Not only is it claimed that the pay and conditions are better, but that working at or from home offers opportunities for self-employment and enterprise in an economy where the prospects for full employment are poor. If it is indeed the case that more work

135

will be home-based in the future then the conditions under which homework is normally carried out and the payment received for it become a matter of more, not less, significance. For we cannot assume that the institutional and ideological framework of home-based work will differ significantly from that which presently exists for homeworking.

This chapter is concerned with the arguments for and against measures to improve the pay and conditions of existing home-workers which have accompanied attempts at reform and organisation. By examining these, conclusions can be drawn not only about the kind of change required but its relevance to other forms of home-based work.

In the 1970s, through the use of the results of official and independent inquiries into homeworking, the Low Pay Unit and other organisations brought the issue of homeworking before the public and produced a relatively large amount of information on pay and conditions which was used to press for improvements. The Low Pay Unit, the Leicester Outwork Campaign and the TUC among others contributed to clarifying many aspects of homeworking, pointing up the inadequacies of conceptions of it used by many official bodies, including the Wages Councils and government departments. Their main work was as pressure groups, informing, questioning and cajoling those in a position to influence legislation and administrative procedures. They assumed, along with Field, that: 'We are a society which still believes, to some extent, that change can be brought about by public debate' (Field, 1976, p. 13). These efforts appeared to find a positive response at the official level. In October 1978 the Department of Employment, with an Under-secretary sympathetic to legislative reform, set up a Home-working Unit, and an Advisory Committee with representatives of employers and trade unions as well as departmental representatives was established to monitor the work of the unit and to draw up proposals for action. In each of the sixteen divisions of the Wages Inspectorate an inspector was made responsible for examining homeworking wages. In February 1979 The Homeworkers (Protection) Bill was introduced into Parliament by a private member, Frank White, to reform the law on homeworking, particularly by granting employee status to homeworkers. This bill was refused a second reading on a technical objection. Despite widespread sympathy the first attempt at legal reform for seventy years was defeated. The Government promised to produce its own bill but before any progress could be made was itself defeated at the May 1979 election.

None of the other initiatives was sustained. The Advisory Committee, though it escaped abolition with the change of government, never met after its second meeting in 1979. The result of the Homework Unit's work was a survey in August 1979 of 106 employers in the clothing industry in four areas of London and the Midlands which claimed that no homeworkers were paid less than the legal minimum rate (Department of Employment, 1980). The resources available for the Wages Inspectorate were subsequently reduced and its capacity to investigate wages in homeworking presumably curtailed.

A House of Commons Select Committee on Employment spent some months collecting evidence on homeworking and in November 1981 published its report (House of Commons, 1981c). While the Minutes of Evidence provide a useful source of information, the recommended actions put forward by the Committee can only be described as minimal. However, even these have so far been ignored by the government and by those departments who were asked to follow through particular aspects of the issue.

Despite these set-backs, the attempts to develop policies on homework continue. Some of these are linked to local government initiatives, which have derived encouragement and funding from the EEC, and many are related to attempts to improve the position of women. For instance, in June 1984, the Third National Homeworking Conference, resulting from inputs from researchers, trade unionists, local authorities and members of parliament, was hosted by the Greater London Council. Contributions were prepared by a large number of individuals, organisations and groups representing homeworkers. The Conference displayed a much greater interest than previously in the international dimension of homeworking, and discussed the setting of campaign priorities and styles of work for organising homeworkers in local areas of Great Britain. In setting out the major areas of concern, there was a clear acknowledgement that it was necessary to prepare the case which would enable a future government not only to restore the benefits and rights of employees, but also to ensure that homeworkers were recognised and included in any legislation and to devise means of realistically implementing it.

The main areas in which legislation is necessary for those engaged in homework production are wages, health and safety, benefits in times of sickness, redundancy, old-age or pregnancy and some regulation to ensure time off for holidays (both annual and statutory), as well as controls on the length of the working week or day. All of these have long featured in the struggles of working people to maintain their standard of living and to improve their working lives. In many, if not all, societies they have become part of the laws of employment which are implemented to varying degrees, depending both on the strength of employee organisations and the creation of bodies to monitor and report to those legally responsible for their enforcement. The ever-present threat to national agreements has led to international agreements, for instance between employers, trade unions and governments under the auspices of the ILO. Such agreements have sought to restrict sweat shops as far as in-workers are concerned, but only very recently has attention been given to homework production.

Whatever gaps and discrepancies exist between societies in relation to their national laws and international agreements, it is the case that homeworkers everywhere are less protected than in-workers. This we would argue is due more to the view that real workers *go out to work*, than to the difficulties of devising and implementing legislation which can be applied to homeworkers. The dilemmas faced by those who campaign to include homeworkers and the main features of the various attempts to do so are outlined below.

But first we present some of our findings on how aware homeworkers were of Wages Councils and their activities and the views they held about possible forms of organisation for themselves, in particular their attitudes to trade union organisation.

Wages

As will be clear from the discussions in Chapters 3, 4 and 5, all the workers in our survey were paid on a piece-rate basis. Their earnings varied, but very few of them could be described as earning anything approaching the rate paid to even the lowest-paid equivalent woman in-worker. The work of only twenty-two out of the ninety homeworkers we interviewed came within the scope of the Wages Councils, which have a duty to ensure that a legal minimum rate is paid. Of these, sixteen were being paid below this minimum and some grossly below (Allen, 1981a, 1982a). This finding was in line with other studies (ACAS, 1978a; Hakim and Dennis, 1982). However, the Select Committee claimed that no evidence was presented to them to indicate that under-payment was substantially higher among homeworkers than among factory workers and pointed out that under-payment in Wages Council trades is not confined to homeworkers (House of Commons, 1981c). While it is clear that the problem of effective regulation of minimum rates is far wider than homework, payment for work done at home appears to present particular problems for those charged with regulating it.

Eighteen of the homeworkers in our survey had heard of Wages Councils and the majority of these gave very general descriptions of their functions, such as 'setting fair wages', 'giving advice on problems with wages', 'fixing a living wage'. One woman had been visited by a Wages Inspector who asked her 'how long it took to do an item and whether she considered it worthwhile'. He did not recommend that her rate, which was 50p an hour, be altered. Another woman working on decorating and packing cards said a neighbour had telephoned the Wages Council about their wage rate, 'but they were not helpful, they said they didn't cover that sort of work'.

Only four of the twenty-two workers covered by the Wages Councils regulations knew of their existence. All four were machinists, one in soft toys and the others in clothing, and their average hourly rate varied from 80p to £1.36. The remaining eighteen were also machinists, three in soft toys and the others in clothing. Seven were Pakistani women, whom it could be argued were not aware of Wages Councils, or minimum rates to which they were entitled, because of their lack of English, but this argument does not hold for the women who were native English speakers. None were new to the work and one had done it for over sixteen years. None worked for more than one supplier. The suppliers varied from one single-handed retailer who operated stalls at several markets to local firms producing for local, national and export markets and also included establishments outside the area using agents or middlemen. The pay of these workers, all of whom qualified for a statutory minimum rate, ranged from 33p to £1.88 an hour, without any clear indication that payment was based on skill or effort differentials. Four of them knew of in-workers doing the same kind of work, but did not know how much they were paid. The Wages Council Inspectorate were either unaware of these workers because the suppliers had failed to register with the appropriate authority, or the rates being paid (less than £1 an hour in eleven cases) were regarded as acceptable by the inspectors.

There were fourteen women who knew about Wages Councils and minimum rates of pay, but whose homework was not covered by them. They did a variety of homework and their earnings ranged from very low to average for homeworkers. Nine of them had had relevant in-work experience and all but one had been trade union members. Most remained in favour of trade union organisation. The experience of trade unionism and their work histories are possibly part of the explanation of how they came to know of Wages Councils. Such information is by no means readily available. It is not surprising that the majority of women who were entitled to Wages Council rates were not receiving them and moreover were in most cases unaware of their rights. Our evidence indicates that the practice of the Wages Inspectorate in implementing minimum rates in those few trades coming within their jurisdiction, fails to meet the legal requirements. Not only are better means of communicating the functions of Wages Councils necessary, but also those suppliers who fail to register their activities need to be brought within the existing law.

Employee rights and conditions of work

In almost all cases the homeworkers in West Yorkshire were concerned with their conditions of work and some gave detailed replies on the changes needed to improve these. Apart from pay, those most frequently mentioned were fair contracts, paid holidays and sickness benefit. Their idea of fair contracts involved agreement on basic earnings, particularly when work was short, an organisation of work which gave them some control over when the work was done, so that night and weekend work was either reduced or recompensed, and some means whereby new or more difficult work was recognised as requiring more effort or skill and a basic rate agreed. Many contrasted the uncertainties of homework with their experience as in-workers in such terms as 'then you knew where you were'.

Many of the women worked in poor conditions with insufficient lighting or heat, inadequate work space or equipment and poor ventilation. Their concerns on health and safety were expressed both on their own behalf and for other members of the family, particularly young children. Their complaints included eye-strain, headaches, backache, worry and tension, the danger of machines or sharp cutting tools, plastic bags and glues and generally the dirt, noise and 'mess'. Some were aware of the fire hazards from bulky inflammable materials stored in the passages, kitchen or living rooms. Others referred to toxic substances or the fluff or hair given off materials with which they worked. Materials which under controlled factory conditions carry little danger to health or safety become highly dangerous in the home, to homeworkers and to young children or elderly relatives sharing living and working space.

Possibilities of organisation

None of the women knew of the National Association of Home-workers or the Homework Campaign, but many expressed interest in learning more about them. As we have seen, few knew about Wages Councils and none had had any advice or help from them. Their grievances over pay or conditions were occasionally taken up with their suppliers, but many referred to 'the take it or leave it attitude' they adopted because they could easily find other women to do the work. Six women who had asked for pay increases reported that they had had to back down, and others who had complained when the type of work was changed unilaterally by the suppliers had been equally unsuccessful. Five women were already working co-operatively, for instance by undertaking to finish work for one another. This occurred especially when sickness of the homeworker or her child would otherwise have prevented completion on time. This co-operation eased their own work lives and met the supplier's demands. Such co-operation was possible because they lived close to one another and were doing the same kind of work. All but one were married to long-distance lorry drivers, whose pattern of work both facilitated and necessitated flexibility from the women. They remained, however, individual workers in relation to the suppliers and the advantages of co-operation were not extended to attempts to improve their pay or change their conditions.

Many women expressed the wish that they could find ways of working more co-operatively with others doing the same work, particularly among those who saw they could market their products directly. The major obstacle was the lack of working capital. One woman, living in a small industrial town, was very interested in setting up a collective for sewers and knitters in her area if the lack of initial capital could be overcome. She had worked full-time for ten years, then as a part-timer. She had been a union member and was in favour of union organisation for homeworkers. Combining homeworking at 80p an hour and registered childminding, she was actively seeking a way out of poorly paid work. Others also saw a clear need for improvements and ridiculed the pay they received. But all returned again and again to the importance of their earnings, however poor, to their households and the measure of independence even this form of paid work gave them. Their realism was based on not only the material conditions of their households but on their long experience as working women in the labour-market and was reflected in their attitudes to trade union organisation for homeworkers.

Attitudes and experience of trade unions

All the women were asked about whether or not they thought trade unions could be helpful either to them personally or to homeworkers generally. As Table 6.1 indicates, there was a marked difference between their answers to the two questions.

Sixteen of the homeworkers had been members of unions when in outside employment and four of these remained members, two in USDAW and two in GMWU. In no case, including those continuing as members, had any trade union attempted to recruit them in their capacity as homeworkers, nor had they received any information on the unions within their trade or industry. When asked if they had ever thought of becoming a member as a homeworker, seventy had not, but eighteeen had. Among the

Table 6.1   *Advantages in union membership (n = 90)*

Response	Homeworkers personally	Homeworkers generally
Yes	4	33
No	81	46
Don't know	5	11

seventy, three were currently union members and three were former members. Ten with union experience had considered joining as a homeworker but only one was a member and this was more related to her part-time outside employment than to home-work. The reasons given for their views on whether or not unions could be helpful make clearer both the obstacles to and the need for organisation. The range of responses is set out in Table 6.2.

It might have been expected that current and former union

Table 6.2 *Personal advantages in belonging to a trade union (n = 85)*

Reasons given	No. of Responses
I. Positive	
Would improve pay	4
Would not be sacked	2
If union specifically for homeworkers	1
	7
II. Negative	
A. Relating to Employers	
Would work be stopped	10
Unions not allowed by firm	6
Employer does not declare work	2
Employer fair	2
	20
B. Relating to Unions	
Unions unable to do anything	6
Unions would not do anything	1
Anti-union	5
	12
C. Relating to Work	
Not a proper job	5
Own boss	1
	6
D. Other	
Do not want trouble	2
Increases would go in tax	2
	4

Table 6.3   *Advantages of union membership for homeworkers generally*
(n = 79)

Reasons given	No. of Responses
I. Positive	
Improve wages	30
Rights and better conditions	19
Could go on strike	2
Everyone should be in	1
	52
II. Negative	
Would be sacked	10
Too many wanting work	3
Unions can't organise homeworkers	10
Not a proper job	5
Nature of job, earnings too low	5
Not worth the trouble	6
Problems with tax	3
Homeworkers don't want it	2
No time for unions	7
Personal choice	4
Accept boss	1
	56
III. Conditional	
Depends on what unions do	6
Depends on your job	5
Depends on which union	1
If everyone in	1
	13

members would have attitudes somewhat different from those with no union experience. This was the case only in so far as they were able to give explicit reasons for their responses, whereas all those unable to give reasons for their views had no union experience. None of the current members saw any personal advantage in belonging to a union as a homeworker. 'I just don't think so, they can't do anything for you when you are at home,' was a common theme. One went as far as to say 'Homeworking is just a job on the side for housewives, it can't be organised'. Only one was positive as far as general advantages were concerned.

The former members of unions were more positive. They saw union organisation as necessary to bring better pay levels and to sort out and improve conditions. It would stop people having to work for 'slave wages' and would mean that 'they could not be sacked' expresses the view of all but two of these women. One of the others felt her family had suffered from the failure of the postal strike in 1971, in which her husband had participated, and the other resented the closed shop. As is obvious from Table 6.2, the negative responses refer to comments on both employers and unions as well as to the work involved. The problem of dismissal for joining a union was, for instance, linked to the recognition that work would be given by suppliers to non-union labour. There was an awareness that employers did not declare the work and the firms did not recognise unions. More generally the view was that unless unions were willing or able to organise *all* homeworkers no advantage could be gained from collective organisation.

The attitude to unions was complex. Some simply saw unions as not interested in homeworkers, but others saw unions as unable to do anything for homeworkers because of their working conditions and lack of any legal protection (see also Hopkins, 1982, pp. 25–6). Only a small minority of our respondents could be described as hostile or anti-union. Hostile attitudes were put forward in highly generalised terms, such as 'they have too much power', or 'they used to be good, but now they go too far'. One homeworker, however, expressed her vehement opposition: 'This is the best paid job of its kind. Sewers don't get as much. They [unions] are as bad as the government, I don't vote anymore. Let them fight it out among themselves. They are all "communists".' Interestingly, the most positive responses towards collective organisation came from those with no union experience. These twenty-two women were clear that unions could and would bring better pay and conditions. Their expectations were not tempered by the experience and knowledge of the limitations of union power or intentions. They lacked an understanding of the way in which unions negotiated on behalf of in-workers, in particular their lack of concern or effectiveness on behalf of poorly paid part-time women. While it is clear that these homeworkers had failed to acquire the general anti-union stance from the media they remained unaware of issues relating to the organisation of casualised workers. The lower expectations of the unionised women reflect a different kind of knowledge of union structures and priorities and of external constraints which make it difficult for unions to organise those subjected to casualised working conditions.

The results of our survey cannot be read as indicating that homeworkers are uninterested in organisation. Many see the limits on trade unions realistically, as concerned with in-workers, particularly full-time, male workers. They appreciate that their casualised working conditions exclude them. Nevertheless they also understand their need for collective organisation and representation if they are to achieve a decent wage and proper working conditions. As one homeworker put it: 'If we got organised like the miners then we could change things.'

A study funded by the Department of Employment presents a different and more negative interpretation of homeworkers' views on trade union involvement. 'The reactions of most respondents to questions on the relevance of Wages Councils and trade unions to homeworkers were either indifferent or defeatist. Many in the sample found the idea of being unionised unattractive' (Cragg and Dawson, 1981, p. 25). This study did not report the reasons for this conclusion.

Interpreting attitudes towards trade unions in contemporary Britain presents difficulties, not the least of which is the media treatment of trade unions and trade unionists. The major popular daily newspapers, those most likely to be seen by homeworkers, and popular television programmes are not noted for their sympathetic or comprehensive presentation of union views or activities. The collective values embodied in trade unionism can be learned only through direct experience. No school or college, apart from a few notable exceptions at tertiary level, provides either factual information or opportunities to consider the collective objectives of working people. The actual experience of union membership or the experience of others in the family or household of homeworkers are the only factors which counter or reinforce the views they adopt.

Efforts at organising

Trade unions and homeworking

The experience of trade unions in organising homeworkers has been limited. There has been a tendency for the existing lack of organisation to be taken as a reflection of disinterest or hostility, or to be seen as a product of particular characteristics such as homeworkers' isolation or fear. One union official, describing the low response of homeworkers to the Hosiery and Knitwear Union's attempt to contact them, said

It was obvious there is a strong element of fear involved where participation is concerned, fear of publicity, fear of being identified, fear of being seen to be involved with the union, all presumably adding up to the fear of losing the job which brings in extra money. (Harrison, 1981)

His view was that trade union organisation is possible only where factories were involved and homeworkers had been employees, and is similar to that in the TUC statement (TUC, 1985). Yet a general enquiry carried out by one union indicated that at least one-third of the homeworking labour force would be willing to join a trade union if one were organised for them (General and Municipal Workers Union, 1977). Moreover, trade union organisation of homeworkers is not unknown.

A branch of the General and Municipal Workers Union was formed specifically for homeworkers making gloves in Devon, with shop steward representatives from the factories involved. The women paid the part-time subscription and half of them joined. Improvements in their pay and conditions followed and the local officials took up the broader questions of their employment status and the disclosure of information by employers. The initiative for the branch had come from homeworkers whose pay had fallen seriously below that paid to in-workers. This branch was unable to sustain its membership and is reported to have folded. No one has made it clear how these workers, as vulnerable as any others in homeworking, decided to seek union assistance, how they managed to get it, or why eventually the homeworkers' branch collapsed. This case could well have been used to explore the particular conditions and attitudes which led to collective organisation.

According to one report, when the industry went out of business the union branch was forced to close (GLC, n.d., p. 10); according to another the branch was closed because homeworkers who had become members resented the fact that the wage increases secured were also being enjoyed by homeworkers who did not pay union subscriptions. Both accounts seem to suggest that the failure of this particular union branch was not due to homeworkers' antipathy to trade union organisation nor to their unwillingness to pay subscriptions. The second account implies that the inability of the union to organise all of the casualised labour force in glove-making was an important factor.

From the mid-1970s homeworking reappeared on the trade union agenda, and resolutions were passed by both the Women's TUC Conference and the main Trades Union Congress. After the failure of the Labour Government to accept the trade union proposals to include homeworkers in the 1975 Employment Protection Act, the Textile, Clothing and Footwear Committee, together with the TUC Women's Advisory Committee, set up a Working Party to draw up a statement on homeworking. The statement issued in 1978 was intended 'to stimulate constructive consideration of the changes which are needed to end the persistent exploitation of an under-privileged group of workers' (Trades Union Congress, 1978, p. 2). A Code of Practice on Homeworking was issued for discussion and action by trade unions, employers and homeworkers. It was intended as guidance to government departments at national and local level, in placing contracts or when giving financial assistance to firms. It advised on monitoring wages, a task falling within the ambit of the Wages Inspectorate. However, despite these efforts little change was achieved.

In 1985 the TUC published a second statement on homeworking, which seems to represent a shift in the importance and publicity it is willing to give to homeworking as a national issue (TUC 1985). It incorporates a more substantial analysis of the place of homeworking in the British economy and recognises that increasing TUC interest is due largely to the claims that there is an expansion of homeworking, particularly in previously highly unionised industries. The creation of local authority projects and programmes to stimulate interest in, and an awareness of, homeworking also seems to have had some impact. For the TUC now tends to see such local organisation as a prerequisite for trade union initiatives, except where in-plant workers already unionised become homeworkers. Whether this development in the approach is to be regarded as a 'let out', a recognition of limited trade union resources, or a realistic appraisal of the limits to trade union organisation, is not clear. Will the unions aid local projects financially when their current funding comes to an end? The statement does not clarify whether unions can justifiably use their resources to promote the interests of home-workers or to provide the means to organise them.

In the Indian state of Gujarat a trade union organiser of some 20-years standing made a break-through in organising casually em-ployed day-labourers and homeworkers, among others. Her efforts helped to create an organisation of these women, founded in 1972. However, it faced immense opposition and was ousted from the textile trade union. Despite this it survived and gained international support. Of the members of this organisation, the lowest-paid women workers, she says

> The experts refer to them as unorganised, informal, marginal, unregulated, peripheral, residual. These are negative terms which give them an inferior and insignificant position in the whole economy, whereas in reality they contribute enormously to the economy . . . To give them positive status and to draw positive attention to them we call them self-employed workers. (Bhatt, 1983, p. 12)

The Self-Employed Womens Association (SEWA) is a challenge to all those who maintain that homeworkers in Britain cannot be organised. Rag-pickers, waste paper collectors and those selling vegetables or second-hand clothes, as well as the homeworkers in textiles, cane and leather work and above all in the cigarette-making industries (*bidi* workers) have been brought together in one organisation, located in Ahmedabad, to fight for better wages and conditions and to obtain fair contracts from the state government. It combines trade union action with development strategies. A women's bank has been established, a co-operative programme which includes training as well as production in rural areas is under way, and facilities for legal aid, health and maternity protection and education are provided (Dholakia, 1984; Jhabvala, 1983). Though its 30 000 members represent only a drop in the ocean of India's estimated 8.8 million workers in household industries (in itself a gross under-estimation), by successfully reaching formerly unor-ganised workers SEWA has lessons for all those concerned to improve the position of homeworkers (Bhatt, 1985).

If, as is being suggested, home-based work is a growth area in Britain and elsewhere, then such issues as the place of organisation and the need for legislation become ever more pressing. Those who assume that market forces will operate to provide decent conditions of work and reasonable standards of living for home-based workers face a wealth of evidence to the contrary. In the contemporary Third World, as well as Western Europe and North America, the existing evidence on homework production indicates that complacency is misguided, certainly as far as women workers are concerned.

Moreover, the historical material from Britain, North America and Western Europe leaves little space for thinking that in the 1980s and beyond new technologies or new ways of organising work will introduce serious shifts in existing power relations sufficient for individuals without collective organisation or legal protection to bargain successfully for better rewards or working lives (Bajohr, 1979; Boston, 1980; Daniels, 1982).

Previous trade union attitudes

The tension between using the authority of the state in the form of the law and developing collective action and organisations to establish the rights of the workers and protect their standard of living, has deep roots in the history of British industrial relations. Previous trade-union policy towards homeworking has been developed against this background. Trade unions, in Britain and elsewhere, have argued that homeworking should not exist and their hostility to homework has at times extended to homeworkers themselves. But whereas in the United States unions in some trades, such as cigar-making and textiles, campaigned vigorously and successfully to prevent homeworking in law, in Britain trade unions have concentrated on improving conditions for factory and office workers, but for the most part have ignored homeworkers (Allen, 1982a). Contrary to many portrayals of unions as all-powerful in setting wages and conditions of workers, they have been in the main responsive organisations attempting to reduce the power of employers and the state. One of the most important ways in which this has been done is by recognising the threat posed by unorganised workers who can be used to undercut wages or worsen conditions. Casualised workers, including homeworkers, have been seen in this way and so long as they remain unorganised have been deemed to be unorganisable. A well-organised, relatively well-paid work-force saw the enactment and effective implementation of legislation to protect or improve workers' rights as predicated on collective organisations. Such a view is not simply a product of narrow, sectional interests, but is well-grounded in historical experience as can be seen, for instance, from the ineffectiveness of Wages Councils to ensure a living wage or even implement the legal minimum rates.

Among male trade unionists – at times perhaps the majority – and particularly among those making policy, there has been a marked tendency to take as given the construction of women's work outside the home as secondary. They have operated exclusionary practices to defend the rights of 'real' workers, sacrificing on innumerable occasions the interests of women workers to secure those of men. As husbands, fathers and sons they have been imbued with the idea that they are the workers, the breadwinners. They have joined with politicians, churchmen, lawyers and employers (and in recent years with psychologists and social workers) in constructing an illusionary world in which their wives, daughters, sisters and mothers are 'at home' providing services for them and the children and not out at work. In doing so they have ignored the realities of the capitalist mode of production and reproduction which incorporates women both as paid and unpaid workers.

Many women too, have become enmeshed in these constructions. They are aware that providing for young children, the sick, handicapped and elderly is either carried out by them or not at all. In addition they are required to service those who go out to work, while their work goes unrecognised, for much of it earns no wage. Their work outside the home is always made conditional on whether they can cope with the domestic labour. Consequently 'choosing' to work at home may appear to offer an option which reconciles the ideological and material contradiction at the centre of women's lives. The price they have paid is to be marginalised yet further by the trade union movement.

In the 1980s the formal position of the TUC and some of the unions affiliated to it is one of support for both an extension of protective legislation and for a policy to organise homeworkers. Stripping away the many layers of the ideological constructions which separate home and work and reinforce the low waged work of women has been left, in the main, to women in the labour movement, supported on occasions by women politicians and researchers. They have historically tried to alter these constructions. Their part in organising against sweated labour, in shops, factories and in homework was one of the most important chapters in securing not only legislation which created Trades Boards and minimum wages but, also, if only briefly, in forcing some recognition of the realities of women's working lives (Boston, 1980; Braybon, 1981; Drake, 1984; Nield Chew, 1982). We have seen in the past few years a resurgence of these same concerns within a context of changes in the law for employees' protection, strengthened in the 1970s by the Equal Pay and Sex Discrimination legislation, and the growth of part-time work for women resulting from labour shortages in the 1950s and 1960s. Although the 1980s have brought reversals, some gains are evident, not least in the heightened awareness among women trade unionists of the many forms of low-paid work and poor conditions experienced by women. This has helped to bring about a changed policy with regard to homeworkers.

Locally-based initiatives

Various local initiatives were established in the 1970s. Saltley Action Centre, for instance, based in an inner city area of Birmingham, enabled the setting up of a small co-operative of Asian homeworkers with child-care facilities provided communally. Community workers, both at Saltley and in Manchester's Moss Side became aware of the low pay and poor conditions of homeworkers in minority groups through direct contact with them. Working within a community work perspective, their energies were put into improvements within the immediate neighbourhoods and gains were made for small numbers of women, but had little effect on the conditions of the majority.

The early 1980s saw an increase in locally-based groups who not only gathered information on the type and conditions of homework production in their areas, but also provided advice and help to homeworkers and sought ways of organising so that the workers themselves had a voice on issues of most concern to them. These initiatives reflected in part a development of the earlier attempts to reform the law and to give an added impetus to the increasing recognition by some unions that the organisation of homeworkers is a necessary part of their work. They also reflected the increasing participation of those involved with women's issues in institutional politics in local government and trade unions. As Labour controlled boroughs and metropolitan authorities began to widen, in some instances, the range of issues they were willing to engage in, particularly in relation to industry and employment an opportunity for homeworking to emerge as a legitimate area of political and economic concern occurred.

In Leicestershire, where outwork has always been a part of the hosiery and footwear trades, and where the Knitwear and Hosiery Workers Union has had a continuing interest in it, the Leicester Outwork Campaign was established in 1980 and in 1981 hosted the Second National Conference on Homeworking (Hopkins, 1982). During the five years of its existence it has developed from being staffed by social and community work students on placement lasting in each case only a matter of months to having seven staff and students. An Inner Area Programme grant provided funding for four years and a full-time Project Organiser was appointed in June 1983. In 1985 County Council funding made possible the appointment of a Women's Employment Adviser for the whole of the county, thus broadening the work beyond the city.

The four basic aims of the Campaign are to provide information, advice and advocacy for outworkers; to undertake research into outworking; to campaign with outworkers at local and national level for better conditions; and to help outworkers get in touch with each other and organise. In the initial years it communicated with homeworkers largely through leaflets, press reports, Fact Packs and a newsletter, *Outworkers Own*, and by responding to telephone requests for information, advice or help. By 1984 it was able to begin to work in inner city neighbourhoods, distributing information through all manner of outlets and working through local organisations to reach homeworkers more effectively and publicise the work of the Campaign (Leicester Outwork Campaign, 1985). Though dependent for part of its funding on local authorities, the Leicester Outwork Campaign, while working closely with or through local authority departments remains an independent organisation with a strongly developed input at the national level.

Many local projects or groups are, however, part of local authority structures. The first local authority to appoint a Homeworking Officer, in 1979, was the London Borough of Hackney. The clothing trades dominated the supply of homework and because of the high demand the officer established a Homeworker's Employment Agency. This was regarded by many as a controversial step seeming to compromise the aims to reform the pay and conditions of homework. But it was argued that the agency would be a vehicle through which the Council could influence the suppliers' employment practices.

Following the recommendations of the London Boroughs Association in 1982, and with the support and funding from the Greater London Council Industry and Employment Committee several boroughs employed officers to stimulate awareness of the conditions in homeworking in London and to facilitate the organisation of homeworkers themselves. Projects were started on the local level, guided by what was seen as a 'new approach' to improving the wages and conditions of homeworkers. Arguing that 'no group of workers has ever made significant and lasting changes in their wages and conditions of work except by organised struggle', organisation by homeworkers is seen as a priority in overcoming the isolation of individual homeworkers, enabling them to share their experiences and organise together for change (GLC, 1983, p. 6. See also Garrett, 1984; GLC, 1985; London Industrial Strategy, 1985; National Homeworking Conference, 1984). Improvement in homeworkers' bargaining position is sought through the provision of training programmes to upgrade homeworkers' skills, develop confidence in seeking work outside the home, improve their English where necessary, and foster the development of co-operatives. In Greenwich, for example, one of the first local authority projects in London to get off the ground, a pilot Fresh Start course was launched funded by the Industrial Common Ownership Movement (ICOM) with money from the EEC. The Greater London Enterprise Board has approved money for the training of homeworkers in the clothing sector, mainly for women from minority groups, as part of a programme aimed at equipping those trained to form independent workshops or co-operatives.

In London, action on health and safety in Greenwich; the collection of evidence on pay and conditions in, for instance, Southwark, Haringey, Hackney and among Bangladeshi women in the East End; and the supply of information to homeworkers on their rights, through Fact Packs similar to those developed in Leicester, indicate a new awareness of the extent of homeworking and the need to develop effective means of organisation and co-ordination. In many other parts of Britain, including Dundee, Wolverhampton, Nottingham and Wales, similar initiatives have been taken, sometimes with local authority support, but also by independent groups. Officers employed by local authorities attempt to influence local authority policies and practices, such as tenancy agreements in Council housing which prohibit paid work in the home and planning regulations which require official permission to carry out homework. These are believed to contribute to feelings of insecurity among homeworkers. Three or four London boroughs and the City of Sheffield have already amended requirements of this kind for homeworkers. Homeworking officers, so far with less success, are also urging authorities to carry out their obligations under the Factories Act 1961, to adapt their training and child-care facilities to meet homeworkers' special needs and to include homeworkers in 'contract compliance' agreements with their own suppliers.

The activities of local homeworking groups represent a significant attempt to address the problems of organising homeworkers and deal with the immediate need to provide advice, support and information. By approaching these within a broad perspective of feminist politics they have reached more homeworkers and they have presented the issues in a different way from that appearing in the studies by the Department of Employment or the statements by the TUC or the House of Commons Select Committee. The focus on collective organisation is justified in part as a return to the methods of traditional trade unionism, but also draws upon the importance given by the women's movement to consciousness raising as a means of mobilisation. Both of these depend for their effectiveness on common interests based on trust, shared experience and a recognition that change is possible.

These local initiatives depend to varying degrees on finance and political support from vulnerable sources. Many initiatives in London were linked to political and financial support from the GLC. In Leicester, the expansion of the Leicester Outwork Campaign activities has been possible through sponsorship by both the City and County Councils. This vulnerability is shared with many other voluntary organisations and is not confined to campaigns on homeworking. Nevertheless the links with trade unions may prove a more stable basis for organising, if the unions at local level can be persuaded to provide financial and political support.

Beyond the local level

After the defeat of the 1979 and 1981 Bills which aimed to give homeworkers, among other things, employee status, and the refusal in 1982 by the government to implement any of the recommendations of the Select Committee Report, there was little activity at regional or national level. The trade unions were faced with the effects of large-scale unemployment, falling membership and subscription income and a government openly hostile to them. The Low Pay Unit's full-time Homeworking Officer had been replaced by a part-timer, reducing its ability to campaign and undertake research.

In the early 1980s the initiative on homeworking therefore passed to local support groups and local authority activities. In London there was some co-ordination of effort through the London-wide Homeworking Group and the Leicester Outwork Campaign attempted to maintain information links with groups throughout the country. It was through their initiative that a national meeting of MPs, representatives of trade unions, local authority and community groups, the Low Pay Unit and researchers, hosted by the Leicester MP, Greville Janner, met in November 1983 to plan and co-ordinate future strategy. The issues of health and safety, employment status, low pay and Wages Councils and the Homeworking Advisory Committee were discussed. It was agreed that an All Party Parliament Group should be established and a national network set up to campaign on these issues. The former is still awaited, but a National Steering Group was formed to organise a Third National Conference which would inaugurate the national network. From this conference came the National Homeworking Group. It was successful in attracting grants and established a national centre in Birmingham in January 1987. Individual membership with a sliding scale of subscription as well as institutional or group membership were adopted. As a national information advisory and campaigning centre with close links with existing groups this is a considerable breakthrough in organising for change in the conditions and status of homework.

Issues in organising for change

At the 1984 conference, a Homework Charter and recommendations on actions to- be taken by a variety of organisations were adopted as policy, and in 1985 a TUC Statement set out its policy proposals (LIS, 1985; TUC, 1985). The Low Pay Unit continued to publish on matters relating to low paid workers, including home-workers (Bisset and Huws, 1985).

All indicate a growing awareness of the many changes needed to 'alleviate the worsening situation of homeworkers' (TUC, 1985) but the emphasis in the Homeworkers Charter has broadened the issues from campaigning for the adoption of a minimum wage, amend-ments to health and safety regulations, and changes in home-workers' employment status to include measures to deal with some of the conditions which it is argued push women into doing homework. Such measures include the free, adequate care of homeworkers' dependants, educational and training opportunities for homeworkers and resources to enable them to meet together both for support and to encourage organisation and campaigning. An even more general aim is to work for the repeal of racist and sexist legislation and against sexist and racist practices which deny women, and especially minority group women, equal opportunities in participating fully in economic and social life. While all those involved in campaigning might agree that 'The denial of economic and social equality to adult women . . . is at the root of the terms and conditions under which it [homework] is done and who does it' (Allen, 1982a) this still leaves open the question of the most effective strategies for bringing about change.

Two issues were of perhaps the greatest importance in the economic and political climate of the mid 1980s, and will be for some time to come. The first is whether, given the scarce resources available, an effective campaign should concentrate on a few, carefully chosen priorities which if successful would bring immedi-ate improvements. Two examples would be the enforcement of safety regulations to control the supply of substances such as solvent-based glue (LIS, 1985, p. 25) and following through con-tract compliance on a systematic basis so that all sympathetic local authorities adopt this as normal practice with regard to homework. Working in close alliance, the National Homeworking Group, local groups and trade unions appear well situated to achieve consider-able advances if agreement can be reached on which issues should be the focus of a national campaign. Such a strategy would not mean that the broader aims were neglected, but they would be carried out through alliances with already existing organisations, leaving the bulk of resources of the homework campaign concentrated on homeworking.

The second issue is whether the campaign for change should shift its focus more in the direction of highlighting who makes the profit out of homeworking, who actually gains from this form of production. Rather than stressing almost exclusively the fear, isolation and vulnerability of 'the homeworker' the emphasis could be put on the suppliers and on retail outlets selling homework products. The campaign could move away from popular stereotypes and towards an analytical appraisal of what and who lies behind the continuing existence and (some believe) considerable expansion of home-based production. Which public bodies, which household names regularly use homework labour? Why do they do it? Such an approach would have the merit of projecting into the centre of the stage those who were at present profit from operating hidden in the wings. No one local campaign, or lone researcher, or trade union can do more than tackle this in a very partial way. Local campaigns working closely with homeworkers rightly base their publicity on the needs and aspirations articulated by their members. But at the national level a shift in emphasis towards those who profit from homeworking could be co-ordinated by the National Homeworking Group.

7

Restructuring and the casualisation of work

In much of this book we have concentrated on analysing the experience of homeworking and on exploring the reasons why firms in a variety of circumstances adopt homeworking for all or part of their production. In this chapter we want to consider similarities between homeworking and certain other forms of employment, so far as conditions of work are concerned. We argue that the restructuring of the British economy is leading to the casualisation of employment for many people, whose terms and conditions of employment are beginning to resemble homeworkers in important ways. Hence it is necessary to broaden the discussion to incorporate a fuller exploration of some of the features of the process of restructuring in Britain and of the rationales which are used to support it.

The casualisation of employment relations

The rights and obligations pertaining to the relation between worker and employer is always historically specific. In Britain the relation is governed partly by common law covering contracts of service, and partly by statute, custom and voluntary agreements. By the late 1970s the rights of employees and the obligations of the employer had been expanded very considerably. Legislation governed employers' obligations regarding health and safety at work, and in industries regulated by the Wages Council enabled minimum rates and paid holiday entitlement to be established. Legislation

159

also modified employers' rights to dismiss workers at will, through the provision of redress for unfair dismissal and notice of and payment for redundancy. It also regularised employment practices for particular categories of workers. After the Second World War, for instance, the practice of hiring dockers on a daily basis was replaced by a scheme which gave a guaranteed basic week. Many of the most comprehensive changes were attempts to equalise the position of men and women in employment, through legislation on equal pay and sex discrimination. In addition, maternity leave made it possible for some women workers to be paid for a number of weeks before and after confinement, and to return to their jobs afterwards.

Other employment practices have been modified through negotiated agreements between employers and trade unions. In Britain paid holidays (apart from statutory bank holidays), the length of the working day and working week, and payments for overtime or unsocial hours have been won for the majority of full-time employees through collective bargaining and are periodically renegotiated. Through the National Insurance system, moreover, employers are obliged to contribute to social insurance covering workers when they are sick, unemployed or retired. These and other measures under which workers enjoy a modicum of employment protection and security have, despite alterations in their details from time to time, regulated the employment of a very substantial proportion of the work-force. There is in addition a body of legislation governing the hours and the kinds of work for young people and for women factory workers.

However, the various measures which regulate employment practices are very unevenly applied. In many respects the rights and benefits to which women are entitled as employees are still comparatively restricted. Where their employment is part-time or broken by periods out of employment women do not enjoy the rights and benefits which accrue to 'permanent' full-time workers as far as pensions and sick pay schemes are concerned, and where they do not work long enough for the same employer do not qualify to be covered by legislation on unfair dismissal. These employment patterns are due not only to their family responsibilities, but also to the fact that women are concentrated in jobs in which turn-over is high. They are also far more likely to be employed in non-unionised sectors and by small firms in which employment practices are not regulated through national agreements between trade unions and employers.

The conditions of employment experienced by homeworkers are a particularly extreme example of women's lesser rights as workers. The rationales usually given to explain this situation have, as we have tried to show, little foundation. Although a substantial proportion of homeworkers work part-time, so do many other workers, particularly women. Homeworkers seek work throughout the year, and many continue in homework, sometimes for the same supplier, for as many years as those who would normally be defined as permanent workers. They work under the control of the supplier, to his or her specifications.

Although homeworkers depend on the supplier for their earnings, and are obliged to take work when it is given and to complete it on time, the supplier has no reciprocal obligations to the homeworker. When a firm supplies former in-workers with work to do at home, or supplies homeworkers with work formerly done in the factory or office, it avoids all the responsibilities which have become associated with the employment of labour. For the firm, labour costs become entirely variable. There are no contracts, labour is purchased only as and when needed, and payment is for work done rather than according to a negotiated hourly, weekly or annual rate. Redundancy pay, paid holidays, extra pay for overtime or unsocial hours, and employers' contributions to National Insurance or pension schemes are all eliminated. Because the employer is not bound by any obligations or commitments to the homeworker the relation between them, and the terms of employment, are casualised. The firm gains total flexibility in its use of labour at the cost of homeworkers' continuity and security of employment.

Employment conditions and social insurance provisions are not therefore, and never have been, uniform, and they have never covered the whole of the working population. But during the 1960s and 1970s, in particular, standards were established which could be used by women in their struggle for equal rights and the recognition of the equal value of their work. During the 1970s those who sought to gain employment rights for homeworkers expected that this would be achieved by defining homeworkers as employees, with all the rights and benefits to which those defined as employees are entitled.

With the end of the period of post-war economic growth and a rising level of unemployment these standards, and the assumptions on which they rest, have been openly challenged in a number of ways. Although the rights and benefits to which full-time employees are entitled have been modified only slightly, it has become much harder for many people to qualify for them. The length of employment needed to qualify for protection against unfair dismissal, for instance, or maternity leave, has increased, the coverage of Wages Councils is being drastically reduced, and the Fair Wages Clause abolished. In addition, jobs defined as temporary, and therefore outside the legislation which still governs the employment of those defined as full-time employees are believed to be increasing rapidly (Manpower Services Commission, 1983). So too are the number of self-employed (MSC, 1985) and the number of those working at or from home (Hakim, 1985a, 1985b), including homeworkers (Mitter 1986). It is now increasingly believed that many workers, men as well as women, adults as well as young people, will experience, in one way or another, casualised employment patterns bringing them closer to those which exist in homeworking.

The extent of these changes is not easily measured. Analytical contributions to debates on the future of work are seriously constrained by inadequate data. For instance, estimates of untaxed earnings in Britain range from 1½ to 15 per cent of gross domestic product, making it impossible to know whether employment opportunities have disappeared or are merely 'hidden' (Rawnsley, 1985). Estimates of self-employment, have been described as a 'back-of-the-envelope' calculation (Hogg, 1985). In some respects official measures of employment and unemployment, like those of homeworking, reflect ideological standpoints. As is well known, the official measures of unemployment do not include large numbers who are seeking work, among others those who do not qualify for benefit. As we discussed in Chapter 2, estimates of homeworking are biased by the definitions adopted in measuring its extent, while the poor records on homeworking in the past make it difficult to adopt a base level from which to measure growth.

The future of work

Restructuring involves not only ways of work but ways of thinking about work. The ideological level of the process of restructuring extends far beyond the enumeration of its extent. Thus the terms used to describe restructuring and its consequences for the workforce are inevitably highly evaluative. Mass unemployment, for instance, has been described by one observer as the 'abolition of work' (Gorz, 1982), while those working at home using new technology are said to be involved in 'telecommuting', 'networking' or 'distance work' rather than homework. What we have described as casualisation is subsumed by some under the more anodyne 'flexible manning' (Atkinson, 1984; IMS, 1984).

While the emergence of the debates on 'the future of work' includes a growing number of contributions from serious scholars on the causes and meaning of shifts in employment, it also includes other contributions which support a not very convincing optimism about current developments. The autonomy and flexibility assumed to be enjoyed by homeworkers are now perceived as becoming more widespread, through the expansion of home-based work, temporary and part-time employment, short-term contracts, fixed-term contracts and self-employment. No longer tied to and constrained by full-time, regular employment, it is argued, people will be able to alter their work commitments as income needs and family responsibilities change, and the alienation of paid labour will occupy a smaller proportion of their lives (Clutterbuck and Hill, 1981; Handy, 1984). Periods of unemployment are seen as enabling people to obtain more training and education in their youth, to engage in constructive, self-generated economic activity in middle age, and to enjoy a longer, more satisfying retirement. This is the silver lining within the cloud of economic recession and mass unemployment.

What does restructuring entail? How are workers affected by it? Is there any possibility of alluring compensations becoming a reality? Given the data on homeworking analysed in this book, there is every reason to believe that they will not.

The restructuring of employment

The restructuring of the British economy incorporates a number of related processes too complex to be more than briefly signposted here. The multinational character of corporate ownership and management, which facilitates the movement of capital across national boundaries, is a crucial component of them. Under the pressure of declining world demand and increased competition from the newly industrialised countries, opportunities for profitable domestic investment are severely squeezed. The international relocation of production, partly to take advantage of lower labour costs, the absence of state regulation and constraints on workers' organisation and militancy, has intensified the decline of investment and employment in the manufacturing sector. Apart from certain consumer goods and services, domestic investment is increasingly concentrated in those sectors which are dominated by, or which service, international capital. They include, on the one hand, oil, chemicals and advanced engineering and electronics, and on the other, banking, insurance and other financial services. However, the adoption of new labour-saving technologies in these sectors severely limits their capacity to absorb those thrown out of work in manufacturing. The service sector, partly through cuts in public spending in the health service and education, for instance, is unable to offset the growing level of unemployment.

The structure of employment and unemployment is also affected by the strategies adopted by capital to meet competition from overseas producers or to increase the profitability of domestic production by reducing labour costs. Attempts to alter the legal framework governing trade union activity or standards of health and safety in the workplace, or to define, identify and eliminate 'overmanning' is sometimes termed 'modernisation'. Ironically enough, it frequently involves a return to methods of production previously discussed as archaic. Whereas firms once sought to regularise the employment of their work-force as a way of increasing worker commitment and productivity, those directly employed by large firms and state corporations and services are increasingly being asked to accept employment on renegotiated terms with various kinds of 'independent' employment agencies or subcontractors. Homeworking, once disregarded as an anachronism, is now viewed as one form of the relocation of production, in this case from factory or office to domestic premises. A range of strategies through which firms are seeking to reduce their obligations to employees, and their consequences for the work-force are discussed below. They suggest that putting work out to homeworkers is only one of several devices with similar rationales and consequences.

Flexible manning

Management consultants believe that flexibility in the deployment of labour is becoming an increasing priority for firms (Atkinson, 1984; IMS, 1984). Market stagnation has already led firms to cut back on permanent personnel, while uncertainty about the pace and level of future growth, the increasing pace of technological change, and a reduction in basic hours of work, mean that firms try to maximise flexibility in the use of labour. While in times of full-employment firms need to 'hoard' labour, high unemployment enables them to take on workers as and when required. High unemployment is also believed to lower worker unity and militancy, allowing firms to offer terms of employment which favour some groups of workers at the expense of others.

The types of flexibility sought by management, and the kinds of schemes which further their goals, have been outlined by Atkinson under the rubric of 'flexible manning' (Atkinson, 1984). The flexibility sought by management, he suggests, can be divided into three distinct categories: functional flexibility in the deployment of workers between tasks, operations, and products; numerical flexibility in altering 'headcount' to meet a changing demand for labour; and financial flexibility in adjusting (that is, lowering) wages in line with increases in the supply of labour. Employment contracts which reduce the firm's commitment to the continued employment of its work-force, such as short-term and temporary contracts, waiver clauses, contracts for set tasks, and the employment of publicly subsidised workers on short training courses, relieve firms of the need to give notice of pay for redundancy and enable hiring and firing to take place 'smoothly' and, of course, more cheaply. Assessment-based pay systems (payment for work done rather than payment for the job) and the negotiation of wage rates at plant level, enable firms to take fuller advantage of regional wage differentials, and those between young and experienced workers and those defined as skilled and unskilled. These 'manpower' policies, Atkinson recognises, intensify existing divisions within the labour force, as between those who are defined as 'core workers', and who are offered full-time, permanent employment, and one or more 'peripheral' groups for whom the firm bears no long-term responsibility. Such policies are most easily implemented when a firm replaces full-time workers, after redundancy, with new workers employed under different terms, especially those with a poorer position in the labour market (women, youth, minorities), or by relocating the work outside its factory or office, to other firms, subcontactors or homeworkers.

The flexibility management gains through these measures has no reciprocal advantage for the worker. This is well demonstrated by the case of homeworkers. The advantages management gains by being able to alter, at will and at no cost, the amount of work, the time given to complete it, and the types of product and piece-rates attached to them is experienced by homeworkers as insecurity and unpredictability. They find it difficult to schedule their other responsibilities around their paid work and are forced to work late into the night and at weekends. They cannot predict their earnings from week to week, and when no work is available they and their families do without basic necessities. Suppliers justify variations in the amount of work and the rates paid by arguing, among other things, that homeworkers work only for extras or in their leisure time, but (as we show in Chapter 3) neither is the case. Homeworkers need their work as a source of income, just like other workers. Otherwise they would not do it.

Similar disadvantages arise from the ways in which the terms of employment of in-workers are being altered. In a detailed study of 4000 men and women who registered as unemployed in May 1980, the Manpower Services Commission found that although 61 per cent were back in employment after ten months, 40 per cent of them had had in the meantime two or more different jobs and 11 per cent three or more (MSC, 1983). As one trade unionist sums up the situation: 'How can workers have the financial security to buy houses and cars and start a family if they are little more than casual labour?' (IMS, 1984, p. 32). Moreover, temporary work or short-term contracts are made available by employers according to their own requirments, and part-time hours are fixed according to production schedules and consumer demand. If they fit in with the workers' other responsibilities or with their preferences, this is coincidental.

The need to earn a regular income at a level to maintain themselves and their dependents is a basic requirement for the majority of the population. It is the only way they have of avoiding poverty. Temporary employment and short-term contracts cannot provide this, and in addition deprive the employee of the means by which pension and other contributory rights can be built up. Even where an adequate income can be earned through successive temporary jobs or short-term contracts, this form of employment uncertainty creates fear among all employees. Workers' needs for flexibility in the timing or duration of their work is far better met through paid maternity, parental and sick leave provisions, by adequate public child-care provisions and care for the elderly, and by more worker participation in the setting of hours of work.

Moves towards what is euphemistically called 'flexibility' are in fact often better analysed as ways of cutting costs or passing them on to other firms, state bodies, or, as in homeworking, workers themselves. These changes are not confined to manual work. School teachers and lecturers in further and higher education, for instance, are increasingly being hired under temporary contracts covering anything from a single term, a part of an academic year, or two, three or five-year periods to perform regular teaching duties. Some lecturers, who are a relatively privileged sector among temporary workers, need to 'sign on' at Christmas, Easter and during the summer – year after year. Many secretarial staff who are regular workers have no employment contract, and may be called for work on a daily or weekly basis. One research institute has been able to retain most of its staff as permanent employees, but only through the novel practice of reducing staff salaries, in the expectation that researchers will make up their own earnings through contracts with international funding bodies. Government cuts in spending on education and research therefore force institutions to reduce costs by evading, reneging on, or refusing commitments to their employees which were previously commonplace in this sector.

Policies like these suggest that measures unrelated to greater 'efficiency' or 'flexibility' are being adopted under these rubrics. Moreover, many of the practices which according to Atkinson are designed to improve firms 'financial flexibility' are far better seen as ways in which work is being intensified. Firms like Rank Xerox, which are encouraging their professional staff to work at home, do this partly to reduce overheads. But they also believe that the sociability inherent in office life is an impediment to increasing the workloads of their managers (IMS, 1984). Firms are seeking the freedom to develop schemes which force their employees to work harder to make up their wages. The use of piece-work and the spread of 'measured effort' schemes into new sectors are examples. Intensification of work is also one of the consequences of putting work out to homeworkers, since it usually involves the replacement of weekly wages with piece-work rates with no guaranteed basic rate.

Terms like 'flexibility' or, as we discuss below, 'autonomy' in work, are used by management to justify changes in employment practices in part by being made to appear to be in the workers' own interests. But they are also promoted as corresponding to the needs of particular sections of the work-force, particularly women. So long as women continue to be depicted as economically dependent 'housewives', their concentration in low-paid, part-time and temporary work will be perpetuated and intensified. 'Core' workers are presumed to be men, and 'peripheral' workers women whose attachment to the labour force is intermittent, whatever their real situation as workers. Atkinson, for instance, rationalises the use of part-time workers by assuming that because turnover among the largely female part-time labour force is high, reductions in 'headcount' can be obtained gently, through natural wastage rather than redundancies. He takes no account of evidence which suggests that turnover rates are related to the nature of the job rather than the gender of the worker (Barron and Norris, 1976).

Once it becomes accepted that lower conditions of employment are permissible for some categories of workers, their numbers are extended through any number of rationales, especially under conditions of high unemployment. Indeed, Atkinson urges firms to distinguish carefully among their workers, retaining employment security for those whose functions are necessary to a firm's long-term viability. In practice it appears that firms do not distinguish between core and peripheral workers on this basis. In the United States, for instance, trade unionists have been asked to accept (and have given their approval of) lower wages and conditions for workers doing identical work in different parts of the country (IMS, 1984). The way in which ideological presuppositions have influenced the definition of 'skill' and the remuneration appropriate to it suggests that the distinctions made between core and peripheral workers is less to do with workers' actual contribution in the labour process than with their social status and bargaining power in the labour-market. Homework is frequently assumed to be confined to unskilled 'auxilliary' tasks in which productivity is low. The skills and commitment homeworkers bring to their work and the value added by it are totally ignored.

The irony is that, despite the hardship created for workers by worsened conditions of work, it is by no means clear that 'flexible manning' necessarily enables firms to become more competitive in the long term. As we have seen, homeworkers are forced to absorb not only overheads, but also the costs arising out of poor management, inefficient marketing, and lack of product innovation. Firms which are encouraged to survive through paying low wages and passing costs on to their workers have no incentive to improve productivity or management efficiency or to increase investment. The schemes mooted in 1986, whereby unemployed workers who accept very low-paid jobs will receive supplementary payments from the state, are wholly indiscriminate in their effects, fostering the growth of the low-wage sector of the economy at the expense of the tax payer who is protecting the inefficient firm as much as, if not more than, the better managed.

Fragmentation of the labour process

Changes which affect employment practices are not confined to firms' personnel policies for in-workers. Firms often decrease their responsibilities for and obligations to the work-force and/or reduce labour costs by re-organising production and fragmenting the labour force. This can include the decentralisation of production, through hiving-off smaller plants to create new subsidiaries; the detachment of units into independent firms tied into the parent firm through franchising or licensing arrangements; and the disintegration of production, through subcontracting or purchasing from outside firms whole goods, components, or services (Schutt and Whittington, 1984). Firms in effect 'externalise' production, 'outsourcing' the goods they sell and contracting out the services they require (Atkinson, 1985; Gerry, 1985; Rainnie, 1984, 1985).

One effect of the increase in subcontracting and outside purchasing appears to be an increase in the number of small firms and an increase in the proportion of workers employed by small firms rather than large corporations. Sub-contracting may also cause a growth in self-employment. The Manpower Services Commission reports that between 1979 and 1984 the number of self-employed rose by some 32 per cent, to one in ten of the labour force (MSC, 1985).

The growth in what is sometimes termed the small-scale sector is welcomed by many who assume gains in autonomy and flexibility. It has been argued by some that the disintegration of large capitalist enterprises and the decline in the number who can expect to be employed by them will permit the emergence of a 'sphere of autonomy', through the expansion of small-scale production based in the home or in geographically dispersed units outside the domination of capital (Gorz, 1982). Others see self-employment, small business and homeworking as avenues for 'autonomous' capital accumulation, or as providing more scope for the expression of initiative, enterprise, and independence outside the restrictions imposed by the state or trade unions on the personnel policies of large firms.

The argument that autonomy is created through decentralisation is highly questionable. As we discussed in Chapter 6, homeworkers as individuals working in their own premises are thought to enjoy more autonomy and flexibility in their work than workers employed in the employers' premises. We showed that their autonomy and flexibility was mythical, for homeworkers are waged workers who are subjected to employer control in a variety of ways. The mechanisms which control the production and innovation of small firms are somewhat different, and derive from the market power of the larger firms. In retailing, for instance, most multiple chains no longer produce the goods they sell, but purchase them from suppliers whose continued viability depends upon meeting the requirements laid down by the purchaser. Marks and Spencer, for example, inspects its suppliers' premises, specifies the exact quality of goods, and even sets its suppliers' profit margins (Mitter, 1986). In general the larger firm maintains its control over the crucial decisions while forcing the smaller firms to bear an increasing proportion of the risks and costs of production.

In fact, some firms appear to be developing highly sophisticated strategies which allow them to decentralise production while maintaining and even increasing their control. An example is the Italian firm Benneton (Mitter, 1986; Murray, 1983). A firm which both manufactures and retails fashion clothing, Benneton has rapidly expanded through a combination of centralised decision-making and the decentralisation of much of its production and distribution to small, nominally independent units. Its retail outlets are franchised, but Benneton expects to link them to head office through computer technology which will enable it to increase the speed with which stocking requirements can be decided and acted upon by the central office. On the production side it is investing in large, capital-intensive factories for the cutting and dyeing of fabrics, but most of the garments are machined by outworkers in small workshops or domestic premises. Its advertising throughout Western Europe portrays an attractive image to young, up-to-date people. Behind this lies long hours of sweated labour.

There is no reason to believe that working conditions in the small firm are preferred. Effective trade union organisation is less likely and this may be one of the attractions for large firms of decentralising work to smaller units. Moreover, in so far as the large firm establishes prices through its monopolisation of the market, small firms can make a profit only by pushing down wages and intensifying work. As the small firms cannot be certain that their contracts will be renewed, they seek to avoid forms of employment which incur obligations to the work-force. Homeworking and other forms of casualised employment are therefore closely associated with sub-contracting, and appear to be a major form through which the cost of labour is reduced without a direct attack on the conditions of work of unionised workers directly employed by the large firm.

Privatisation

Analogous developments are taking place in the public sector through privatisation. When public services put out to tender work which was previously undertaken by a directly employed labour force, this leads not only to redundancies but the wage rates and conditions of service are no longer the concern of public employers. Well-established negotiating machinery between them and the trade unions can therefore be by-passed. Instead these become subject to the cost-cutting policies inherent in the move towards privatisation. The wages of already poorly paid workers are forced down, paid holiday entitlement cut and the amount of work expected intensified.

Privatisation is also affecting predominantly male workers formerly employed by the state-owned industries. At British Steel, for instance, thousands of workers were made redundant, but much of the work they previously undertook still needs to be done. Redundant supervisors now compete as sub-contractors for it (IMS, 1984; Fevre, 1986). They employ workers on a casual basis, do not supply adequate protective clothing and serious industrial accidents go unreported by those who fear that future work opportunities for themselves or their friends will be affected.

Privatisation can be only partly justified in terms of the reduction of state expenditure. Fevre has argued that at the British Steel's Port Talbot plants falling standards of work mean that productivity is actually falling and costs thereby increased in the longer term. The situation in the health and education services is not dissimilar. The privatisation of laundry work, cleaning and catering has led to a number of allegations of lower standards of cleanliness and poorer diets and the loss of the commitment and care for patients which was a valuable if less easily measured contribution made by domestic workers employed directly by hospitals.

Fevre has argued that sub-contracting at British Steel is primarily a consequence of bias towards private enterprise. It can be seen as part of the more general extension of investment opportunities into profitable areas previously under the control of the state sector. The autonomy of these enterprises, like those selling to private firms, is partly illusory, for their viability depends on obtaining contracts made available in the state sector. In the case of British Steel, for instance, the new contractors benefit because their workers' wages are topped-up by payments made by the state to firms which employ former workers, as part of the original British Steel redundancy package. This has meant that long-established contractors with British Steel are no longer able to compete successfully for the work.

Self-employment

Self-employment, whether or not it takes place in the home, is characterised by quite different social relations from those of waged homework. But it can share important characteristics with the forms of casualised waged work discussed above, and therefore needs to be considered within this context. Whereas 'permanent' employees usually receive a guaranteed basic wage while they are in work and can claim redundancy pay and unemployment benefit if they lose their jobs, the situation of self-employed workers is similar to that of temporary and seasonal workers. The self-employed have no employment rights, as they have no employer against whom to claim. The work of many of the self-employed may be low-paid, irregular and intermittent. This makes it impossible for them to maintain the level and continuity of earnings which may have previously obtained as employees. In addition they have difficulty in maintaining their national insurance payments.

Given these problems, it is surprising that very little is known about the new self-employed. Some are young people who have never been able to obtain employment, while others are workers who have been forced through redundancy to replace comparatively secure, well-paid employment with an economically precarious existence (Gerry, 1985). In the American construction industry, it has been argued that self-employment appears to vary cyclically with the level of unemployment, rising when waged employment is unobtainable and falling when more regular waged work becomes available on the labour market (Linder, 1983). This indicates that self-employment reflects a low demand in the labour-market. In Britain, evidence provided by the Manpower Services Commission survey on self-employment (MSC, 1985) claims that nearly 40 per cent of the self-employed employ other workers. This rise in the number of self-employed has been accompanied by a rise in the number of self-employed workers who work only part-time and may indicate that many of the new unemployed are unable to obtain sufficient work.

Anecdotal evidence indicates that for the self-employed who work at or from home the situation is particularly dire so far as levels of earnings are concerned. Postgate's account of sixteen individuals who are involved in 'home-based economic activity' indicates that most could not expect to support themselves from their work. The fourteen self-employed individuals who were working at or from home – including a dressmaker, a disabled electrician, a shoemaker and a graphic artist, as well as individuals who were doing car repairs, running employment agencies and teaching adult education classes – were very rarely able to support themselves by this work. Their experience contrasts markedly with the rewards recounted by those in the survey who themselves employ outworkers and homeworkers (Postgate, 1984). For many, so far as remuneration is concerned, self-employment is not so much a choice as a 'rubbish dump' for those whose labour is relatively surplus to capital's present requirements (Gerry, 1985).

At the most general level, Gerry has argued, new growth in self-employment and small business takes place as the result and by-product of the overall strategies of large, international capital. Mechanisms of exploitation, including chain sub-contracting, out-working and monopolistic sub-contracting between one large buyer and many micro-enterprises, are being resuscitated and revitalised. As he points out, capital may encourage the growth of the small-scale sector for both material and ideological reasons, but it is unlikely to permit it 'a degree of real (rather than merely formal) autonomy which might prejudice the benefits which the ruling class gains from its economic and juridicial relations with small units of production' (Gerry, 1985, p. 311).

The encouragement and growth of the small-scale sector is part and parcel of the more general casualisation of employment, through which capital invites workers of many different kinds to assume a greater share of the costs or production and/or reproduction and to accept a lower return on their labour. The petty trader or craftsperson is in effect asked to provide for or to supplement the costs of his or her own reproduction, saving the state all or part of these costs.

Among the categories we have been discussing, homeworkers are distinctive in that their labour is remunerated through the wage labour contract, and the controls exercised by the supplier are identical to those exercised by the employers of in-workers. The return on labour of the self-employed and those running small businesses is established by capital differently, through the price mechanism, but it is readily cheapened through competition. The self-employed and small business entrepreneurs are subject to the compulsion of the market-place, which enforces standards of quality and efficiency. In addition, however, they are subject to the particular requirements of larger firms, as a condition of obtaining work from them and being paid on its completion. Clients and customers who monopolise outlets for goods and services produced in the small-scale sector are in a position to exercise very consider-able control on both prices and standards of work. Highly depen-dent, dispersed units of production, sub-contractors and the self-employed are competing among themselves for work from large corporations and the state, forcing them to keep their prices down and to absorb a wide range of costs previously borne by the large employer.

When formerly waged or salaried workers are forced to sell their labour as freelancers, or to tender for the work they did previously as employees, their bargaining power can be reduced with no corresponding enhancement of their autonomy in work. Whereas many once enjoyed – or on joining the labour force could have expected – waged and salaried employment in which a degree of control could be exercised through trade union membership, they are now subjected to a market over which they have no control. Whenever possible, they pass the costs they are forced to bear on to their own employees, including homeworkers, and maintain profit margins by paying low wages. But relative to the large corporations or state services which supply their work their autonomy remains minimal.

Neo-familialism

Many observers have suggested that an expansion in the activities of the family will help people to deal with the consequences of high unemployment and the reductions in state expenditure. But is this in fact a viable strategy, given what we know about relations between family members and between family and society? The data on homeworking analysed in this book suggests that domestic production is not only unable to provide a substitute for formal employment, but cannot be conceptualised as a separate realm.

The kinds of activities which families are expected to take up, and the analytical framework which underpins them, has been analysed as 'a kind of 'neo-familism' (Godard, 1985). They are based on the notion that the family's role in reproduction can be extended into areas previously located in the market sphere. Some see the family evolving into a 'new work collective' through the expansion of home-based work in the 'electronic household' that is being created by new technology (Toffler, 1980). Others have argued that households already provide for themselves substitutes for the services which used to be located in the commercial domain, using their own privately-owned tools and machinery (Gershuny, 1979, 1985; Gershuny and Pahl, 1979/80. This argument is pushed further by those who claim that a decommodification of economic activity is taking place, in which households exchange services without entering into the market, or provide more goods and services for their own use through a development of self-provisioning and an expansion of domestic labour. In all these ways, it is argued, they will be able to provide alternatives to the income and identity formerly associated with waged employment.

As part of this neo-familial perspective, the family is also being asked to provide alternatives to services provided by the state as well as those produced for or purchased in the market. Since 1979 government has sought to impose or re-impose on the family responsibilities which were formerly undertaken by the state. Cuts in social services and welfare benefits, reinforced by the ideology of community care, assume that families will care for the sick, handicapped and elderly, and will support young people who, through unemployment or low wages and state regulations, are unable to live separately and maintain themselves (Allen, 1982f; Henderson, 1985).

This emphasis on the capacity of the family to take on these obligations is justified in several different ways (Godard, 1985). It is argued that since people prefer to offer and receive mutual aid within the family and that working in the household enhances personal autonomy this is a positive development. A second view is that since the household is a highly efficient unit for the pooling of resources and the allocation of labour between the private and public domain it is necessary to further harness its possibilities during economic recession. In a more pessimistic vein, the incapacity of the market to generate employment, or of the state to finance public services, simply forces families to take on as best they can, all manner of tasks in the interests of the survival of their members.

Whatever the justification adduced, the capacity of the family to expand its activities is rather more problematic than these propositions imply. It can be argued that in so far as the family is able to absorb these expanded activities, it is at the cost of personal autonomy for some of its members, particularly women. The ability to do so is in any case highly variable as between households. The assumptions that households can simply revert to older patterns of reproduction, intensify their present ones or adopt new ones are highly questionable, particularly if the implications for the wider economy are taken into account.

How far families are capable of absorbing the effects of economic recession, and whether or not increases in caring and servicing enhance personal and family autonomy are not matters merely of interpretation or speculation. Our analysis of homeworking is directly relevant to arguments about the home as an area of autonomy and freedom. It suggests that the meaning of work in the domestic domain is highly specific to gender. Whereas there are indications that for men doing a few hours' paid or unpaid work at home may be experienced as a welcome release from office or factory life, enhancing their sense of personal autonomy and allowing more time to spend with their children (Olson and Primps, 1984), for women work at home is different. Few in our sample expressed a preference for paid work at home, and many turned to it only as a last resort. They did not believe that as compared with going out to work it allowed them to spend more time with their children. It was apparent that the absence of any separation between unpaid and paid labour led to extreme stress and over-work, for while the female homeworker must meet her obligations to the employer, she experiences no corresponding reduction in her responsibilities to other family members. Indeed, their expectations may be increased since she is 'at home anyway'.

One advice manual on working at home correctly perceives the conflicting demands experienced by women, but sees the solution in terms of a division of household space between 'office' and 'home', with the implication of a correspondingly simple division of her time and attention (Gray, 1982). In fact, for homeworkers such a division is rarely practicable, because of the lack of space at the women's disposal and because of the power relations within the household and their impact on women's labour time. The data analysed in Chapter 5 clearly demonstrate that husbands' views regarding meals, cleanliness and child-care duties constrain women's work options and the use of their time in the home. No models of the allocation of labour by family members can ignore the wider sexual division of labour and the highly personalised form in which it is experienced in individual households.

It was also clear that working at home leads as often to anger, tension and conflict as to co-operation and mutual aid (see Chapter 5). Arguments between husbands and wives were reported to take place over the presence of homework, and over the allocation of responsibility for the work between them. Some husbands objected not only to the mess and inconvenience, but to seeing their wives occupied in this way. Women did not find it easy to engage their husbands' help in their work. Although it was frequently forthcoming, requests for help had to be carefully negotiated. Envisioning the home as a unit of production, whether for the market, reciprocal exchange, or own use, involves questions about the bases on which the right to use and direct the labour of other family members is assumed and exercised. 'Mutual aid' is a mystification of existing patterns of power with and between households.

Our data also show that homeworking creates inconvenience, mess and in some cases health and safety hazards. Others have demonstrated that even among white-collar and professional workers, men and women working at and from home absorb the space needed for shared family recreation (Postgate, 1984). While some of those with paid employment outside the home may well enjoy using their spare time to enhance their standard of living, particularly where they have no responsibility for unpaid reproductive labour, for others, particularly women, dependence on the home as a work-place is not associated with increased personal autonomy and may decrease further their claims to any autonomy. Homeworking is undertaken partly as a consequence of women's subordination in the labour-market and to the wishes and needs of others in the family for whom they have life-long responsibilities.

Somewhat different questions about personal autonomy arise in relation to the intensification of responsibilities for dependants within the household through cuts in social services. In addition to the impact on the autonomy of women, who undertake by far largest burden of physical care, multi-generational families do not necessarily experience this as enhancing personal autonomy. The lack of personal autonomy experienced by most young adults forced to remain in their parents' home is so obvious that it immediately reveals the very partial picture of family life adopted by those who promote mutual aid within the family. Less obvious are research findings which suggest that when the elderly are forced to accept care from an adult child this can exacerbate the loss of status and independence associated with old age (Henderson, personal communication).

Whether or not families are *capable* of absorbing the effects of economic recession raises more complex questions. Both historical and statistical evidence is relevant. The survival strategies in which households engage includes a complex and historically changing mix of waged, informal, subsistence and 'normal' domestic work (Mingione, 1985; see also R. E. Pahl, 1984). Households cannot simply shift from one mix to another. Their capacity to adopt new strategies depends upon the composition of households, the character of relations with kin and neighbours, the productive resources at their disposal, and the level and types of state provision, including income maintenance benefits and public services. In Southern Italy, for instance, household strategies which included a high proportion of informal work were moderately adequate for a minimum level of survival while awaiting or planning migration to Northern Italy or abroad, but they cannot provide a livelihood for the large numbers of households who can no longer escape poverty through this route. Such families, Mingione argues, have reached a cul-de-sac, with no viable strategy available to them.

A full understanding of the situation in Britain would require a historical analysis of the creation of state income-maintenance schemes and public services and the struggles to obtain them. These were created, after all, because private family solutions to the care of the elderly or the provision of income in times of unemployment or sickness were inadequate. Today the expectation that families can absorb the costs of their unemployed members, or that some adults require only temporary or occasional low-paid work, assumes a conjugal household and a husband/father breadwinner paid a family wage. This is not the reality. Even at present conjugal households require the earnings of both husband and wife, and very long hours of work, paid and unpaid, on the part of both. For the growing number of lone-parent families, and the elderly living alone, such a strategy is in any case ruled out. Nor can it be assumed that families will be willing or able to support their unemployed members. There is evidence which suggests that even when parents are able to aid their unemployed children financially both parents and children believe that this undercuts the independence appropriate for adult children (Allatt and Yeandle, 1986). It must also be remembered that all the evidence that made the case for paying child benefit to mothers, as well as academic research, has indicated that in important respects household income is not shared among household members according to need (J. Pahl, 1983).

When it comes to the role of informal work and self-provisioning as a hedge against declining, uncertain earnings, the most telling evidence has been uncovered by research conducted in the Isle of

Sheppey, which included detailed accounts of the mix of work activities engaged in by households (R. E. Pahl, 1984; Wallace and Pahl, 1985). These show that it is those households with one or more persons in full-time employment who are involved in the exchange of unpaid services between households, and who engage in a variety of self-provisioning activities. Both waged and non-waged work opportunities are not evenly distributed between households, but are concentrated in 'busy' households with more than one earner. Those who lack regular employment are dependent on state benefit. The only form of home-based economic activity available to the poor was homeworking in manufacturing, similar with respect to both pay and lack of autonomy to that found in West Yorkshire.

A final consideration is that even were it possible for households to extend the range of their unwaged activities, this would have repercussions on the demand for marketed goods and services, with implications for both the level of employment and for the state's capacity to generate income through taxation for those public services and benefits which remained. This is one more indication that the neo-familial perspective is deeply flawed by its isolation of the family in a privatised cycle of production and reproduction. It fails to consider the links and dependencies which characterise relations between household, economy and the state in industrial societies. Those who now look to the family to provide for its own needs have quite correctly begun to challenge the model of a household in which only one individual, the husband/father, is assumed to be 'working', and have begun to recognise women's unpaid labour in the home as a form of work. But they fail to take account of the relation between women's paid labour and purchases on the market, or women's already heavy burden of unpaid and paid labour. Given the working days of the homeworkers described in Chapter 5, one is hard put to see that their labour can be stretched very much further. It is readily apparent that there is a widening gulf between the kinds of solutions offered by some social theorists and policy-makers and the actual experience of households increasingly subjected to low wages, unemployment and the curbs on their rights of access to state financial or service provision.

Conclusions

The changes reviewed in this chapter are increasingly recognised, discussed in the press and on television as well as social science journals. Indeed, some change is so rapid that discussion of it can be outdated by the time it is published.

The reasons for considering some aspects of these changes in the context of homeworking are threefold. First, we seek to ensure that in the discussion of casualised employment homeworking does not, as so often in the past, remain invisible. Secondly, homeworking provides a very good example of the implications of casualisation for workers themselves. It is a particularly important example in showing how assumptions about gender are, on the one hand, used by firms and others to explain and justify low pay and employment insecurity and, on the other, conveniently ignored when claims about the benefits of home-based work are made.

Finally, and in some ways most importantly, we are arguing that casualised employment does not constitute a solution to economic recession, but is in fact one of its symptoms. Our analysis of the cost-cutting aspects and the processes of deregulation involved in casualised employment is in some respects similar to that of those who support such measures as a way of increasing the competitiveness of British firms. But the evidence on homeworking suggests that these are effective in maintaining profitability only where firms can pass on costs to their workers, not only in the form of low wages, but also in terms of the costs of production and reproduction of the work-force. Such a strategy is relevant only where employment is available to some sectors of the working population, who can then directly subsidise the reproductive activities of households carrying such costs or dependent on casualised employment. It is not a strategy for economic recovery at a national level. This would require a reconsideration of the relationships between capital, labour and the state taking full account of the structures of oppression and exploitation in the sexual division of labour as these have developed in the family and labour-markets of industrial capitalism.

8
The way forward

Where do we go from here? In Britain and many other countries, including some in the Third World, there now exists sufficient information to frame legislation on homeworking and to press for its enactment. We have presented evidence primarily on homeworking in Britain, concentrating on its extent, the ways it is organised, its similarities to other forms of casualised employment, and some of the proposals which have been made to bring about improvements for homeworkers, as well as the more commonly addressed aspect, the character of the labour force. In these conclusions we set out some of the aspects of homeworking on which further research is necessary and consider the main policy implications to emerge from research to date.

Our main goal has been the development of a more adequate analysis of homeworking. However, policy proposals to improve homeworkers' pay and conditions are not so far removed from this concern as it might appear. This is because the present lack of regulation is closely related to conventional assumptions about work. These both influence and are themselves constructed out of the character of existing employment legislation, the statistical recording of employment and social scientific analyses of work and employment. All these tend to make homeworking either invisible or to marginalise its part in production. Despite the contribution homeworkers have made and continue to make to the economy as producers and to their households as breadwinners their work is consistently ignored. In the 1980s, as in the past, outrageously low wages, long hours of work, unpredictable earnings and injury to the health and safety of homeworkers and their families go largely unquestioned. We have tried to show that one cannot document conditions in homeworking, or its extent, or which firms use it and why, without challenging conventional approaches to the sexual division of labour and the location of work.

However, reformulating basic assumptions is only a starting point. We have tried to provide the reader with detailed empirical data on homeworking, not simply on homeworkers themselves but on homeworking as a method of production. One of the strengths of this approach is that it draws attention to the suppliers of homework. This is one of the most neglected aspects of investigation so far and one that needs to be extended further.

With a few exceptions the investigation of homeworking has so far concentrated on homeworkers themselves and their characteristics. We have tried to set this kind of information in context. Explaining homeworking in terms of the characteristics of homeworkers mistakes cause for effect. It leaves out of the analysis the social divisions and social processes through which the labour force is constructed and differentially allocated to jobs which command different levels of remuneration and different conditions of work. Involvement in homeworking can only be properly understood as part of the segmentation of labour-markets, the sexual division of labour, the privatisation of responsibility for the care of children and other dependents, and state income maintenance policies. The association between homeworking and women of child-rearing age is, as we showed in Chapter 3, at least partly true, but needs to be considered in this wider context.

We have argued, further, that the ideological and practical constraints on women's paid employment do not constitute an adequate explanation of homeworking. Rather, such constraints are used to justify the construction of women as an appropriate labour force and to legitimate a method of production which persists primarily because of its benefits to employers. Homeworkers are not people who would otherwise be unemployed, but those who are employed in a particular location because of the advantages this provides the supplier. We discussed these in some detail in Chapter 6.

Further research on the suppliers of homework is vitally necessary. The fear is often expressed that protective legislation, existing or proposed, would increase suppliers' costs and put homeworkers out of work. To meet this objection we need to know much more about the economics of contemporary homeworking. The Department of Employment's analysis of employers' use of homework (Hakim, 1985) concluded, significantly, that firms using outworkers and freelancers were more profitable than those that did not. This suggests that those who supply homework could bear higher costs and still remain profitable. But the confusion in the Department's survey between different types of off-premises work and the nature of the sample involved means that its findings cannot be taken as definitive.

There is some evidence that the decision to use homeworkers is not based entirely on relative cheapness. Along with Rubery and Wilkinson (1981) Wray has shown that a wide range of factors lead firms to use homeworking when the necessary capital equipment can be fitted into domestic premises. In her study of the hosiery and knitwear industry she found that several product and labour-market factors encouraged the use of homeworkers. These include small-sized bottlenecks, short-lived bottlenecks, shortage of factory space, shortage of in-workers with appropriate skills and a shortage of time to train inexperienced in-factory applicants (Wray, 1985, p. 17). It has also been suggested that in some product markets, such as high fashion clothing, homeworking is preferred to overseas factory production because of the short lead time between the identification of current fashions and getting products into the shops. Other industries will differ in detail, but product and labour-market factors will enter into employers' decisions on whether to use homework labour if protective legislation is introduced. Until further investigation is undertaken the bold claim that firms will dispense with homework remains simply guesswork. Very similar objections have been raised against many legislative innovations including legislation on equal pay, where it was argued that women would lose out to men, but these objections ignored segmented labour-market factors as well as short-term competitive factors.

A related area in which further research is necessary is that of homeworking among disabled people. The fear is expressed that protective legislation would deprive many, who due to mental or physical disability are unable to leave their home or are incapable of performing at the level of ordinary workers, of the opportunity of doing paid work. Whether or not this is true for even a minority of disabled homeworkers is not known, however, and even were it the case would not be an adequate reason for denying people with disabilities the same employment rights enjoyed by others. Such assumptions are all too similar to those made about homeworkers who are responsible for dependants. If one does waged work at home it is simply assumed that one is incapable of working outside. We have tried to show that in many cases this is fallacious. Many homeworkers seek work outside the home but are unable to obtain jobs.

If we examine the question of disabled people's need for paid work, it is abundantly clear that an evaluation of homeworker schemes for them, such as those run by the MSC or Remploy or those for blind workers, is long overdue. The majority of disabled homeworkers fall outside these schemes, and there is little information on their situation. We came across several disabled people doing homework during our research, but this was fortuitous and we did not have the resources to conduct a proper investigation into disabled homeworkers. We were, however, informed on many occasions of how widespread this was and could not fail to recognise its importance.

Little is known about the work preferences of disabled people or the alternatives to homework which could be made available to them. We cannot assume that those who prescribe homeworking for them are right. It is an easy option, but one which leads disabled workers into grossly exploited work. Indeed, even the Manpower Services Commission has said that they do not see homeworking as a policy priority, but rather as 'something of a fall back where mobility and other problems are such that people cannot participate in a more normal working environment' (House of Commons, 1981d, p. 90).

Legislation to protect homeworkers could worsen the position of disabled people only if they were excluded, for whatever reasons, from its provisions. To use them in objecting to protective legislation runs counter to their long-term interests. But much more research is necessary to make visible their situation, especially in relation to the adequacy of state income maintenance levels.

We argue, then, that homeworking persists because of its advantages to the supplier rather than its supposed advantages to the worker. Consequently research must explore the linkages between suppliers in long sub-contracting chains, so that it will be easier to locate the responsibility for compliance with future protective legislation on those who at present profit from it, but whose involvement is obscured. Another goal should be the identification of additional ways of improving homeworkers' situation, including alternatives to homeworking. In this connection the 'action research' sponsored by local authorities on, for instance, questions of health and safety and alternative employment and training initiatives is a step in the right direction. Its stress on identifying alternatives and providing spaces to campaign for legal change makes a welcome contrast to research which implies, through a spurious circular reasoning, that because those who work at home either prefer it or have no alternative nothing can or should be done. Fears of possible untoward effects of protective legislation raise genuine concerns and need careful consideration. As such they point to the need for soundly-based research and rigorous analysis, but should not be used as an excuse for inaction.

Policy implications

How can research on homeworking contribute to the formulation of policy on homeworking? The relationship between research and policy initiatives lies at the heart of much applied research and is an important consideration for many feminist researchers, but it is rarely discussed as an issue in its own right. Nor are we able to undertake this task here. But it needs to be stated that it would be irresponsible to document the condition of homeworkers without drawing attention to a range of measures which could bring about an improvement.

Our analysis of homeworking gives particular importance to the ways in which existing employment law provides scope for firms to define homeworkers as self-employed, and thus to evade obligations which are owing to employees. The absence of any kind of standardised employment conditions in homeworking means that market forces are permitted to push down wages and conditions to even lower levels, and to enable firms to undercut the wages and conditions of in-workers. Those firms which would wish to ensure that their employees, including homeworkers, are able to earn a living wage under decent conditions are unable to compete with the less scrupulous. As Churchill pointed out ninety-five years ago in introducing legislation to establish the Trades Boards, 'where you have no organisation, no parity of bargaining, the good employer is undercut by the bad and the bad employer is undercut by the worst' (Low Pay Unit, 1983).

In Chapter 6 we considered some of the demands, past and present, which have been made by the trade unions and those concerned with low pay, women's employment and homeworking. As we pointed out, in the mid-1980s several important policy documents were issued which identified initiatives which could be taken. The Homeworkers' Charter, adopted by the National Homeworking Group, demands significant changes in the underlying conditions which it believes prevent homeworkers from seeking work outside the home or pressing for better wages and conditions as homeworkers. It also includes a number of more immediate practical demands. These were supplemented by the British Trades Union Congress Statement on Homeworking. The demands and proposals of both documents are reproduced in Appendices A.1 and A.2. Although they arose at a particular juncture in the movement to improve conditions in homeworking, they are unlikely to become outdated until appropriate measures are taken. Along with our own supplementary proposals, listed in Appendix A.3., they highlight the scope of measures which must be taken if homeworking is to be brought within the framework of state regulation in Britain. The concrete detail and comprehensiveness of these proposals refutes the claim that nothing can be done and shows, by contrast, the vacuousness of much existing legislation.

While clearly these demands and suggestions could not be applied elsewhere without some modification, they are a pertinent indication of the kinds of changes necessary well outside Britain. The International Labour Office has conducted a survey of statutory provisions in a number of countries and reviewed the existing ILO instruments which bear on homeworking. It has been suggested that a new instrument dealing specifically with the protection of domestic outworkers should be promulgated, and that a Code of Practice for multinationals operating through subcontractors in the developing countries and the Free Trade Zones is necessary (M. Owen, 1985).

A recognition of homeworkers' status as waged or salaried employees, differentiating them from self-employed, is the first requirement for improvements in their position. Although much is made of the legal difficulties involved in legislation those who have investigated homeworking have found, almost without exception, that homeworkers see themselves as employees and are treated as such so far as the control of their work is concerned. The supplier of work would become legally what he/she is at present, the employer. The responsibility to implement all the relevant aspects of protective legislation would follow. Agents and middlemen would act on behalf of the firm or oganisation, but the legal responsibility would remain with the firm who was the ultimate supplier. The latter would then be forced to stipulate the conditions of employment in awarding contracts to sub-contractors.

Locating the responsibility of the employer clearly would also increase the possibility of effective implementation of legislation. This requires registration and monitoring wherever homeworking labour is used. The failure of registration, which was first required as far back as 1895 in some trades and most recently under the 1961 Factories Act, has been due in part to a failure to identify clearly where the responsibility lay. Non-compliance with the regulations has involved both the lack of realistic penalties for the supplier and the failure of the enforcing authority to monitor and report on homeworking in their areas of responsibility. While some of this was due to inadequate resources, much can be attributed to the marginalisation of homework as a productive economic activity. The second requirement is therefore adequate sanctions and resources.

Legislation which recognised homeworkers as employees would be a major step forward. Nevertheless it would leave many wider issues unresolved. These include poor pay, legal cover for part-time work and state policies on income maintenance, all of which are of particular relevance to homeworkers. Women figure disproportionately among the low-paid. In 1984/5 of the 3.9 million full-time workers estimated to be low-paid, 2.4 million were women and three-quarters of women employed part-time were also low-paid (Byrne, 1984, p. 7). The issue of low pay is a general one, but any steps such as national minimum wage which might be taken to tackle it would include homeworkers more effectively if they were given the status of employees. Much the same can be said of any efforts to cover adequately part-time workers, whose position in full of anomalies (Gill and Whitty, 1983). Without employment status part-time homeworkers would not gain from such improvements.

Measures like these, we would argue, are as vital for those using new technologies as those doing 'traditional' homework. Some people see new technology homework as a novel opportunity for more interesting, better-paid homework having nothing in common with sweated labour. But women need to be aware that it raises many of the same problems for those who do it. Rather than enhancing autonomy at work, new technologies provide yet more sophisticated mechanisms for the control and intensification of work. The health hazards are only beginning to be explored. The problems of combining care for family members, cooking and housework and paid labour are identical.

The optimism about new technology repeats popular ideas about the benefits of working at home, such as those which appear in advice manuals for women seeking paid work at home. Along with their lists of opportunities to be grasped, such books have usually pointed, realistically, to some of the difficulties paid work at home poses for women in particular. But like those who extol the virtues of new technology homework, they have no cutting edge, for they never challenge the constraints which unpaid labour imposes on women's employment options, the limited and declining opportunities for work outside the home, or the coercive character of the social relations which control women's labour in both paid and unpaid work.

The reforms outlined above would lessen some of the grosser aspects of the exploitation associated with homeworking. In addition to pressing for practical measures which are possible within existing social relations, however, much more far-reaching changes are required for homeworking to become the positive choice which it is sometimes portrayed to be at present. Changes not only in the sexual division of labour but in the power relations between men and women, in the division between public and private responsibilities, and the resources available to households engaging in productive activities, including the design and amount of domestic space available to them, would be part of this agenda. Beyond this, changes relating to the labour-market, including better access to training for available jobs and a reduction in the level of unemployment, are required. But while we recognise the need for such fundamental alterations in the underlying conditions, there are changes which could be more rapidly and easily implemented and these must be taken up as the starting point.

Appendix A.1
TUC policy proposals*

The TUC wishes to direct these proposals towards trade unions, local authorities, sympathetic political parties, the Health and Safety Commission, local support groups, and all those who are committed to improving the situation of homeworkers.

The TUC also hopes that homeworkers themselves will read, or be made aware of them. Some of the proposals, such as on legislation to confirm employment status, require action by the government of the day.

Trade Unions

133 Union[s] should seek to achieve employee status for homeworkers, with the company concerned making deductions for PAYE, national insurance contributions, and employer and employee pension contributions.

134 Trade unions should seek to include terms and conditions for homeworkers in collective agreements:

* rates of pay for homeworkers the same (pro rata for part-time workers) as on-site employees doing the same work, or work of equal value.
* piecework prices for homeworking that are comparable with those in the factory.
* homeworkers should receive sick pay, holiday pay and maternity/paternity leave pro rata to full time employees.
* in addition homeworkers should receive allowances for overheads such as lighting, heating and power for machines.
* unions might also consider pressing firms for childcare facilities so that homeworkers who would rather work on-site have the opportunity to do so.
* homeworkers should be included in profit – sharing and/or share option schemes.
* employee pension rights must be protected if on-site workers switch to homeworking.

*Excerpted from the *TUC Statement on Homeworking*, 1985, pp. 26–9.

135 Trade unions should obtain from employers details of the volume and type of work put out to homeworkers, possibly using the ACAS Code of Disclosure of Information.

136 Unions should remind safety representatives that, under the Code of Practice on safety representation, employers are required to make available to them information on articles or substances which an employer issues to homeworkers.

137 Unions may wish to consider setting up groups or committees in companies using homeworkers to monitor the volume, type and frequency of working being put out and the terms and conditions of homeworkers.

138 The names and addresses of homeworkers should be obtained from the employer.

139 All union publications, leaflets, etc. whether national, local or in-company should be sent to homeworkers.

140 Contact should be made with homeworkers wherever possible. Unions may wish to recommend to lay representatives from the company concerned that they carry out this task.

141 Contact with homeworkers can be made through links with local authority homeworking officers and local support groups where these support trade union membership.

142 Trade unions will need to examine their structures to see if they are conducive to homeworkers, particularly women, playing an active part in them. This examination would be in line with the TUC recommendations contained in the TUC publication *Equality for Women within Trade Unions*.

Unions may also wish to consider a different level of subscription for homeworkers. They may also wish to consider establishing separate sections to provide a special identity and to cater for homeworkers' specific problems.

143 Unions may wish to make an official responsible for the recruitment of homeworkers and to conduct special recruitment campaigns.

144 All trade unions, whether organising in homeworking industries or not, should seek to make their members aware of the problems of homeworkers and of the potential for the spread of homeworking.

Local Authorities

145 Local authorities can take practical steps which materially benefit homeworkers, in particular through ensuring registration of home-workers in their area and by appointing homeworking officers. They should also seek to cooperate with the appropriate local union organisation.

146 Local authorities should insist that all suppliers tendering for orders inform them if they employ homeworkers and whether or not they are employees with PAYE and tax deducted at source.

147 Local authorities should insist that all contractors comply with Section

133 of the Factories Act and register their homeworkers with the Environmental Health Department.

148 Contractors should also be asked to guarantee that they observe Wages Councils' Orders where appropriate, or that pay and conditions for their workers are not less favourable than the general level of wages and conditions observed by other local employers engaged in a similar trade.

149 No firm should be granted financial assistance including rent free or subsidised premises by a local authority unless it complies with the above.

150 Local authorities should adopt a contract compliance policy which would help to ensure that firms meet these conditions. Unions should be supplied with names and addresses of homeworkers, on the understanding that unions will first inform local authorities of their intended recruitment methods, in particular which individual contacts would be attempted. Unions could also inform local authorities which listed homeworkers have been contacted in this way.

151 Local authorities should consult with the local branches of the appropriate union before placing orders.

152 Local authorities should review their policy criteria in areas such as tenancy agreements and planning permission to ensure that homeworkers are not being disadvantaged.

153 Local authorities' services, such as childcare and training should be reviewed to see if these meet the special needs of homeworkers.

154 Local authorities in areas where homeworking is carried on should consider appointing a homeworking officer, if they have not already done so.

Government Action:

Legislation

155 Some of the measures which need to be urgently taken to lessen the plight of homeworkers, and ensure them adequate protection can only be introduced by Government. In particular there is now a widespread recognition that homeworkers must have employee status.

156 Therefore the Government should introduce legislation to extend statutory protection of employment to homeworkers.

157 Such legislation would need to set out a legal definition of a homeworker. Reproduced below is a definition which originates with the Private Members' Bill, the Homeworkers (Protection) Bill, which was unsuccessfully introduced in 1979 and 1981. The definition in its present form was included in the Sex Equality Bill introduced by Jo Richardson MP in 1983:

'homeworker' means an individual who contracts with a person, not being a professional client of his, for the purposes of that person's business, for the execution of any work (other than the production or creation of any literary, dramatic, artistic or musical work) to be done in domestic premises not under the control or management of the person with whom he contracts, and who does not normally make use of the services of more than two individuals in the carrying out of that work, and in this Act work contracted to be executed by a homeworker is referred to as 'homework'.

158 The Government should also amend the Equal Pay Act so that differences in the location of work are not defined as 'material differences'. Homeworkers would then be able to claim equal pay with on site workers engaged in like work or work of equal value. The Sex Equality Bill includes this as follows:

Work done by a homeworker may be regarded as like work to work done by another person who is not a homeworker, not withstanding that the work is executed at a different time or place or that the homeworker is, but the other person is not, free to delegate the execution of the work. Differences between work which a homeworker does and like work which another person who is not a homeworker does, which arise necessarily from the fact that the work is executed at a different time or place, or from the fact that the homeworker delegated the execution of some or all the work, are not to be treated either separately or in combination as a difference of practical importance in relation to terms and conditions of employment.

The fact that a person is a homeworker does not constitute, either alone or in conjunction with any other matters which result from the fact, a material personal difference between the case of the homeworker and that of another person who is not a homeworker.

Wages Councils

159 The Government immediately increase the numbers of the Wages Inspectorate, and require them to make more visits to premises and reports on their findings. It should also revive the Homeworking Unit within the Inspectorate to monitor the work of Wages Inspectors in this area and ensure that local authority lists are available to them. Homeworkers should receive all the rights given to Wages Council workers, and there should be adequate protection for those who bring complaints.

Penalties

160 The Government should review and update the penalties charged on employers and suppliers of work who evade legal requirements so that these are made an effective deterrent.

Homeworkers' Advisory Committee
161 An indication that the Government takes seriously the situation of homeworkers would be for it to reconvene the Homeworkers Advisory Committee which has not met since 1979. This Committee, consisting of employer, trade union and independent members could then begin the work of advising Government on appropriate policy steps.

Health and Safety Commission
162 At present homeworkers are effectively excluded from the cover of health and safety legislation. The Health and Safety Commission should act to bring pressure on Government to bring about long overdue reform in this area. Legislation is needed to:
163 Put a general duty on those giving out homeworking to make six monthly returns to local authorities giving details of where work is placed and information on the type of work and the materials and equipment involved.
164 The above information should be open to authorised trade unions.
165 Prohibit dangerous equipment and hazardous materials which present risks which cannot be controlled in the home.
166 Update and extend the existing list of dangerous materials.
167 Ensure adequate inspection and enforcement arrangements by expanding the number of inspectors and providing them with the necessary back-up facilities.

Appendix A.2

Policy adopted by the 1984 National Conference on Homeworking*

Homeworkers' Charter

The demands contained in this Charter are those made by homeworkers. The vast majority are women who suffer the triple burdens of childcare, housework and paid employment. Homeworkers are caught in the poverty trap and as such provide cheap, unorganised labour, especially for the sectors of industry which perpetuate the worst employment practices. Homeworking, especially in the new technology industries, both in manufacturing and the provision of services, is on the increase; it is now being promoted as the way of working in the future even by multinational concerns. It is clear that the bad employment practices of traditional industries are being imported into the newer ones to the detriment of worker organisation. Homeworkers, who are particularly vulnerable to racist and sexist exploitation, subsidise their employer's profits and there is no doubt that given better opportunities few homeworkers would work at home.

This Charter therefore demands that:

1. FREE ADEQUATE CARE OF DEPENDANTS IS AVAILABLE FOR HOMEWORKERS

A majority of homeworkers say that they are forced to work at home in order to look after children, or sick, elderly or disabled dependants, and that if adequate care were freely available this would enable them to work outside the home.

2. RESOURCES ARE PROVIDED TO ENABLE HOMEWORKERS TO MEET TOGETHER FOR MUTUAL SUPPORT, ORGANISATION AND CAMPAIGNING

Homeworkers live and work in isolated conditions with little or no opportunity for exchanging information with each other, or for recreation. If homeworkers are to improve their economic status these resources must be available.

3. EMPLOYEE STATUS IS GIVEN TO HOMEWORKERS

Lack of clarity about employment status of homeworkers has resulted not only in the casualisation of homeworkers' labour but also in the loss of other

* Excerpted from London Industrial Strategy, *Homeworking*, 1985, pp. 28–9.

195

rights and benefits which depend on proof of employment status: e.g., sick pay, Unemployment Benefit, Maternity Benefit, Family Income Supplement, pensions, etc. In addition, homeworkers subsidise their employer's business by paying rent, rates, heating, lighting, running and maintaining their machines. The employer also does not pay any staffing costs, thus avoiding capital and revenue outlay.

4. AN END TO RACIST AND SEXIST PRACTICES AND THE REPEAL OF RACIST AND SEXIST LEGISLATION
The isolation and fear which homeworkers suffer are compounded by the laws, attitudes and practices of a society which is essentially racist and which denies the right of all women to participate socially and economically in it. Institutional racism and sexism informs the attitudes and procedures which exclude women and black and minority ethnic people from the benefits of the community to which they contribute.

5. THE ADOPTION OF A NATIONAL MINIMUM WAGE
The adoption of a national minimum wage for all workers is essential in order to end the super-exploitation of homeworkers, people with disabilities and other unprotected groups. One national minimum wage will eliminate the problems associated with the complicated Wages Council Orders and their present lack of enforcement.

6. THE AMENDMENT OF RELEVANT REGULATIONS TO ENSURE THAT HOMEWORKERS AND THEIR FAMILIES DO NOT SUFFER INJURY, DISEASE OR SICKNESS AS A RESULT OF THEIR WORK
Homeworkers use dangerous substances such as glues, fixes and solvents, unguarded machinery and VDUs in their home without the protection afforded all other workers. They carry the responsibility for the health and safety of themselves and their families which should by right be that of their employer. The Health and Safety at Work Act must be amended to include all homeworkers.

7. COMPREHENSIVE TRAINING AND EDUCATIONAL OPPORTUNITIES FOR HOMEWORKERS
Given the opportunity homeworkers prefer to work outside the home. Some lack the necessary skills and education to participate in the labour market; some are skilled in one process or [sic] production which may well be in a rapidly changing industry; some skilled workers may have been out of paid work while raising children and their skills need upgrading; some have never had the opportunity.

Recommendations by the National Steering Group on homeworkers
These were accepted by the 1984 National Conference, for action by the following organizations:
Trade Unions should:
–   include homeworkers in all procedural agreements and those concerned with pay and conditions
–   include homeworkers in all childcare demands and provision
–   ensure the proper payment of nursery and other childcare workers

- monitor the introduction of new technology and control its devolution from workplace to home
- employ appropriate full-time female organisers to encourage membership of trades unions amongst homeworkers
- work with appropriate community organisations in promoting the interest of homeworkers
- examine the need for trades unions' structures to be more accessible to homeworkers

Local Authorities should:
- relax planning regulations to allow homeworkers to work at home
- where homeworkers are tenants of the local authority not treat homeworking as a 'business' by unreasonably withholding consent
- incorporate in the agreements for supplies and service the stipulation that homeworkers employed by the contractor or sub-contractor should be given terms and conditions no less favourable than their factory-based counterparts
- provide specialist advice and information for homeworkers in the forms relevant to homeworkers and in community languages
- when employing homeworking officers, employ women particularly from minority ethnic communities
- continue to fund voluntary sector projects promoting the interests of homeworkers
- provide acceptable childcare facilities for homeworkers
- provide appropriate access to alternative training and education facilities for homeworkers
- ensure proper payments for childcare workers
- carry out obligations under the Factories Act 1961

Grant-aided women's and homeworkers' organizations should:
- recognise the compounded problems of homeworkers and train themselves accordingly
- work with trade unions, community groups, women's groups, etc. in helping homeworkers organise, e.g., in producing homeworker-specific information etc., on benefits, health and safety, etc.
- work with trades unions, community groups, women's groups to present homeworkers' demands to local authorities, etc.

Community Groups should:
- recognise the economic/social needs of women/homeworkers represented by/in the group
- provide resources for women/homeworkers to organise separately
- be prepared to support women/homeworkers in presenting their demands to local authorities, etc.
- facilitate the access of women/homeworkers to trades unions, women's groups, etc.
- address the needs of homeworkers in their own areas of work

The Labour Party should:
–   include in the manifesto the extension of employment protection to homeworkers
–   amend the regulations and procedures under the Health and Safety at Work Act to protect homeworkers
–   adopt a basic minimum wage which will benefit homeworkers in all industries
–   retain the Wages Councils and extend their power to enable a better implementation of their Orders
–   reconvene the Homeworking Advisory Committee and ensure that homeworkers are properly represented on it
–   extend childcare facilities bearing in mind the needs of homeworkers
–   extend access to training and educational opportunities for homeworkers
–   work locally with trade unions, community groups, funded agencies, etc., in helping homeworkers to organise
–   ensure that local authorities provide for the stated needs of homeworkers, e.g. childcare, training, etc.
–   commit resources to implementing policies which benefit homeworkers

Academics and Researchers should:
–   in creating their methodology recognise the need to work as part of a community-based project/organisation or through local community workers who have the appropriate languages
–   ensure that the results of their work are made available to those working with homeworkers
–   continue where possible to contribute to the well-being of homeworkers by keeping in touch with the projects and homeworkers with whom they work

Appendix A.3
Policy recommendations

1. Employment status:
   a. That the definition of homeworking adopted in the Homeworkers (Protection) Bill 1979 be adopted.
   b. That homeworkers so defined be granted employment status, including protection against unfair dismissal.
   c. Employers be required to inform homeworkers of their employment status in writing.
2. Registration:
   a. An employer of homeworkers be required to register with the Local Office of the Department of Employment. (Employer to include sub-contractor or agent as well as direct employer.)
   b. Such employers to make regular returns to the local Department of Employment on the numbers of homeworkers employed at six monthly intervals.
   c. The returns to list the names and addresses of homework employees, which shall be made available to Environmental Health Officers, designated trade unions, the Health and Safety Officials, Wages Inspectorates and local employers' associations.
   d. An officer within the local authority be appointed to assist employers in meeting their requirements on registration and to facilitate access to lists by those designated in clause (c).
3. Statistical Records:
   a. Local Department of Employment officers to compile on a regular basis statistics on employers and homeworkers within their area. These statistics to be publicly available.
4. Wages
   a. The establishment of a statutory national minimum wage and Wages Inspectorate machinery to ensure its enforcement.
   b. A regional inspectorate adequate to monitor wages paid to home-workers in all industries and services, with powers to inspect records, visit homeworkers and employers, investigate complaints and prosecute for illegal underpayment.

199

   c. All employers of homeworkers to keep records of work done and wages paid.

   d. Such records to be made available to the Wages Inspectorate, local Department of Employment officers, employers' associations and trade unions.

   e. Wage rates for homeworkers to be equal to comparable in-workers, where these exist.

   f. Where in-workers do not exist, a rate be set based on a simulation of the work under factory conditions or on an investigation of the time taken by a number of homeworkers. The Wages Inspectorate and the Local Authority Homeworking Officer, together with the employer and a representative of the appropriate trade unions to monitor the rates being fixed.

   g. Supplementation to cover the additional costs borne by homeworkers be paid by the employer. Rates of supplementation to be agreed by the Local Authority Homeworking Officer and the appropriate trade union.

5. Health and Safety:

   a. The Health and Safety at Work Act to be effectively applied to homework.

   b. The Health and Safety Commission to be responsible for the health and safety of homeworkers:

      i. by establishing adequate machinery at national, regional and local level for the enforcement of the law, including regular and spot inspections,

      ii. by listing and reviewing on a regular basis all hazardous materials and dangerous equipment, taking fully into account the additional problems for health and safety imposed by domestic locations,

      iii. to prohibit, without exception, the supply of certain hazardous substances for homework purposes.

   c. All employers of homeworkers to make half yearly returns to the Local Authority Homeworking Officer on the type of work, materials and equipment involved and listing addresses to which they are supplied.

   d. These returns to be available for inspection by officials of the Health and Safety executive, trade unions and employers associations.

   e. All employers to provide homeworkers with written information on health and safety matters prepared by the Health and Safety Executive.

References

Abidi, Nigar Fatima (1985), 'Home Based Production – Women Weavers of Eastern Uttar Pradesh' (New Delhi: Asian Regional Conference on Women and the Household), mimeo.

ACAS (1978a), *Button Manufacturing Wages Council: Report of an Inquiry* (London), Report no. 11.

ACAS (1978b), *Toy Manufacturing Wages Council: Report of an Inquiry* (London), Report no. 13.

Alexander, Sally (1980), 'Introduction' to Marianne Hertzog, *From Hand to Mouth: Women and Piecework* (Harmondsworth: Penguin).

Allatt, Patricia and Susan Yeandle (1986), 'It's Not Fair, Is It? Youth Unemployment, Family Relations and the Social Contract' in S. Allen *et al.* (eds), *The Experience of Unemployment* (London: Macmillan).

Allen, Sheila (1980), 'Women in Local Labour Markets: Results, Problems and Research Strategies' (London: SSRC Workshop on Local Labour Markets, 10 March).

Allen, Sheila (1981a), *Homeworking in the West Yorkshire Connurbation: SSRC Final Report*, September.

Allen, Sheila (1981b), 'Invisible Threads', in Kate Young and Caroline Moser (eds), 'Women in the Informal Sector', *Institute of Development Studies Bulletin*, Special Issue, XII, 3.

Allen, Sheila (1982a), 'Domestic Production and Organising for Change', *Economic and Industrial Democracy*, III, 4.

Allen, Sheila (1982b), 'Gender Inequalities and Class Formation', in Anthony Giddens and Gavin MacKenzie (eds), *Social Class and the Division of Labour* (Cambridge University Press).

Allen, Sheila (1982c), 'Perhaps a Seventh Person,' in Charles Husband (ed.) *'Race' in Britain: Continuity and Change* (London: Hutchinson).

Allen, Sheila (1982d), 'Waged Labour in the Home: The Myth of the Separation of Home and Work for Women in Britain', in Kirsten Hvidfeldt *et al.* (eds), *Strategies for Integrating Women into the Labour Market*, European Women's Studies in Social Science, No. 1 (Copenhagen: Women's Research Centre in Social Sciences).

Allen, Sheila (1982e), 'Women in Local Labour Markets', J. Laite (ed.), *Bibliographies on Local Markets and the Informal Economy* (London: Social Science Research Council).

201

Allen, Sheila (1983a), 'Casualised Working Relations: A Discussion of the Sociology of Work' (Oxford: British Sociological Association Sexual Divisions Study Group), mimeo.

Allen, Sheila (1983b), 'Production and Reproduction: The Lives of Women Homeworkers', *The Sociological Review*, XXXI, 4, November.

Allen, Sheila (1985a), 'The Labour Process and Working at Home' *Social Scientist* (New Delhi), XIII, 10–11, October–November.

Allen, Sheila (1985b), 'Protective Legislation for Home-based Production' (New Delhi: Asian Regional Conference on Women and the Household), mimeo.

Allen, Sheila and Julia Graham (1981), *Memorandum of Evidence to the Select Committee on Employment*, mimeo.

Allen Sheila, Alan Waton, Kate Purcell and Stephen Wood (eds) (1986), *The Experience of Unemployment* (London: Macmillan).

Allin, Paul and Ray Thomas (1984), *Statistical Needs on Attitudes to Work and Employment* (Bradford: British Sociological Annual Conference), unpublished paper.

Anthias, Floya (1983), 'Sexual Divisions and Ethnic Adaptation: The Case of Greek-Cypriot Women', in Annie Phizacklea (ed.), *One Way Ticket: Migration and Female Labour* (London: Routledge & Kegan Paul).

Armstrong, P. (1982), 'If it's only women it doesn't matter so much', in Jackie West (ed.), *Work, Women and the Labour Market* (London: Routledge & Kegan Paul).

Arnow, Harriet (1972), *The Dollmaker* (New York: Avon Books).

Anwar, Muhammad (1979), *The Myth of Return* (London: Heinemann).

Atkinson, John (1984), *Flexibility, Uncertainty and Manpower Management* (Sussex: Institute of Manpower Studies), Report no. 89.

Bajohr, Stefan (1979), *Die Hälfte der Fabrik*, Verlag Arbeiterberegung und Gesellschaftswissenschaft (Marburg: West Germany).

Baldamus, W. (1961), *Efficiency and Effort: An Analysis of Industrial Administration* (London: Tavistock Publications).

Ballard, Barbara (1984), 'Women Part-time Workers: Evidence from the 1980 Women and Employment Survey', *Employment Gazette*, XCII, 9.

Baud, I. (1983), *Women's Labour in the Indian Textile Industry* (The Netherlands: IVO).

Baud, I. (1985), 'Industrial Sub contracting: Effects of Putting Out System in India' (New Delhi: Asian Regional Conference on Women and the Household), mimeo.

Barker, Diana Leonard and Sheila Allen (eds) (1976), *Dependence and Exploitation in Work and Marriage* (London: Longman).

Barrett, Michèle (1980), *Women's Oppression Today* (London: Verso).

Barron, R. D. and G. M. Norris (1976), 'Sexual Divisions and the Dual Labour Market', in Diana Leonard Barker and Sheila Allen (eds), *Dependence and Exploitation in Work and Marriage* (London: Longman).

Baxi, U. (1985), 'State, Seths and Siksha: The Saga of Satteora' (New Delhi: Asian Regional Conference on Women and the Household), mimeo.

Beale, Sally (1978), *A Study of Homeworking in a Limited Geographic Area* (University of Bath: School of Management) unpublished M.Sc. dissertation.

Bell, C. (1982), 'Work, Non-Work and Unemployment', in R. G. Burgess (ed.), *Exploring Society* (London: British Sociological Association).

Bhatt, Ela (1983), 'Address at the Thirteenth World Congress of The ICFTU, Oslo, June 23–30, 1983', in *We, The Self Employed* (Ahmedabad, India: SEWA).

Bhatt, Ela (1985), 'The Invisibility of Home-Based Work: The Case of Piece Rate Workers in India' (New Delhi: Asian Regional Conference on Women and the Household), mimeo.

Bhatty, Zarina (1985), 'Economic contribution to the Household Budget: A Case of the Beedi Industry' (New Delhi: Asian Regional Conference on Women and the Household), mimeo.

Bissett, Liz and Ursula Huws (1985), *Sweated Labour: Homeworking in Britain Today* (London: The Low Pay Unit), Low Pay Pamphlet no. 33.

Bolton, Brian (1975), *An End to Homeworking?* (London: Fabian Society), Tract no. 436.

Boston, Sarah (1980), *Women Workers and the Trade Union Movement* (London: Davis Poynter).

Bowey, A. M. *et al.* (1982), *Effects of Incentive Payment Systems, United Kingdom 1977–80* (London: Department of Employment), Report no. 36.

Bradby, Barbara (1977), 'The Non-Valorisation of Women's Labour', *Critique of Anthropology*, III, 9/10.

Braverman, Harry (1974), *Labour and Monopoly Capital: The Degradation of Work in the Twentieth Century* (New York: Monthly Review Press).

Braybon, Gail (1981), *Women Workers in the First World War* (London: Croom Helm).

Bremen, J. A. (1976), 'A Dualistic Labour System? A Critique of the Informal Sector Concept', *Economic and Political Weekly*, 2, pp. 48–50.

Bromley, Ray and Chris Gerry (eds) (1979), *Casual Work and Poverty in Third World Cities* (Chichester: John Wiley & Sons).

Brown, Marie (1974), *Sweated Labour: A Study of Homework* (London: Low Pay Unit), Pamphlet no. 1.

Burns, S. (1977), *The Household Economy* (Boston: Beacon Press).

Byrne, D. (ed.) (1984), *Cheap Labour: The Current Crisis* (London: Low Pay Unit), Low Pay Review no. 20.

Bythell, Duncan (1978), *The Sweated Trades: Outwork in the 19th Century* (New York: St. Martin's Press).

Campbell, Beatrix (1978), 'Lining Their Pockets', *Time Out*, 13/19 July.

Cavendish, Ruth (1981), *Women on the Line* (London: Routledge & Kegan Paul).

Child, John (1986), 'New Technology and the Service Class' in Kate Purcell *et al.* (eds) *The Changing Experience of Employment: Restructuring and Recession* (London: Macmillan).

Clutterbuck, David and Roy Hill (1981), *The Re-Making of Work:*

Changing Work Patterns and How to Capitalise on Them (London: Grant McIntyre).

Cockburn, Cynthia (1986), 'Women and Technology: Opportunity is Not Enough' in Kate Purcell *et al* (eds) *The Changing Experience of Employment: Restructuring and Recession* (London: Macmillan).

Commission on Industrial Relations (1973), *Pin Hook and Eye and Snap Fastener* (London: HMSO), Report no. 49.

Commission on Industrial Relations (1974), *Clothing Wages Councils* (London: HMSO), Report no. 77.

Counter Information Services (1981), *CIS Report: Women in the 80s* (London: CIS).

Coyle, Angela (1982), 'Sex and Skill on the Organisation of the Clothing Industry', in Jackie West (ed.), *Work, Women and the Labour Market* (London: Routledge & Kegan Paul).

Coyle, Angela (1984), *Redundant Women* (London: The Women's Press).

Cragg, Arnold and Tim Dawson (1981), *Qualitative Research among Homeworkers* (London: Department of Employment) Research Paper no. 21.

Craig, C., J. Rubery, R. Tarling and F. Wilkinson (1980), *Abolition and After: the Cutlery Wages Council* (London: Department of Employment), Research Paper no. 18.

Craig, C. *et al.* (1982), *Labour Market Structure, Industrial Organisation and Low Pay* (Cambridge University Press).

Crine, Simon (1979a) *The Hidden Army* (London: Low Pay Unit).

Crine, Simon (1979b) *Final Report to the Nuffield Foundation* (London: Low Pay Unit), unpublished.

Crine, Simon (1980a), *Pickpocketing the Low Paid* (London: Low Pay Unit) Report no. 1.

Crine, Simon (1980b), *Who are the Low Paid?* (London: Low Pay Unit) Bulletin no. 31.

Crine, Simon (1981), *The Pay and Conditions of Homeworkers: Submission to the House of Commons Select Committee on Employment* (London: Low Pay Unit).

Dale, A., G. N. Gilbert and S. Arber (1985), 'Integrating Women into Class Theory', *Sociology*, IXX, 3, August, pp. 384–408.

Daniels, Cynthia (1985), 'Working Mothers and the State' University of Massachusetts, unpublished Ph.D.

Delphy, C. (1981), 'Women in Stratification Studies', in Helen Roberts (ed.), *Doing Feminist Research* (London: Routledge & Kegan Paul).

Department of Employment (1980), 'Statutory Wage Relations in 1979', *Department of Employment Gazette*, LXXXVIII, 7.

Department of Employment (1985), *Consultative Paper on Wages Councils* (London: HMSO).

Dex, Shirley (1985), *The Sexual Division of Work* (Brighton: Wheatsheaf Books).

Dholakia, Anila R. (1984), 'Rural Women in White Revolution', UNICEF Seminar on Women's Dairy Co-operatives, New Delhi, May (Ahmedabad, India: SEWA).

Drake, Barbara (1984), *Women in Trade Unions* (London: Virago Press). Original edition, Labour Research Department, 1920.

Dube, Leela (1985), *Women and the Household, Report on Regional Conference for Asia* (New Delhi).

Dundee Inner City Neighbourhood Action Centre (1984), *Working at Home: A Feasibility Study into the Extent, the Problems and the Future Requirements of Homeworkers in Dundee* (Dundee).

Evans, Alistair (1975) *Homeworking in a London Borough* (University of Warwick: Industrial Relations Unit), Project Report.

Ewing, K. D. (1982), 'Homeworking: A Framework for Reform', *The Industrial Law Journal*, II, 2.

Fevre, Ralph (1986), 'Contract Work in the Recession' in Kate Purcell *et al.* (eds), *The Changing Experience of Employment: Restructuring and Recession* (London: Macmillan).

Field, Frank (1976), *Seventy Years On: A New Report on Homeworking*, Low Pay Bulletin no. 10/11, August–October (London: Low Pay Unit).

Field, Frank (1984), 'A Minimum Wage is not Enough', *The Times*, 5 September.

Finch, Janet (1983), *Married to the Job: Wives' Incorporation in Men's Work* (London: George Allen & Unwin).

Forester, Tom (1975), 'The Home Workers', *New Society*, 4 September.

Freeman, Caroline (1982), 'The "Understanding" Employer' in Jackie West (ed.), *Women, Work and the Labour Market* (London: Routledge & Kegan Paul).

Friedman, Andrew (1977), *Industry and Labour: Class Struggle at Work and Monopoly Capitalism* (London: Macmillan).

Gamarnikow, Eva, David Morgan, June Purvis and Daphne Taylorson (eds) (1983), *Gender, Class and Work* (London: Heinemann).

Garrett, Maureen (1984), *Homeworking in Southwark: A Report from the Southwark Employment Unit* (London).

General and Municipal Workers Union (1977), *Annual Conference Report* (London).

General Household Survey (published 1980, 1983, 1984) surveys for 1978; 1981; 1982 (London: HMSO, Office of Population Censuses and Surveys, Social Survey Division).

Gerry, Chris (1985) 'The Working Class and Small Enterprises in the U.K. Recession' in Nanneka, Redclift and Enzo Mingione (eds), *Beyond Employment* (Oxford: Basil Blackwell).

Gershuny, J. I. (1979), 'The Informal Economy: Its Role in Industrial Society', *Futures*, II, 1, February.

Gershuny, J. I. (1985), 'Economic Development and the Change in the Mode of Provision of Services', in Nanneka Redclift and Enzo Mingione (eds), *Beyond Employment* (London: Macmillan).

Gershuny, J. and R. E. Pahl (1979/80), 'Work Outside Employment: Some Preliminary Speculations', *New Universities Quarterly*, XXXIV, 1, Winter.

Gibb, Frances (1984), 'Homeworkers Get Job Protection', *The Times*, 4 May.

Gill, Tess and Larry Whitty (1983), *Women's Rights in the Workplace* (Harmondsworth: Penguin).

Godard, Francis (1985), 'How do Ways of Life Change?', in Nanneka Redclift and Enzo Mingione (eds), *Beyond Employment* (London: Macmillan).

Goldthorpe, J. (1983), 'Women and Class Analysis: In Defence of the Conventional View', *Sociology*, XVII, 4, pp. 465–88.

Goldthorpe, J. H. and K. Hope (1974), *The Social Gradings of Occupations: New Approach and Scale* (Oxford: Clarendon Press).

Gorz, A. (1982), *Farewell to the Working Class* (London: Pluto Press).

Government Statistical Services (1981), *White Paper* (London: HMSO) Cmnd 8236.

Gray, Marianne (1982), *Working from Home: 201 Ways to Earn Money* (Loughton, Essex: Judy Piatkus).

Greater London Council (1983), 'A Strategy for Homeworking in London: Report by the Director of Industry and Employment', 13 December.

Greater London Council (1985), *Report of the National Homeworking Conference 1985* (Greater London Council, Industry and Employment Branch).

Greenwich Homeworkers Project (1984a), *Annual Report* (London).

Greenwich Homeworkers Project (1984b), 'A Brief Report on the Project' (London: National Homeworking Conference) mimeo.

Guardian Women (1985), 'Letters', *Guardian*, 23 April.

Hackney–Islington Partnership (1980), *Clothing and Footwear Industry Sector Study* (London: The Inner City Unit).

Hakim, Catherine (1980), 'Homeworking: Some New Evidence', *Employment Gazette*, LXXX, 10, pp. 1105–9.

Hakim, Catherine (1984a), 'Homework and Outwork: National Estimates from Two Surveys', *Employment Gazette*, XCII, 1, pp. 7–12.

Hakim, Catherine (1984b), 'Employers' Use of Homework, Outwork and Freelances', *Employment Gazette*, XCII, 4.

Hakim, Catherine (1985), *Employers' Use of Outwork: A Study Using the 1980 Workplace Industrial Relations Survey and the 1981 National Survey of Homeworking* (London: Department of Employment) Research Paper no. 44.

Hakim, Catherine and Roger Dennis (1982), *Homeworking in Wages Councils Industries: A Study Based on Wages Inspectorate Records of Pay and Earnings* (London: Department of Employment) Research Paper no. 37.

Handy, Charles (1984), *The Future of Work: A Guide to a Changing Society* (Oxford: Basil Blackwell).

Harrison, Barbara (1981), 'Health Hazards and Homeworking', *Labour Research*, LXX, 6.

Hart, Keith (1973), 'Informal Income Opportunities and Urban Employment in Ghana', *Journal of Modern African Studies*, XI.

Hartmann, Heidi, I. (1981), 'The Family as the Locus of Gender, Class and Political Struggle: The Example of Housework', *Signs*, VI, 3, Spring, pp. 366–94.

Head, P. (1961), 'Putting Out in the Leicester Hosiery Industry in the Middle of the Nineteenth Century', *Leicester Archeological and Historical Society Journal*, XXXVII, 3, pp. 44–59.

Health and Safety Commission (1976), *Consultative Document: Work in Domestic Premises*.

Health and Safety Commission (1979), *Consultative Document: Homeworkers Draft Regulations*.

Henderson, Janet (1985), 'By the Community: An Ideological Response to the Crisis in the Welfare State?' (British Society of Gerontology Annual Conference, University of Keele, 27–29 September.

HMSO (1979), *Homeworkers (Protection): A Bill to Amend the Law to Provide for the Future Protection of Homeworkers, etc.*, 29 February.

Heyzer, Noeleen and Kate Young (n.d.), 'Women and the Working Poor: Towards a Framework of Analysis' (Brighton: Institute of Development Studies) unpublished paper.

Hindess, Barry (1973), *The Use of Official Statistics in Sociology* (London: Macmillan).

Hogg, Sarah (1985), 'Making Sense of the Jobless Numbers', *The Times*, 24 June.

Hope, Emily, Mary Kennedy and Anne De Winter (1976), 'Homeworkers in North London', in Diana Leonard Barker and Sheila Allen (eds), *Dependence and Exploitation in Work and Marriage* (London: Longman).

Hopkins, Mary (1982), *Homeworking Campaigns Dilemmas and Possibilities in Working with a Fragmented Community*, MA dissertation, University of Warwick (Leicester Outwork Campaign).

House of Commons Select Committee on Employment (1981a), *Homeworking*, CBI Wages Councils (Employers') Consultative Committee Memorandum (London: HMSO) 7 April.

House of Commons Select Committee on Employment (1981b), *Homeworking*, Minutes of Evidence (London: HMSO).

House of Commons (1981c) *Homeworking*, First Report from Employment Committee (London: HMSO) HC 39.

House of Commons Select Committee on Employment (1981d), *Homeworking*, Memorandum submitted by the Manpower Services Commission and Minutes of Evidence, 17 March (London: HMSO).

Hunt, Pauline (1980), *Gender and Class Consciousness* (London: Macmillan).

Hurstfield, Jennifer (1980), *Part-time Pittance* (London: Low Pay Unit) Review no. 1.

Hussain, Hameeda (1985), 'Capitalist Penetration into Handicraft Manufacture: An Historical Review of Women's Work for the Market' (New Delhi: Asian Regional Conference on Women and the Household), mimeo.

Hutchins, B. L. (1907), *Home Work and Sweating* (London: The Fabian Society).

Huws, Ursula (1984a), 'New Technology Homeworkers', *Employment Gazette*, XCII, January.

Huws, Ursula (1984b) *The New Homeworkers: New Technology and the Changing Location of White Collar Work* (London: Low Pay Unit) Pamphlet no. 28.

Hvidtfeldt, Kirsten, Kirsten Jorgensen and Ruth Neilsen (eds) (1982), *Strategies for Integrating Women in the Labour Market, European Women's Studies in Social Science*, no. 1 (Copenhagen).

Institute of Manpower Studies and Manpower Limited (1984), *Flexible Manning – The Way Ahead: Report of a Joint Conference* (Sussex: Institute of Manpower Studies) Report no. 88.

International Labour Office (1972), *Employment, Incomes and Equality: A Strategy for Increasing Productive Employment in Kenya* (Geneva: ILO).

Irvine, John, Ian Miles and Jeff Evans (eds) (1979), *Demystifying Social Statistics* (London: Pluto).

Jackson, B. (1976), 'Childminding: The Breakthrough Point in the Cycle of Deprivation', in Department of Health and Social Security, *Low Cost Day Care Provision for the Under-Fives* (London: DHSS).

Jackson, Brian and Sonia Jackson (1979), *Childminder: A Study in Action Research* (London: Routledge & Kegan Paul).

Jenkins, C. and B. Sherman (1979), *The Collapse of Work* (London: Eyre Methuen.

Jhabvala, R. (1983), 'The Home-Based Workers', *We, The Self-Employed*, (Ahmedabad, India: SEWA) October.

Jordan, David (1977), *The Wages of Uncertainty: A Critique of Wages Councils Orders* (London: Low Pay Unit).

Jordan, David (1978), *The Wages of Fear: A 1978 Report on Homeworking* (London: Low Pay Unit), Bulletin no. 20.

Keller, Bill (1984), 'At the Centre of New Fight: Home Work', *New York Times*, CXXXIII, no. 46050, 20 May.

Land, Hilary (1980), 'The Family Wage', *Feminist Review*, 6.

Leeds Trade Union and Community Resource and Information Centre (1984), 'Background Report on Homeworking for Leeds City Council', unpublished paper.

Leicester Outwork Campaign (1985), *Annual Report 1984–5*.

Leighton, Patricia (1982), 'Employment Contracts: A Choice of Relationships', *Employment Gazette*, XC, 10, pp. 433–9.

Leighton, Patricia (1983a), *Contractual Arrangements in Selected Industries: A Study of Employment Relationships in Industries with Outwork* (London: Department of Employment) Research Paper no. 39.

Leighton, Patricia (1983b), 'Employment and Self-Employment: Some Problems of Law and Practice, *Employment Gazette*, XCI, 5, pp. 197–203.

Leighton, Patricia (1984), 'Observing Employment Contracts', *Industrial Law Journal*, XIII, 2, pp. 86–106.

Linder, Marc (1983), 'Self-Employment as a Cyclical Escape from Unemployment: A Case Study of the Construction Industry in the United States during the Post-War Period', in I. H. Simpson and R. L. Simpson (eds), *Peripheral Workers: Research in the Sociology of Work*,

A Research Annual (London: JAI Press) vol. II pp. 261–74.

Littek, Wolfgang (1986), 'Rationalisation, Technical Change and Employee Reaction' in Kate Purcell *et al.* (eds), *The Changing Experience of Employment: Restructuring and Recession* (London: Macmillan).

Llewelyn Davies, Margaret (ed.) (1977), *Life as We Have Known it, by Co-operative Working Women* (London: Virago) original edition 1931.

London Industrial Strategy (1985), Section Five: Sweated Trades and Services *Homeworking* (Greater London Council, Industry and Employment Branch).

Longmate, N. (1973), *How We Lived Then* (London: Arrow Books).

Low Pay Unit (1983), *Who Needs the Wages Councils?* (London: Low Pay Unit) Pamphlet no. 24.

McKee, Lorna and Colin Bell (1986), 'His Unemployment; Her Problem: The Domestic and Marital Consequences of Male Unemployment' in S. Allen *et al.* (eds), *The Experience of Unemployment* (London: Macmillan).

MacLennan, E., C. Pond and J. Sullivan (1983), *Low Pay: Labour's Response* (London: Fabian Society) Tract 488.

MacEwan Scott, Alison (1979), 'Who are The Self-Employed?' in Ray Bromley and Chris Gerry (eds) *Casual Work and Poverty in Third World Cities* (Chichester: John Wiley).

McNally, Fiona (1979), *Women for Hire: A Study of the Female Office Worker* (London: Macmillan).

Maher, Vanessa (1981), 'Work, Consumption and Authority within the Household A Moroccan Case' in Kate Young Roslyn McCullagh and Carol Wolkowitz (eds), *Of Marriage in the Market: Women's Subordination in International Perspective* (London: CSE Books).

Manpower Services Commission (1983), 'Special Feature: Patterns of Unemployment', *Labour Market Quarterly Report* (Sheffield).

Manpower Services Commission (1985), 'Special Feature: Self-Employment', *Labour Market Quarterly Report*, February (Sheffield).

Martin, J. and C. Roberts (1984), *Women and Employment: A Lifetime Perspective* (London: HMSO).

Marriott, R. (1957), *Incentive Payment Systems: A Review of Research and Opinions* (London: Staples Press).

Marx, Karl (1958), *Capital*, vol. I (Moscow: Foreign Languages Publishing House).

Mendels, F. F. (1972), 'Protoindustrialisation: The First Phase of the Industrialisation Process', *Journal of Economic History*, XXXII, pp. 241–61.

Meissner, M. *et al.* (1975), 'No Exit for Wives: Sexual Division of Labour and the Cumulation of Household Demands', *Canadian Review of Sociology and Anthropology*, XII, 4, pp. 424–39.

Middleton, C. (1974), 'Sexual Inequality and Stratification Theory', in Frank Parkin (ed.), *The Social Analysis of Class Structure* (London: Tavistock Publications).

Mies, Maria (1982), *The Lace Makers of Narsapur: Indian Housewives Produce for the World Market* (London: Zed Press).

Miles, Ian (1983), *Adaptation to Unemployment?* (Sussex: Science Policy Research Unit) Occasional Paper Series, no. 20.

Miles, Ian and John Irvine (1979), 'The Critique of Official Statistics', in John Irvine *et al.* (eds), *Demystifying Social Statistics* (London: Pluto).

Mingione, Enzo (1985), 'Social Reproduction of the Surplus Labour Force: The Case of Italy' in Nanneka Redclift and Enzo Mingione (eds), *Beyond Employment* (London: Macmillan).

Minns, R. (1980), *Bombers and Mash: The Domestic Front 1939–45* (London: Virago).

Mitter, Swasti (1986), 'Industrial Restructuring and Manufacturing Homework: Immigrant Women in the U.K. Clothing Industry', *Capital and Class*, 27.

Mohiuddin, Yasmeen (1985), 'Women's Employment in Handicrafts: A Case Study of Sind, Pakistan' (New Delhi: Asian Regional Conference on Women and the Household), mimeo.

Moser, Caroline (1978), 'Informal Sector or Petty Commodity Production: Dualism or Dependence in Urban Development', *World Development*, VI, 9/10, pp. 1041–64.

Murray, Fergus (1983), 'The Decentralisation of Production – The Decline of the Mass-Collective Worker' *Capital and Class*, 22, Spring.

National Board for Prices and Incomes (1969), *Pay and Conditions in the Clothing Manufacturing Industries* (London), Report no. 110.

National Homeworking Conference (1984), *Reports of Local Authority Projects*, (London: Greater London Council, 2 June), mimeo.

New Delhi (1985) 'Women and the Household: Asian Regional Conference', 27–31 January, unpublished papers.

Newton-Moss, Janie (1977), *Homeworkers: A Study of Women Working at Home* (University of York: Diploma in Social Administration), unpublished dissertation.

Nield Chew, Ada (1982), *The Life and Writings of a Working Woman* (London: Virago Press).

Oakley, Ann and Robin Oakley (1979), 'Sexism in Official Statistics', in John Irvine *et al.* (eds), *Demystifying Social Statistics* (London: Pluto).

Oliver, Judith (1983), 'The Caring Wife', in Janet Finch and Dulcie Groves (eds), *A Labour of Love – Women, Work and Caring* (London: Routledge & Kegan Paul).

Olson, Margrethe and Sophia Primps (1984), 'Working at Home with Computers Work and Non work Issues', *Issues*, XV pp. 97–112.

Owen, Margaret, (n.d.), 'Rationale for an International Instrument to Protect the Home-based Producers', unpublished draft.

Owen, Margaret (1984) Private Communication.

Owen, Margaret (1985), 'Legal and Policy Issues Relating to Homebased Producers' (New Delhi: Asian Regional Conference on Women and the Household), mimeo.

Owen, Tim (1980), *Wrong Side of the Tracks: Low Pay in British Rail* (London: Low Pay Unit) Pamphlet no. 14.

Pahl, J. (1983), 'The Allocation of Money and the Structuring of Inequality within Marriage', *Sociological Review*, XXXI, 2 pp. 237–62.

Pahl, R. E. (1980), 'Employment, Work and The Domestic Division of Labour', *International Journal of Urban and Regional Research*, IV, 1, March.

Pahl, R. E. (1984), *Divisions of Labour* (Oxford: Basil Blackwell).

Pahl, R. E. and Claire Wallace (1985), 'Household Work Strategies in Economic Recession', in Nanneka Redclift and Enzo Mingione (eds), *Beyond Employment* (Oxford: Basil Blackwell).

Parsons, Talcott (1943), 'The Kinship System of the Contemporary United States', *American Anthropologist*, XLV, 1.

Pearson, Ruth (1986), 'Multinational Companies and Women's Labour' in Kate Purcell *et al.* (eds), *The Changing Experience of Employment, Restructuring and Recession* (London: Macmillan).

Phillips, Anne (1983), *Hidden Hands: Women and Economic Policies* (London: Pluto).

Phillips, Anne and Barbara Taylor (1980), 'Sex and Skill: Notes towards a Feminist Economics', *Feminist Review*, no. 6.

Phizacklea, Annie (ed.) (1983), *One Way Ticket: Migration and Female Labour* (London: Routledge & Kegan Paul).

Playford, Clive (1980), *In the Shadow of Decline* (London: Low Pay Unit) Pamphlet no. 16.

Pond, Chris (1980), *Low Pay and Unemployment* (London: Low Pay Unit).

Pond, Chris (1981), 'Low Pay – 1980s Style', *Low Pay Review*, 4, March.

Pond, C. (1985), *No Return to Sweatshops: Government Economic Strategy and the Wages Councils* (London: Low Pay Unit) Pamphlet no. 37.

Pond, Chris and Steve Winyard (n.d.), *The Case for a National Minimum Wage* (London: Low Pay Unit) Pamphlet no. 23.

Portes, A. and J. Walton (1981), *Labour, Class and the International System* (New York: Academic Press).

Poster, Mark (1978), *Critical Theory of the Family* (London: Pluto).

Postgate, Richmond (1984), *Home: A Place for Work? Possibilities and Snags Explored* (London: Calouste Gulbenkian Foundation).

Posthuma, Anne (n.d.), 'High Tech Job Wars', unpublished paper.

Printing World (1984), 'U.K. Typesetters: What Price Competition?', *Book Production*, (Supplement to *Printing World*), Spring, pp. 20–4.

Pugh, H. S. (1984), *Estimating the Extent of Homeworking* (London: City University Social Statistics Research Unit) Working Paper no. 15.

Purcell, Kate, Stephen Wood, Alan Waton, and Sheila Allen (eds) (1986), *The Changing Experience of Employment: Restructuring and Recession* (London: Macmillan).

Rainnie, A. F. (1984), 'Combined and Uneven Development in the Clothing Industry: The Effects of Competition on Accumulation', *Capital and Class*, 22, Spring.

Rainnie, Al (1985), 'Small Firms, Big Problems: The Political Economy of Small Businesses', *Capital and Class*, 25, Spring.

Rao, V. R. and S. Husain (1983), 'Invisible Hands: Women Workers in the Garment Export Industry' (New Delhi: ICSSR, Indo-Dutch Programme).

Rao, Rukmini and Sahba Husain (1985), 'Invisible Hands: Women in Homebased Production in the Garment Export Industry, (New Delhi: Asian Regional Conference on Women and the Household), mimeo.

Rawnsley, Andrew (1985), 'Well-Met by Moonlight', *The Guardian*, 27 November.

Redclift, Nanneka and Enzo Mingione (eds) (1985), *Beyond Employment: Household, Gender and Subsistence* (Oxford: Basil Blackwell).

Robinson, Olive and John Wallace (1984), 'Growth and Utilisation of Part-time Labour in Great Britain', *Employment Gazette*, XCII, 9.

Roldán, M. (1985), 'Industrial Outworking: Struggles for the Reproduction of Working-Class Families and Gender Subordination' in Nanneka Redclift and Enzo Mingione (eds), *Beyond Employment* (Oxford: Blackwell).

Rose, Richard (1983), *Getting By in Three Economies* (Strathclyde: University of Strathclyde Centre for the Study of Public Policy).

Roy, Donald (1952), 'Quota Restrictions and Gold Bricking in a Machine Shop', *American Journal of Sociology*, LVII, pp. 427–42.

Rubery, Jill and Frank Wilkinson (1980), 'Homeworking in Ex-Wages Council Industries: Report to the Department of Employment', unpublished draft.

Rubery, Jill and Frank Wilkinson (1981), 'Outwork and Segmented Labour Markets', in F. Wilkinson (ed.), *The Dynamics of Labour Market Segmentation* (London: Academic Press).

Rubery, Jill, Roger Tarling and Frank Wilkinson (1984), 'Labour Market Segmentation Theory: An Alternative Framework for the Analysis of Employment Systems' (Bradford: British Sociological Association Annual Conference) unpublished paper.

Saifullah Khan, Verity (1979), 'Work and Network: South Asian Women in South London' in Sandra Wallman (ed.), *Ethnicity at Work* (London: Macmillan).

Samuel, Raphael (1977), 'Workshop of the World: Steam Power and Hand Technology in mid-Victorian Britain', *History Workshop*, 3, Spring.

Scase, Richard and Robert Goffee (1982), *The Entrepreneurial Middle Class* (London: Croom Helm).

Scase, Richard and Robert Goffee (1983), 'Business Ownership and Women's Subordination: A Preliminary Study of Female Proprietors', *The Sociological Review*, XXXI, 4, November.

Schutt, J. and R. Whittington (1984), 'Large Firms and the Rise of Small Units' (Nottingham: Small Firms Research Conference) mimeo.

Shah, Samir (1975), *Immigrants and Employment in the Clothing Industry: The Rag Trade in London's East End* (London: The Runnymede Trust).

Sharpe, Sue (1984), *Double Identity: The Lives of Working Mothers* (Harmondsworth: Penguin).

Smith, Roger (1976), 'Sex and Occupational Role in Fleet Street', in Diana Leonard Barker and Sheila Allen (eds), *Dependence and Exploitation in Work and Marriage* (London: Longman).

Stanworth, M. (1984), 'Women and Class Analysis: A Reply to John Goldthorpe', *Sociology*, XVIII, 2 pp. 159–70.

Stedman-Jones, Gareth (1976), *Outcast London* (Harmondsworth: Penguin Books).

Sulaiman, H. (1985), 'The Productive Activities of Malaysian Women in the Market and Household Production Sectors' (New Delhi: Asian Regional Conference on Women and the Household), mimeo.

Telecommuting Review (1985) 'Colorado Legislature Passes Pro-Homework Resolution', September.

Thomas, Pat (1978), 'Homework: Beyond the Fringe of the Labour Market – A Study of Homework in Great Britain' (Brunel University) unpublished dissertation.

Thompson, E. P. (1967), 'Time, Work Discipline and Industrial Capitalism', *Past and Present*, 38.

Thompson, Paul (1983), *The Nature of Work: An Introduction to Debates on the Labour Process* (London: The Macmillan Press).

Tilley, C. and R. Tilley (1971), 'Agenda for European Economic History in the 1970s', *Journal of Economic History*, XXXI, pp. 184–98.

The Times (1984), 'Law Report: 'Home Workers Have Status of Employed Persons', 4 May.

Toffler, A. (1980), *The Third Wave* (London: Collins/Pan Books).

Townsend, Peter (1974), 'Poverty as Relative Deprivation: Resources and Style of Living', in Dorothy Wedderburn (ed.), *Poverty, Inequality and Class Structure* (London: University of Cambridge Press).

Townsend, Peter (1979), *Poverty in the United Kingdom* (Harmondsworth: Penguin).

Townshend-Smith, Richard (1979), 'Law of Employment: Recognising a Contract of Employment – II', *New Law Journal*, CXXIX, 5926, 18 October, p. 1022.

Toynbee, Polly (1985), 'Guardian Women', *The Guardian*, 15 April.

Trades Union Congress (1978), *A Statement on Homeworking* (London).

Trades Union Congress (1985), *Homeworking: A TUC Statement* (London).

Wallace, Claire and Ray Pahl (1986), 'Polarisation, Unemployment and All Forms of Work', in S. Allen *et al.* (eds), *The Experience of Unemployment* (London: Macmillan).

Watanabe, S. (1972), 'International Subcontracting, Employment and Skill Production', *International Labour Review*, CV, 3.

West, Jackie (ed.) (1982), *Work, Women and the Labour Market* (London: Routledge & Kegan Paul).

Westwood, Sallie (1984), *All Day Every Day: Factory and Family in the Making of Women's Lives* (London: Pluto).

Winyard, Steve (1976), *Policing Low Wages* (London: Low Pay Unit) Pamphlet no. 4.

Wix, D. H. C. (1984), *Bygone Quorn in Photographs*, Portrait of an Urban Village (Loughborough: Rawlins County College).

Wootton, Barbara (1955), *The Social Foundation of Wage Policy* (London: George Allen & Unwin).

Wray, Kathy (1985), *The Demand for Labour in a Textile Local Labour Market with Particular Reference to Twilight Workers and Homeworkers*

(University of Loughborough), unpublished Ph.D.

Young, K. (1978), 'Modes of Appropriation and the Sexual Division of Labour: A Case Study from Oaxaca, Mexico', in Annette Kuhn and AnnMarie Wolpe (eds) *Feminism and Materialism* (London: Routledge & Kegan Paul).

Young, Kate (1981), 'Domestic Out-work and the Decentralisation of Production: A New State in Capitalist Development' (Mexico: Paper for the ILO Regional Meeting on Women and Rural Development, August 24–28).

Young, Kate and Caroline Moser (eds) (1981), 'Women and the Informal Sector', *IDS Bulletin*, XII, 3.

Author Index

215

218   *Author Index*

Subject Index

219